ENDLESS APPETITES

Since 1996, Bloomberg Press has published books for financial professionals, as well as books of general interest in investing, economics, current affairs, and policy affecting investors and business people. Titles are written by well-known practitioners, Bloomberg News® reporters and columnists, and other leading authorities and journalists. Bloomberg Press books have been translated into more than 20 languages.

For a list of available titles, please visit our Web site at www.wiley.com/go/bloombergpress.

ENDLESS APPETITES

How the Commodities Casino Creates
Hunger and Unrest

Alan Bjerga

Alan Bjerga
Hettinger, ND
6-4-12

BLOOMBERG PRESS
An Imprint of
**WILEY**

Published by John Wiley & Sons, Inc., Hoboken, New Jersey.
Published simultaneously in Canada.

For general information on our other products and services or for technical support, please contact our Customer Care Department within the United States at (800) 762-2974, outside the United States at (317) 572-3993 or fax (317) 572-4002.

Wiley also publishes its books in a variety of electronic formats. Some content that appears in print may not be available in electronic books. For more information about Wiley products, visit our web site at www.wiley.com.

Library of Congress Cataloging-in-Publication Data:
Bjerga, Alan.
    Endless appetites : how the commodities casino creates hunger and unrest / Alan Bjerga. — 1st ed.
      p. cm. — (Bloomberg ; 151)
    Includes index.
    ISBN 978-1-118-04323-3 (hardback); 978-1-11-16959-9 (ebk); 978-1-118-16961-2 (ebk); 978-1-118-16960-5 (ebk)
    1. Food prices.   2. Food security.   I. Title.
    HD9000.4.B485 2011
    363.8—dc23

                                                 2011029936

Printed in the United States of America

10 9 8 7 6 5 4 3 2 1

To the family,
and the farmers.

Contents

Author's Note

My own experience of farming, growing up on 80 acres near the center of Minnesota, was radically different from those experienced in the countries whose farms I traveled to—Ethiopia, Kenya, Thailand, and Nicaragua—for the writing of this book. And in other ways, not so different.

My parents' sheep farm, and the corn and dairy farms nearby, used different technology, had different weather, and in a lot of ways had many advantages over the farms I visited for this book. But farmers everywhere share similar worries, as well as a similar pride in producing crops from land that nourishes life itself. The weather, is always fickle, the harvest is always uncertain, and the balance between investing to be a better farmer and avoiding debt that can wipe out a family is shared the world over.

The farms of the United States today are prospering in global markets. That wasn't the case in the 1980s, when I was growing up. The last world food-price crisis, in the 1970s, brought prosperity that U.S. farmers naturally followed with more planting; when production overmatched world markets the next decade, prices, and farms, collapsed. American farmers, in a way, were their own worst enemies—they'd become so productive that not as many of them were needed. The federal government tended not to help matters much. A U.S. grain embargo against the USSR was one of the first news stories I remember—you'd hear about it on *The Farm Today*, the midday news show on the local TV station, and you'd hear about it at church, when families gathered for coffee and cinnamon rolls after the service. Corn prices were dropping, and that was only the start of the most difficult decade any U.S. farmer today can remember.

Foreclosure auctions and tense conversations weren't unusual in Minnesota where I grew up. Near Ruthton, a small town in the southern part of the state, a farmer and his son killed two bankers. You'd hear about "nickel auctions" where friends of a farmer about to lose his property would make sure that no one bid more than a nickel on any item for sale, forcing the auction to close. You'd hear about tractorcades and rallies at the capital for more farm support, and you'd know more farm families going to food shelves over the holidays because their own land couldn't support them. And of course, you'd hear the John Mellencamp songs on the radio, rains on scarecrows, and sons whose farms of their childhoods would only live as memories.

The government shoveled out record farm aid in response to the crisis, but in the end it took a shakeout of food markets to stabilize U.S. agriculture. A lot of farmers left the business. Those who survived did so either by getting bigger, buying out their neighbors and farming ever-larger plots of land, or by moving into niche crops and livestock. Ethanol, first supported by the government as a way to give farmers another market for excess corn, helped a lot of families prosper as it became more popular, and it's still a job-creator in a lot of small towns even as it drives up the price of their neighbors' hog and cattle feed. Globalization has been good for U.S. agriculture sales—record exports and rising farm incomes aren't a coincidence. Subsidies are still railed against by budget watchdogs and trade organizations, but they're actually much lower than even a few years ago. To a large extent, U.S. farmers are more market-centered than ever, feeding America and much of the world.

Farmers today grow for markets that want their goods. Given where food prices are now, and with reason to believe this increase won't be followed by a collapse like last time, there's room for more of them. U.S. farmers today are the most efficient, most productive farmers the world has ever known. They're also the least indebted they've ever been—those who remember the 1980s are slow to take on debt that might hurt them later. *The Farm Today* was cancelled decades ago, and many farmers and small towns still struggle— weather and economics ensure there will always be hardships to overcome, and good jobs, which many farmers need to stay afloat, are hard to come by. Rural life has changed, becoming more diverse, and in many ways more complicated, than it was decades ago. But U.S. farming isn't going away, and the work of U.S. farmers is more important to the planet than ever.

My parents weathered the storms well. Mom kept track of every dollar, Dad worked overtime for the Minnesota State Patrol—always the real source of income—and we didn't go too far on family vacations. A lot of our food was our own and from our neighbors' farms, and it was better than what was found in the grocery store: fresh strawberries and rhubarb for pies. Blueberries and raspberries. Potatoes, cucumbers, and carrots. Fresh chicken, fresh beef, fresh venison during deer-hunting season, fresh turkey at Thanksgiving; and pickled, canned, and deep-frozen everything during the winter. My parents sold the farm after I'd left for college. They were ready to live by water, which many Minnesotans do when they get older. My dad used to say the family needed to keep our land because someday I'd want to come back to run the farm. We all knew it was a joke. I clearly had no future in agriculture. My brother, a Future Farmers of America state-contest perennial, was the real farm help—I got stuck shelling peas from my mother's giant garden on August afternoons, with no entertainment options other than reruns of *Jeopardy!* and *The Beverly Hillbillies.*

Success seemed to mean getting far away from home. I wrote about ethanol in newspaper stops in Sioux Falls and Wichita, but it wasn't until I moved to Washington that I embraced farm writing—and, in a sense, my own background. Arriving in September 2001, just as the 9/11 attacks occurred, I was thrown into stories that hardly seemed real. But somebody had to cover the farm bill then making its way through the House of Representatives, and as the youngest, least experienced reporter in the Knight-Ridder bureau, I drew the short straw. I found it fascinating—familiar, yet because of just how broad the world's agriculture really is, with something completely different to learn nearly every day. Apparently, some of the knowledge overheard from *The Farm Today* and church coffees had sunk in without me knowing it. I moved to full-time farm-writing at Bloomberg in 2006, and the opportunities have only continued to blossom. As I've told my father, "Isn't it great that someone in our family actually made money from farming?" He laughs, then goes back to fixing whatever car he's restoring in his retirement. Really, though, that's not the kind of wealth I'm talking about—there's so much more to appreciate, every day.

A billion people may go hungry this year, but that's not the farmers' fault. They can feed the world—and even help clothe it and fuel it—if the market's working right. People with one acre in Ethiopia, or 10,000 acres in North Dakota, can co-exist, and contribute, and learn from one another, and grow our way out of the food shocks we're seeing. What follows are a few things I've learned on a journey I set out upon for this book in the fall of 2010, just as prices started rising again, and continued into the middle of 2011, and will continue well beyond its publication. I don't claim expertise on anything, and I suspect I'll change my mind some as the journey continues. I do know I've met many hard-working people who are trying to ensure that hunger goes away. This book is about their fields, informed by the one I knew best. They are not just memories, now or ever.

May 11, 2011

Prologue

The headlines of July 20, 2011, were typical fare for a summer news cycle. Congressional leaders and President Barack Obama were negotiating an agreement to forestall the forecast calamity of breaching the U.S. government debt ceiling. Embattled News Corporation Chairman and CEO Rupert Murdoch was fighting to keep his company's phone-hacking scandal under control, and British Prime Minister David Cameron was trying to limit his own entanglement. Financial markets ended the day with slight declines. Corn prices fell because of hopes that rain would limit a heat wave.

Less prominent, though still in the headlines, was the United Nations declaration of a famine in southern Somalia as the Horn of Africa experienced its worst drought in six decades. Food assistance is a way of life for many in that part of the world, the result of poor rains and poorer people, but a famine is a problem of a higher order; for a United Nations famine designation, malnutrition rates among children in an area have to exceed 30 percent; more than two people per 10,000 must die from hunger-related causes each day; and people have to be unable to access food and other basics of life because they're either nonexistent or simply too expensive.

The Dadaab refugee complex in neighboring Kenya, built for 90,000 people, was caring for more than 400,000. Across the Horn of Africa, more than 11 million people were threatened as farms failed and food costs tripled. Tens of thousands had already died before the declaration was made. Aid appeals ranged from $120 million to $300 million to $1.6 billion. Distribution of aid would be difficult, given the civil war raging in Somalia, a nation that hasn't had a functioning central government for two decades.

Maybe that's why the famine in Somalia wasn't the top news that day. Famine and warfare in Africa: Where's the surprise? Suffering is easier to forget when it seems constant. In the rush for the newest scandal or the latest score, the everyday tragedy of worldwide hunger may fade into the background. An overcrowded camp holding the equivalent of the population of Wichita, Kansas, and a population equal to that of Ohio being threatened with starvation are both depressing, but seemingly far away from the citizens of a well-fed nation. Maybe it's seen as inevitable, yet malnutrition is unnecessary today. Each person on the planet can be fed with existing agricultural production. With the right decisions, people threatened by famine today could even feed themselves—and help out the rest of us tomorrow, when we will need one another to thrive on a crowded planet.

This is a book about globalization—its (intended and unintended) consequences, its challenges, and its opportunities. It is about violent collisions and everyday hopes. It is a journey into hunger, wild markets, and the global food business, featuring the world's most humble farmers and its most powerful leaders, all seeking answers in an increasingly uncertain world. And it's about how new connections being forged can make famine a memory.

To feed everyone, we need everyone. To make famine a memory, we first must stop forgetting about it. And we have to understand and explore the ties that bind the fortunate to the famished.

We begin.

CHAPTER 1

Floors, Fields, and Famines

Greg O'Leary is walking the Chicago Board of Trade wheat pit near the close of a day's session in mid-December, 2010. Prices are up today. Egypt, the world's biggest wheat buyer, has bought 110,000 tons of hard-red winter wheat from the United States, which ships more of that crop than any other country. Jordan has bought another 150,000 tons. Exports have boomed since a summer drought pushed Russia, Egypt's main supplier, to slap an export ban on its harvest. That's driving North African and Arab nations to U.S. sellers to stave off food shortages and higher prices.

The day's most traded wheat contract, the one that requires delivery in March, ends the session up one-and-a-half cents, closing at $7.6475 a bushel—the exactness of buyer-and-seller haggling in Chicago means futures prices are rounded to the hundredth of a cent. It's an up-and-down day in the pit. Prices had been as high as $7.71 earlier, which would have been the biggest jump in a week. Then the dollar started strengthening, and that made buyers worry that the exchange rate may make U.S. wheat less competitive than Canada's or Australia's.[1] Wheat prices are up 41 percent for the year, and investors who had stayed on the sidelines during the global financial crisis are piling back in. After the market closes, Barclays Capital will announce that commodity assets under big-bank management have reached a record $354 billion.[2] That's one-third more than one year ago and four times what it was five years ago. The world economy is growing again. That means more meat, more metal, and more gasoline as the world's producers try to meet the planet's endless appetites.

1

O'Leary is on the floor partly to make money, partly to share market gossip with his friends, and partly out of nostalgia. He started working in the pit in 1980, a farm kid from Newton, Illinois, fresh out of high school, running messages for a trader. The frenetic pace didn't leave time for college—"I went to the college of the Chicago Board of Trade," he says—but over three decades he accomplished something much more difficult than what many degrees require. He mastered markets—the math, the methods, and the willpower needed to successfully buy and sell soft-red winter wheat, the variety of the grain traded in Chicago.[3]

O'Leary makes his money watching the spread in prices among different wheat contracts, looking at the differences between March, May, July, September, and December prices and pouncing when one seems out of line with another. Profits off the spread can be very small, but they add up over time. Chicago trading is all-consuming and high-risk, with fortunes made and lost in a day—as long as you can keep your accounts in order, you can keep playing, and for more than 160 years, it's been a way of life. Collectively, the bets average out into some of the most stable food prices in the world. The runner from Newton became an independent broker in 1993. Today O'Leary heads his own firm, a member of the world's most important commodities exchange. He takes his spot in the octagon, gets an employee's update on the flow of the market, and readies for the close.

He doesn't actually have to do any of this.

Electronic trading has swallowed open outcry in the Board of Trade futures pits. On a platform where more than 150 traders used to elbow one another for position in the terraced octagon where they stand to make their bids and their offers for wheat, maybe one-tenth that many are present for today's 1 P.M. close, which, along with the opening bell, is the most heavily traded period. The pits where traders buy and sell options contracts, a more-complex instrument that's tougher to translate to the electronic world, are still close to full. In the adjacent futures pit some traders are sitting on the top step, reading newspapers, chatting, or gazing elsewhere, counseled by their thoughts. All of them, including O'Leary, have wireless laptops slung over their shoulders so they can buy and sell electronically—which they do in their offices, at home, and on their vacations—while anticipating a stray offer to be made on the physical floor.

Commodities exchanges from Sydney, Australia, to Minneapolis, Minnesota, have ended open outcry altogether. Chicago's remaining pit traders also trade electronically, where more volume and greater volatility—and thus greater potential for profit and loss—awaits. O'Leary says the floors still serve a purpose. Sometimes a seller doesn't want the electronic universe to immediately know he's selling grain. Sometimes, a seller just wants to negotiate with another human being.

"Some days I get mad and I'm like, I'm not even going to go electronic," O'Leary says. "I'm just going to bid and offer. I don't want to play pinball."

He sighs. "Eventually it's all going to be gone. You'll reach a point where you're not going to be able to sell it the way we do it."

A bell rings to note that closing is moments away. O'Leary leaps to place his bids, and for two minutes, sales fly fast, like old times. Trading closes. Everyone goes back to their e-mail, except for a couple younger brokers who have challenged one another to a ping-pong game upstairs. Chicago is covered in snow. The market settles its last contracts, and the floors are swept of a court of confetti-like receipts, artifacts of momentary profits and losses. Traders linger at their desks, mull their fortunes or lack thereof at nearby bars, and step into the cold Lake Michigan air, hustling home through the holiday night.

■ ■ ■

Chicago is asleep. Morning is warming Tunisia. Mohamed Bouazizi, who supports his mother, uncle, and younger siblings by selling produce from a street cart in Sidi Bouzid, a four-hour drive from the capital, Tunis, begins his daily walk from his three-room stucco house to the market in his hometown, where nearly one-third of the workforce is unemployed and the nearest movie theater is 80 miles away. Bouazizi buys produce from farmers and sells it to passersby. Sometimes his sales are stymied by authorities, who harass him and block his efforts to sell fruit, saying he doesn't have a proper permit. Today his food, which he bought on credit, is confiscated. His mother later says her son is publicly humiliated by a city official, a woman who slaps him when he tries to protect his apples. His scale is taken, too, and his cart is overturned, scattering its contents.[4]

Food prices are rising in Tunisia, a country that imports more than twice as much grain as it produces. Bouazizi has had enough. He heads to the local government office to complain. No one listens to him. Outraged by his treatment, shortly before noon he douses himself with paint thinner and sets himself on fire in protest. The fire sears his clothes onto his body and burns off his lips. He lingers in his hospital bed while his rage at Tunisia's government sparks nationwide protests against high unemployment, political repression—and the high cost of the food sold from street carts and supermarkets. The protests spread. President Zine El Abidine Ben Ali, for more than two decades the strongman of Tunisia, unsuccessfully attempts to defuse the disturbances by announcing a massive jobs program to lower youth unemployment, belatedly visiting Bouazizi at his bedside, and feigning sympathy for the frustration his own government has created.[5] The protesters greet his gesture with derision, attacking police stations and government offices.

Bouazizi dies of his burns in less than three weeks. Ben Ali's regime outlives Bouazizi by 10 days. The street vendor's death intensifies the protests, and the violence, and the president flees the country. Riots spread to Algeria, shortly to be followed by protests in Egypt, where an annual $3 billion in subsidies for food-buyers isn't enough to curb outrage at rising bread prices. Tensions are building in Libya, which imports 90 percent of its grains.[6] Bread becomes a common theme of the North African and Middle East revolutions that erupt. Baguettes are held aloft by protesters. Frying pans, tin-pots and water buckets are the new suits of armor—an unleavened pancake taped across one's head is useless against a bullet but powerful as a symbol.[7] Chicago wheat is still rising. The United Nations has officially put world food prices at a record high. In Tunisia, Algeria, Egypt, Syria, and Yemen, throughout North Africa and the Middle East, bloodshed is an additional cost.

■ ■ ■

The price of food—the cost of a loaf of bread in a supermarket, brought to you via a global system of farmers, purchasers, processors, distributors, retailers, and consumers—some with more money than others—some with more information than others—some with more varieties than others—the system that in many ways decides who gets to eat and who doesn't—the system that connects Greg O'Leary, to a family budget, to Mohamed Bouazizi, to a revolution, to you—starts with a simple question:

What's it worth?

For Hugo Alejandro and his buyers, it's worth the long haul.

The white-gravel road from Estili, Nicaragua, grinds nerves and revives old injuries. The drive to the tomato farm is supposed to take 20 minutes. I've spent more than an hour veering among outcroppings of white-chalk rocks and ribbons of pavement that are modern for one mile and moonscape the next, trying not to crack my skull against the ceiling of the SUV—a veteran of the winding roads of rural Nicaragua—and still, no tomato farm in sight. Just rocky road and mountains and endless, disorienting turns.

Santos Palma, the Catholic Relief Services manager driving the SUV, jokes that the drive will do me good. "*Tienes que ver el campo para saber donde comprar su finca en Nicaragua,*" he says—you have to see the countryside so you know where to buy your farm in Nicaragua. My Spanish is limited, so

I don't try to tell him I've heard a variation of his joke before. I fiddle with my camera, which isn't working right, and hope this ride ends soon. This is the last day of my five-month, four-continent quest for answers. I would like to end it with bones intact.

We're wondering if we'll have enough gas to get back to Estili. I am not looking forward to being stranded on an isolated rural road the night I'm to leave Managua. Santos is unworried—of course, he started his Catholic Relief work as an emergency coordinator immediately after Hurricane Mitch hit in 1998, so he's dealt with bigger concerns than my red-eye flight. Just when we start serious discussions about turning back, we arrive at the farm of Hugo Alejandro. The farmer grows six acres of tomatoes, corn, cabbages, and onions in a field nestled in the sparsely populated highlands of northern Nicaragua. He's lived in the region his entire life, and he carries a daily reminder of its turbulence: a wrist that bears a silver-dollar-sized lump that's the legacy of a *Contra* rebel bullet that pierced his body and ended his two years as a draftee in the Sandinista army during the 1980s, fighting for control of the country. When asked to sign his name, Alejandro, now in his mid-forties, hands the notepad to his wife. He has never spent a day in school.

And until four years ago, his tomatoes seldom traveled far from his farm.

Alejandro has become an expert in the latest methods of growing tomatoes, as have his children, all of whom have made it through at least sixth grade. The perishable, but profitable, fruits and vegetables he grows are aided by drip-irrigation technology that reduces energy and water use, and they're being sold in supermarkets owned by a new buyer that demands consistent quality and exact food-safety standards—Walmart, which has expanded into groceries in Latin America. ACORDAR, a U.S. Agency for International Development project with partners that include Catholic Relief Services and Lutheran World Relief, is helping Alejandro's family with training and financing.

The spring harvest is beginning. Alejandro is holding ripened tomatoes in his stronger right hand. "We have to produce better vegetables if we want the supermarket to buy vegetables from us," he says in Spanish. "People who buy in the supermarket have money, and they want quality for their money."[8]

We spend about half an hour on his property, talking about irrigation, his children, and how the new supermarkets give him extra income he uses to buy fertilizer to boost yields of the crop that feeds his family as well as the grocery shoppers of Estili and Managua. Time is short because the drive took too long, and it's best to be on the highway before dark. We settle in for another bone-rattling hour, likely the last I ever spend on this road. Tomorrow I'll be back in the United States at a reception toasting press freedom near the U.S. Capitol dome. Alejandro will have his harvest, and these roads.

To haul tomatoes.

■ ■ ■

Abebech Toga, an Ethiopian farmer and mother of six living in the country's Southern Nations region, wants to send her children to college. She markets her corn and her fair-trade coffee through her local cooperative, and she studies market trends everywhere from the local outdoor bazaar in her town of Sodo to the Chicago Board of Trade. She hears the latest prices over the radio and through her cell phone, and the information— soon, she hopes, to be accompanied by better roads—connects her to the local, regional, national, and international marketplace that needs her crops.

Like Alejandro, Toga is a smallholder farmer, called such because she farms a small plot of land in places where subsistence production and incomes are common. The walls of her mud-hut home are decorated with posters of the Periodic Table, the English alphabet, and President Barack Obama, all meant to inspire her children. She is the designated trainer of other farmers in her village, showing them how to reduce moisture in their crops and prevent losses after harvest through an initiative offered through the World Food Programme called Purchase for Progress. The initiative attempts to create a market for growers of corn like Toga who need reliable buyers for the surplus they don't consume themselves. Eventually, when the program exits her area, the hope is that she will have the training and experience to sell high-quality corn at fair market prices to become a competitive businesswoman in a better-fed Ethiopia.

"A farmer needs a market," she says.[9]

Toga and Alejandro are trying to do what every human tries to do—stay nourished, be healthy, and create a better life for their families. For many of the world's poorest people, many of them farmers in rural areas but also living in cities, many of them living in impoverished nations but some of them in the richest nations on earth, that task is becoming more difficult. For nearly one billion, it is at times impossible.

The world is in a new era of rising and shifting food costs that thwart solutions even as suffering increases around the globe. Hunger that declined for decades now stubbornly refuses to fall further as high prices and turbulent weather have stopped three decades of progress in its tracks.

In 2009, hunger affected a record number of people as costs fluctuated after a price spike that began in 2007 started pushing more people into poverty. Another surge in 2010 sent prices to a new record early the next year, at levels twice where they were five years earlier.

From 2007 to 2009, more than 60 food riots erupted worldwide, leading to violent deaths in Egypt, Cameroon, and Haiti and putting the number of global hungry on a trajectory that, in 2009, topped a billion for the first time.[10] (See Table 1.1.) The food-price spike of the past decade has returned in this one. Starting with the drought that withered wheat in nations of the former Soviet Union in 2010, a new round of unrest began with food riots in Mozambique in September, gained traction in Tunisia, and ultimately became a crucial part of the volatile blend of youth unemployment, long-simmering dissatisfaction with corrupt rulers, and political awakening that has touched off demonstrations from Morocco to Oman, toppled dictators in Tunisia and Egypt, and fed civil war in Libya. Frustration with the price of bread, gasoline, and other consumer staples fed the riots, with governments unable to calm the discontent. Low-income countries are especially vulnerable to instability when food prices rise and have been for decades, a 2011 International Monetary Fund report found; more frequent rises in food prices creates more frequent unrest.[11]

Dissatisfaction with the price of groceries, and its part in an explosive mix of politics and outrage in developing regions, has brought crop supply-and-demand, normally the realm of agricultural economists, to public attention. By April 2011, World Bank President Robert Zoellick warned that the planet was one more shock away from a full-blown food catastrophe. As high food prices pushed an estimated 44 million people into poverty, according to the World Bank, forecasts for global hunger were rising, and the United States,

TABLE 1.1 Number of Undernourished People in the World (in Millions) and Proportion of Undernourished People in Developing Countries

Year	1969–71	1979–81	1990–92	1995–97	2000–02	2005–07	2008	2009	2010
Number of undernourished people	878	853	843	788	833	848	921	1023	925
% share of under-nourished	33	25	20	17	17	16	17	18	16

Source: "The State of Food Insecurity in the World," United Nations Food and Agriculture Organization, 2010.

food supplier to the world, struggled through a flooded spring and scorching summer just to keep up with demand.[12]

The losses due to hunger aren't only today's. Malnutrition stunts children's growth, weakens immune systems, and permanently lowers mental development, ending what little chance poor economies may ever have of developing their human capacity and competing with the rest of the world, according to Jeffrey Sachs, head of the Earth Institute at Columbia University and former director of the UN Millennium Project, which fights poverty in famine-prone regions.

"This isn't a short-term problem or fluctuation," he said. "The effects of hunger now last for generations. What we have right now is a large and rapidly growing world economy that is pressing against its limits. We're facing a world of scarcity."[13]

The failure to bring food security—the condition in which people know they will have reliable access to affordable nutrition—to the world isn't presently a failure of having enough food. World agriculture produces more calories per person, per day, than it did in the 1970s, even as the planet's population doubled.[14] Crop and livestock production today is adequate to feed everyone, with food to spare—the world produces almost 2,800 calories per person each day, well above the 2,100 needed for adequate nutrition.[15] Hunger comes from a lack of available food, caused by the disruption or disappearance of supplies or an inability to buy what's in stores. In a cruel irony, the people most trapped by hunger are often farmers themselves, stuck at subsistence levels that tip toward famine when crops fail and money is unavailable for necessary nutrition.[16]

Uncertainty over one's next meal isn't strictly a developing-world problem: About one in six Americans struggled to have enough food at some point in 2009.[17] Hunger in richer nations, however, is less connected to volatile prices than in poorer regions. Food is more available in developed nations, as evidenced by the coexistence of hunger with obesity, which affects more than one-third of the U.S. population and more than 20 percent of the population in a half-dozen other countries.[18] Problems with food waste, a major factor of inefficient food distribution, are also different. Rich countries throw away food bought from a store, while in poorer places food never even gets there because of inadequate storage. About 40 percent of food waste in sub-Saharan Africa happens in farms or warehouses.[19] Better storage alone would save up to 20 percent of African grain production that is lost to microbes, pests, and lack of access to markets, according to a U.N. study.[20]

Hunger may worsen in coming decades. The world's population, topping 7 billion in 2011, is expected to rise to 9 billion by mid-century and surpass

10 billion by century's end.[21] Food demand will rise more steeply—70 percent by 2050.[22] More people will want more food. They will also want better-quality nutrition, more convenient access to it, and more variety in their diets, as poor consumers become middle-class consumers in China, India, Brazil, and other emerging countries.

Bigger crops that can stave off famine will need to be grown without major expansion of land devoted to farming. Global growth in farm yields that averaged 2 percent per year from 1970 to 1990 have since stalled at just over 1 percent. Stagnant growth may continue as climate change and soil degradation trump new technology in the struggle for more productive land.[23] Much of the additional land that is available is in sub-Saharan Africa, the world's most hunger-prone region. Still, about 90 percent of food increases will have to come through intensification higher yields on efficiently used cropland, much of it already under cultivation, according to the UN.[24] Exhausted soils, depleted water, and pests will require sustainable farming practices, the UN said: "The food price spike of 2008 and the surge in food prices to record levels early in 2011 portend rising and more frequent threats to world food security."[25]

A globalized economy is interdependent, with more people wanting more food from beyond their own borders. Most of the food shipped around the world still is sent from the world's richer nations—the United States, the European Union, Canada, Australia—to the poorer, while rising powers like Brazil become more important. Go to a G-8 summit of the world's leading economies, and the people there will look very, if not exceedingly, well-fed. This global food market has brought wealth to some places—U.S. farmers in 2011 may see both record exports and profits.[26] Farmers today produce greater varieties of food for ever-more-diverse diets, from more meat in Asia to organic foods in the European Union and fresh-food farmers' markets of locally grown goods across the developed world. Yet, more than half of respondents in a global survey conducted in mid-2011 said they had changed their diets in the previous year because of higher food prices, in some cases by cutting back on fruits and vegetables.[27] Malnourishment is making a comeback.

■ ■ ■

Evidence of the market turmoil is the volatility of global commodity prices that's rising just as millions of investors have found new ways to speculate in crop prices, ironically in a quest for financial stability. Global financial instability and volatile markets are "contaminating" commodity prices, the newly elected head of the United Nations Food and Agriculture Organization, Jose Graziano da Silva of Brazil, said in his first press conference after being selected to head the agency starting in 2012.[28] World prices set on trading floors that smoothed prices for decades are exporting volatility and creating unrest, even as a new class of investors—us, through our 401(k) plans and mutual funds—tie the fortunes of rich-nation wealth seekers to poor-nation consumers and farmers who struggle to feed themselves. Investment in vehicles tied to commodities prices—the energy, food, and metals that comprise the raw materials of human life—by early 2011 was 55 times larger than in 2000, directly connecting rich-world investors to volatile food costs. The effects of commodities trading on food prices is controversial. Regardless of cause, the price swings of global crop and energy markets have turned a quarter-century of stable food costs into a marketplace casino where demand pushes prices higher—and droughts drive them higher still—while a cooling economy or an unexpected gain in supplies cascade them down faster than any changes in how much people actually eat. From mid-2007 to mid-2008, world food prices rose 46 percent, then plunged 34 percent in the second half of that year, bottoming out in February 2009, even as U.S. prices, where commodity-price increases are more smoothly integrated into grocery costs, rose more slowly and steadily. From June 2010 to 2011, prices rose another 39 percent (see Figure 1.1). High prices are more harmful in countries that depend on imports for food and where poorer citizens spend a larger percentage of their income on food. The U.S. share of income devoted to food is less than 10 percent. People in impoverished nations may spend 70, 80 percent on a meager diet.

FIGURE 1.1 U.S., World Food Costs

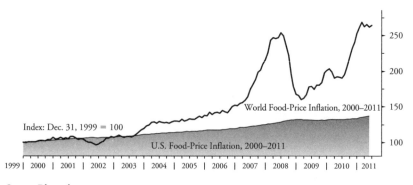

Index: Dec. 31, 1999 = 100

World Food-Price Inflation, 2000–2011

U.S. Food-Price Inflation, 2000–2011

1999 | 2000 | 2001 | 2002 | 2003 | 2004 | 2005 | 2006 | 2007 | 2008 | 2009 | 2010 | 2011

Source: Bloomberg.

Our appetite for food is accompanied by a thirst for energy, which raises food-transport and processing costs. The price of a barrel of oil, barely over $10 at one point in 1998, reached more than $147 a decade later, placing an added tax on nutrition. Efforts to combat climate change and encourage alternatives to oil have increased production of biofuels, whose backers promise freedom from energy dependence while drawing acreage and production away from food in pursuit of that goal. As those demands increase, so does their pressure on food prices.

Weather has always been central to food markets; in the past century, everything from floods in South Asia to multiyear Dust Bowl droughts in the United States have crimped supplies. In a world of rising populations and food needs, destructive weather creates supply swings and trade disruptions that shutter borders and throw prices into chaos. Globally, changes in weather patterns may double food prices by 2030, with half of the increase attributable to climate change.[29] Water requirements may rise 40 to 100 percent, numbers that have been boosted by global warming.[30] Irrigation has been crucial to increasing food supplies, but it's being used inadequately in some regions while in others—including Saudi Arabia—over-reliance on irrigation depletes water tables and creates food-security mirages that won't last another generation. In 2000, half a billion people lived in countries short of water. By 2050, it will be 4 billion.[31]

Governments also contribute to higher, volatile prices, erecting trade barriers that inhibit the flow of goods from places of surplus to places of need. And in the most direct expression of the go-it-alone approach, some of them have turned to snapping up land in less-developed countries to grow food for their own consumers, a new land grab of questionable benefit to poorer nations. The list goes on. Declining crop surpluses have made food prices more sensitive to small shifts in supply and demand as a just-in-time model of food inventories leaves the planet vulnerable to shortfalls between harvests. A weaker dollar, the global food trade currency, raises export costs.

In the past half-decade food prices have spiked twice—in 2008 and in 2011—with riots and revolutions as results. The farmers who underpin global food security can raise production in response to higher prices and, over time, lower consumer costs while lifting themselves. But the fast ups and downs of the market add risk that poorer farmers can't take on. And so riots rise again, in Algeria, and Tunisia, and Egypt, in Oman, in Bahrain, in Uganda. . . .

■ ■ ■

Globalized supply and demand turns problems in one region into crises in others. Still, from that failure comes a chance for solutions that can help lift millions of the world's poorest people from poverty—with the right access to markets and incentives. Today's casino is tomorrow's opportunity for the world's smallest farmers, its biggest businesses, and the consumers in between. The casino can be tamed, the planet can be fed, and famine can be banished to the past.

In Sabasaba, Kenya, a new agribusiness center is creating a gathering place for storing and selling bananas to shoppers in Nairobi and other growing Kenyan cities. Rebecca Wairimu Njoroge sells her fruit at the Sabasaba Agribusiness Centre in the Muranga'a region and helps organize sales for her self-help farmers group, which local growers formed to bunch their bananas and finance investments in higher production.

"People are waking up, because what happened before was that we had produce, but we had no market," she said.[32] She and her fellow farmers now benefit from connections to one another and to other customers, she said. Njoroge, whose education was limited at first because her brothers' training came first, eventually became a nurse. "In the old days, the girl had nowhere. It was not necessary to educate that girl. The boy was preferred. But today they are equal, even in job opportunity," she said. Now retired and returned to farming, she has extra money she uses to visit her son, who is a minister. In Ohio.

In Nakhon Sawan province, in the heart of Thailand's rice bowl that feeds hundreds of millions around the world, Ronnachai Ruasrichan left nine years at a Taiwan factory making air-conditioning units for cars so he could return to the rice-growing he learned as a child. "I didn't want to live overseas as I got older," he said.[33] His paddies, on which he has learned to grow high-quality rice varieties, have yielded him enough income to buy additional land and an Isuzu pickup truck. He's wondering now how he can sustain his fortunes as grain prices rise and fall.

And in Soddo, Abebech Toga is showing her fellow farmers how to grow more crops, getting them beyond the age-old famine fears to using their potential to prevent it among others. All of them need a better market. But how to build it? The first clues are found on the floor—the trading floor, in Chicago.

CHAPTER 2

Chicago Makes a Market

The Chicago Board of Trade is a colorful place, with a colorful history.

Traders at the CBOT bring more than a century and a half of tradition to their jobs. The pits, where buyers and sellers match orders and haggle contracts, have been shaped like octagons since the 1800s, creating a corner for each contract that's bought and sold. Elaborate hand signals, called the "arb" for arbitrage, serve as shorthand for buyers and sellers who need to communicate orders quickly across the pits. Palms facing toward the body mean buying, as in bringing something toward you. Palms outward means sell—you're pushing the products away. To show numbers one through five, you hold your fingers straight up; six through nine, hand sideways. Zero is a clenched fist. The pits themselves are terraced to improve sight lines, and have been that way since the Gilded Age. Red, green, and yellow contract prices for each agricultural commodity offered by the Chicago Mercantile Exchange (CME), the CBOT's owner, flash above the traders, along with listings of other company products, equities indexes, and large-screen TV monitors scrolling headlines from financial news networks and The Weather Channel. The adjacent financial trading floor, where exchange rates, stock-index values, and other financial instruments are bought and sold, are the Board's bread-and-butter volume generators. Still, agriculture futures built the Chicago Board of Trade and are what's most commonly associated with the exchange.

The sales slips and newspapers cast onto the floor add a ticker-tape-festive feel to the chaos; the shouting and jockeying for position looks like dozens of pickup basketball games in which everyone's calling for the ball, but no one has it. Only the players know whether they're winning or losing. And most of the action takes place in the first and final five minutes of the game.

But at least they all have uniforms. At the Board of Trade, a cow-print jacket is acceptable work wear.

Each company registered with the Board can offer its own distinct jacket, letting potential customers know on-sight who they're dealing with—even though, in reality, many of these traders have been working the floor for decades and know every nervous tic, fear, and weakness of fellow traders, who serve as trusted ally one moment and fierce competitor the next. Competition to be seen ups the color quota further. Greg O'Leary is of average height and build, and wouldn't necessarily stand out in a crowd; his orange-and-green jacket, based on the Irish flag, is a signature calling card in the pit. One of his traders has one-upped his boss today by wearing an "England Out of Ireland" button on his lapel.[1] I have arrived in a suit. I've written about the Board of Trade for years, but this is my first visit to the floor, and I'm overdressed. The minders the CME have sent—first to get me onto the floor smoothly, then to find out exactly who I'm talking to and why—tell me to be aware that my odd appearance may distract the traders. No one pays any attention to me— including the minders, who after a few minutes have other things to do than lead around the square in the suit at a financial-world Grateful Dead show. I pick up a few receipts to decipher the language written on them, one man gathering what another has spilled.

The Chicago Board of Trade is only one of dozens of commodities exchanges worldwide, and each one on the map has its legends. Chicago's influence, history, and volume make it the most important food-trading center on Earth. The CBOT's 605-foot Holabird & Root Art Deco building on West Jackson Street, built in 1930, was the city's tallest for its first 35 years. It's capped by a three-story statue of Ceres, Goddess of Agriculture, who holds a sheaf of wheat in her left hand and a bag of corn in her right. Ceres' home today sets global benchmarks for corn, wheat, soybeans, oats, and rice, affecting prices quoted to farmers, importers, and exporters from Toledo to Tunisia. The Board of Trade is a treasure to the local businesses that founded and nurtured it, though it's no longer independent since the Chicago Mercantile Exchange bought it. The nearby CME, a shareholder-owned, for-profit corporation originally called the Chicago Butter and Egg Board when it started in 1898, offers contracts in cattle, hogs, and dairy and forest products. The longtime Board rival surpassed it in volume in 2001, aided by the rise of its Eurodollar contract. The CME took over in 2007. With its other acquisition—the New York Mercantile Exchange, a trading venue for cocoa, coffee, cotton, sugar, and, most importantly for food prices, oil—the combined, Chicago-based CME Group is the world's largest platform for futures and options contracts.

Even when its trading floors are closed, companies, investors, and speculators can buy and sell the group's products online, worldwide, around the clock. Still, its early development was nothing more than an attempt to link farmers in a developing nation—the United States of America—to markets. As it improvised its path to greatness, it gave lessons about prices, supply, and demand that shape the world food market today.

■ ■ ■

The nineteenth-century U.S. dash westward quickly created a problem that threatened the nation's growth. The settlers filling the rich farmland near the Great Lakes, extending into the Midwest and stretching toward the tall-grass prairies of the Plains, needed a central place to sell their grain and ways to get it there. Water passages helped farmers get their crops to eastern population centers. The Mississippi River nourished settlements from Minnesota to Louisiana. The Erie Canal made Buffalo, New York, an early hub for inland goods to get to the East Coast. But as populations kept pushing west and cities kept growing on the eastern seaboard, much of the country needed a faster, less expensive option for getting grain than the Gulf of Mexico, the destination for goods grown along the Mississippi River, or the northern route to Buffalo. Left unsettled, the problem of how to exploit the burgeoning Midwest breadbasket would leave the vast middle of the United States sparsely settled and scarcely developed, filled with small farmers who would grow enough to feed themselves and not much else.

U.S. history is populated with boomtowns and bust cycles of cities built with high hopes that faded. Some gently evolved into small towns with tiny high schools and impressive local-heritage festivals. Others grew into regional hubs, eventually developing interstate highway nodes, local industries, and pro sports teams. A few succeeded spectacularly, enriching the nation, the city's citizens, and its boosters—to their great relief, since most of them were heavily invested in local real estate. In many cases the successes were aided greatly by a new invention, the railroad, that could connect cities to water and with one another, cutting transportation time so dramatically that not only could staple grains like wheat, corn, and oats get to market quickly, even cattle and dairy products shipped from one region could help feed another, with proper refrigeration.

Chicago capitalized.

The site on Lake Michigan had been eyed by explorers since the 1600s as a potential link between the Great Lakes and Mississippi River water systems. The village of Chicago, organized with fewer than 100 people in 1833, showed grand ambitions from the get-go. By 1840 it had more than 4,000 people. As it grew, sacks of grain started piling up for shipment as farmers led wagons along wooden-plank roads to the port. By decade's end it was clear that Chicago was becoming the essential distributor for Midwest grain, and Midwest grain was necessary to feed America.

Modern Chicago was born in 1848. While socialist revolutions raged from Brazil to Hungary, Marx and Engels were writing *The Communist Manifesto*, women were gathering in New York to demand the right to vote, Mexican War hero Zachary Taylor was being elected president, and an anti-war Illinois politician named Abraham Lincoln was ending his only congressional term in failure, the City on the Lake was opening for business, linked by rail and water. The Illinois and Michigan Canal running between Chicago and La Salle–Peru on the Illinois River that connected the Great Lakes to the Mississippi River and the Gulf of Mexico, and the Galena & Chicago Union Railroad, the city's first rail line, both were completed that year. And on April 3, in a meeting above a flour store at 105 South Water Street, 83 businessmen determined to make their city the hub of a trading network from New Orleans to New York held the organizational meeting of the Chicago Board of Trade.[2]

Presumably, none of them were communists.

The Board of Trade organized the business community of a now 20,000-strong city, which was already a commodities center, complete with enterprising meatpackers, warehousers, and shippers setting up shop convenient to roads, rails, and Lake Michigan. It also, in large part, was set up to decide how to handle the grain onslaught arriving in Chicago for export, as rail and waterways made the city a logical shipping point.

The Board was set up to be private and self-regulating while it stayed closely tied to the city. Chicago surpassed New Orleans as the top crop shipper to the East Coast in 1854, and the 1 railroad line had multiplied to 30 by 1860. Water and rail traffic grew, and the boosters of Chicago and the Board found themselves at the center of a developing new world. But solutions to old problems create new ones. Illinois, Indiana, and Wisconsin farmers were becoming the world's most productive, and their ranks were swelling with settlers from Minnesota, Iowa, and points west and south, shipping more of their grain to Chicago. Storage warehouses sprang up all along the transportation routes, allowing farmers to hold off on selling until they got a better price. Yet harvests are unreliable, crops that sit in warehouses for too long deteriorate, and business transactions involving faraway customers required trust that was hard to establish in short times over long distances. Food-buyers in New York or Philadelphia, or even a miller in Chicago or Buffalo, couldn't know for sure that a bushel of corn from Iowa wasn't two-thirds corn and one-third insects. They couldn't ensure they could get flour when they needed it. And if all the farmers decided they didn't like the price they were being offered and wanted to keep their products off the market, there was little that buyers could do. Unreliable crop quality and wild price fluctuations threatened to throw Chicago's markets into chaos, just as city leaders were realizing their dream.

Ever-intrepid Chicago had an answer.

The Board of Trade half-planned, half-stumbled its way into becoming the world's first modern commodities market, the one after which all other exchanges in physical goods have patterned themselves. The key was to create a market that fit everyone's needs. Chicago warehouses were haphazardly empty or full depending on whether or not farmers wanted to keep their crops there or upriver. They also were prone to wild quality variations, as some farmers carefully dried their grains and removed impurities while others chose to test the market price for wheat-and-insect blends. The Board began to create grading standards for wheat, sharing those grades with buyers who wanted reassurance of quality. Impartial, third-party grading standards were attractive to companies that weren't nearby and couldn't physically inspect the grain they were buying. The Board started attaching grades to its warehouse receipts, a document that gives proof of ownership of a commodity stored somewhere for safekeeping, in 1857. The bins quickly filled with high-quality grain that pleased the millers, and mothers, of the expanding East Coast population.

Yet another new invention, the telegraph, let buyers and sellers negotiate prices and delivery dates for those receipts while the grain was in storage and without having to ever examine the commodity itself. A food company in New York could buy corn from Iowa while Chicago made sure grasshoppers weren't included in the sale. Canals and railroads took bulk goods where they needed to be, quickly. The exchange made crop pricing more efficient and transparent by creating a standard set of trading practices that could be applied across markets, said David Lehman, who heads research and product development for the CME Group. Other parts of the world with rich natural resources—Ukraine most immediately springs to mind, he said—didn't have the same fortunate combination of well-developed market institutions supporting its agriculture that the United States has. That's a big part of why the United States became the world's biggest crop shipper while rivals flailed, he said.

"There are other areas of the world that have the kind of natural resources that we do," he said. "They don't have quite the transportation infrastructure. They certainly don't have the legal and financial infrastructure that we have in the U.S. But I think because of having these transparent, well-functioning, really well-regulated markets in the U.S., that led to the ability to develop as a supplier to the world."

The Board's health has ebbed and flowed with the U.S. farm economy. Contracts evolve over time. The Board of Trade introduced ethanol futures in 2005, anticipating biofuels demand, while in July 2011 the CME retired the venerable pork-belly futures that dated to 1961, since no one had bought or sold one since February. Charles Carey was chairman of the Chicago Board of Trade when it merged with the CME. He started trading in Chicago on the smaller, less-expensive-to-join MidAmerica Commodity Exchange in 1976, and joined the CBOT in 1978. He's a third-generation commodities trader, and his family's fortune rose and fell with the exchange. In 1929, right before the Great Depression, a seat on the Board of Trade could cost more than $60,000, he said. In World War II, when the government set commodity prices, membership could be had for $25. He calls the 1970s the "Golden Years," when the exchange aggressively started to expand its products beyond crops, linking more closely with other bourses on other continents and beginning to resemble today's 24/7 market. Today's CME is in no danger of being eclipsed in importance anytime soon, even as rivals emerge in Asia and Europe, he said. Companies, investors, and producers of raw goods to manage risk will only want more reliability as the world grows more complex, he said.

"A contract is a contract, and we haven't had a default since 1848," he said. "We are the reflecting pool. We are the transparency that allows people to make decisions, and we actually lower the cost of production and of merchandising grain because people transfer their risk to this commodity exchange.

"The whole world sees our prices, and the whole world reacts to our prices."

■ ■ ■

And when people saw the success, they wanted in.

The new trading system gave farmers a guaranteed price for their crops, helping them finance their fields and not be forced to sell at harvest, when annual gluts drive down prices. Food buyers liked the exchange because it smoothed out their cash flow and kept farmers from hoarding when food was scarce. The market also created opportunities for people who wanted to make money off crops without growing or selling food. Someone who didn't ever want to accept delivery of actual grain, using receipts, could still benefit from the burgeoning markets. A speculator could buy food from Minnesota, hold onto that receipt while it sat in a Chicago warehouse, and then sell it to someone in New York later at an advantageous price.

Speculators are useful because they bring extra money to the market, smoothing out situations when buyers and sellers can't agree on a price—*liquidity* is the financial term. Producers and users of farm goods have traditionally eyed them with suspicion as interloping middlemen who could manipulate markets for their own benefit and distort prices if they aren't properly watched. In the worst case, a speculator with enough resources and not enough scruples could try to "corner" the market, buying up the complete supply of a crop, then holding onto it and dictating the price of bread. The tension between the farmer, the merchant, and speculators comes to a head whenever price gyrations throw food prices into turmoil.

The Civil War put the first big strain on the new way of crop trading. Traders did their part to win the war for the North, first by recruiting a Board of Trade Battery that saw action in Chickamauga and Atlanta and more importantly by helping ensure that Union troops were better fed, with Chicago-traded grain, than their Confederate counterparts. Contract terms evolved as the war continued, fitting the needs of buyers and sellers who wanted protection from prices, driven as much by setbacks and successes on the battlefield as by showers and shortages of rain. Sellers wanted to lock in a good price to manage their harvests. Buyers wanted to make sure they'd be able to get grain 10 days, one month, two months into the future. The Board regularized the contracts as demand grew, formally offering its first "futures" in 1865. Futures contracts weren't unknown in human history—the Dojima Rice Exchange in Osaka, Japan, had futures in the eighteenth century. The system collapsed after volatile prices, food riots, starvation, panic among samurai who were paid in rice, attempted price manipulation by speculators, and frequent intervention by the government's shogun left Japanese rice trading in tatters.[3]

Safely shielded from samurai and shoguns, Chicago policed its markets. Farmers and customers could better manage their risks, and speculators could profit, sometimes to the chagrin of other traders. Some speculators became wealthy. Others went broke. Still others did both, depending on the week.

Benjamin "Old Hutch" Hutchinson, a failed shoemaker from Massachusetts, bought a Board of Trade membership for $5 in 1857 and held a fortune topping $20 million by the 1880s. He profited spectacularly in Civil War wheat and profited again by squeezing higher prices out of his fellow traders in an 1888 buying binge. Ira Munn, a one-time Chicago

Chamber of Commerce president and warehouse tycoon, faked his grain-storage capacity and threw into question the integrity of warehouse receipts in 1872. He fled the city to escape arrest, resurfaced in Denver, started the first sawmill in the mining town of Ouray, Colorado, and died as one of its leading citizens. James Patten, called "The Man Who Raised the Price of Bread" by *Harper's Weekly* in 1909, was indicted by a federal grand jury for violations of the Sherman Anti-Trust Act and pleaded guilty of conspiring to buy the previous year's U.S. cotton crop and withhold it from markets. After his plea bargain and a wrist-slap fine, he traveled the world and donated millions to Northwestern University and the fight against tuberculosis, the disease that had killed his father.

The money sloshing through Chicago, and its potential impact on farmer profits and consumer food prices, inevitably drew the attention of government officials. Federal authorities became more active in monitoring and limiting activity deemed to harm market efficiency and the public's interest in reasonable prices for physical goods as Chicago gained wealth. Ira Munn inadvertently furthered the public interest—likely not his original goal—via a Supreme Court case that established a government role in regulating business when its activities intersect with the public interest; the *Munn* case became bedrock U.S. business regulation. Other bouts of volatility and public outcry over alleged manipulation prompted passage of landmark federal laws overseeing commodities trading—the Grain Futures Act of 1922, the Commodities Exchange Act of 1936, and the amendment to that act that created the Commodity Futures Trading Commission, today's commodities regulator, in 1974.

Chicago prospered through it all, surviving fire, Depression and war as a great world city founded and strengthened by trade. The Board of Trade, and later the Merc, helped make the United States the biggest exporter of corn, wheat, and soybeans on the planet. It indirectly fostered rural prosperity that set the stage for the emergence of the industrial Midwest early in the twentieth century, creating the wealth that fueled urban development. And with the United States likely to remain the top shipper of major world foodstuffs for the foreseeable future, the exchange—and its role in the daily struggle to set market prices that determine who gets to eat what—will remain crucial to global food prices for decades.

■ ■ ■

What's it worth? For food, ask Chicago. The question is answered there more than anyplace else.

But the more things stay the same, the more things change.

Crop trading, dominated for more than a century by grain merchants like Cargill Inc. or Archer Daniels Midland Co., and leavened by Chicago-based speculators like O'Leary, has been transformed since the 1990s by two trends that in some ways have reinforced one another: around-the-clock, around-the-globe electronic trading and the rise of a new kind of speculator, the worldwide financial institution with trading desks that reach far beyond commodities, able to shift money from crops to currencies to metals to bonds to energy to stocks and back with the click of a mouse. The conduit broadens speculation beyond Old Hutch and adds a new source of funding that dwarfs anything seen before on global crop markets: Us.

Physical goods have an obvious appeal to investors: Unlike a company that could go out of business or a country that could default on its debt, corn will always have some sort of value as something people can eat to stay alive. And every day more children are born who will need corn or some other crop to eat, unlike an Internet startup the world decides it doesn't need at all. Ever-higher demand attracts investors, especially when supplies fluctuate from year to year and supply increases aren't certain to keep pace with global needs.

For decades, anyone who wanted to enter the potentially fortune-making world of commodities faced potentially high obstacles to entering the market.

First, proximity. A person didn't have to be in the wheat pit to trade wheat in Chicago, but it was a lot easier and faster on the floor. That tilted market participation toward local trading experts and outside companies that had the resources to maintain trading arms of their global operations.

Another problem was physical ownership. Unlike shares of company stock, which someone can buy and hold onto forever without taking any action until it's sold, a futures contract for a bushel of corn in Chicago, or a barrel of oil traded in New York, or any other commodity, comes with an expiration date, after which the product has to be paid for and stored somewhere. If someone decides to buy 5,000 bushels of wheat—the standard size of a contract—for March 2012 delivery, a buyer either needs to get rid of that contract before March or find someplace to put 150 tons of grain. Contracts aren't small, or cheap. At $6 a bushel, a single contract costs $30,000, more than most small investors would want to put into a single product that could lose half its value in weeks.

The final problem was that commodities markets, as regulated by the federal government, were always meant primarily to help producers and buyers find the proper market price for the products that sustained their livelihoods rather than to make a fortune for speculators. Middlemen were tolerated as long as the trading was honest and didn't distort the primary function of finding an appropriate price for the food people eat, but commodities trading was explicitly not for everyone. The Commodity Futures Trading Commission (CFTC), set up to police markets, limited speculation. "The capacity of any contract market to absorb the establishment and liquidation of large speculative positions . . . is not unlimited," the agency wrote in 1981.[4] Rules dating to 1936 limited the number of contracts speculators could buy, restricting the role investment banks, pension plans, and other potentially big investors could play in crop markets. U.S. wheat fields were fenced off from global investment flows, deemed too different and too central to people's everyday lives to be part of the booms and busts to which other, easier-to-enter markets were prone, and which unregulated crop markets themselves frequently had been.

Speculation limits didn't eliminate wild price swings in food markets. World events, weather, and economic disruptions gave commodities plenty of reasons to go up and down. The two World Wars saw dramatic spikes in crop and energy prices; adjusted for inflation, corn reached what today would be $25 a bushel in the first war and $20 a bushel in the second, the former figure being three times higher than anything touched in the twenty-first century. In the first half of the 1970s, when the U.S. currency started floating freely, the Soviet Union made massive grain purchases, and the OPEC oil embargo ended price stability in energy, prices spiked at levels that wouldn't be touched again for more than three decades. In the last two decades of the twentieth century, when stock markets started a quarter-century climb, crops stagnated. The Dow Jones Industrial Average tripled in the 1980s; a bushel of corn lost exactly 49.5 cents for the decade, about one-fifth of its value. (See Figure 2.1.) U.S. production kept up with global trends of supply and demand, making more production, not higher prices, the key to farmer income. That's in keeping with long-term agricultural economics. Food tends to become less expensive to produce over time, as better yields

FIGURE 2.1   U.S. Corn, Wheat, and Soy (Prices in Cents)

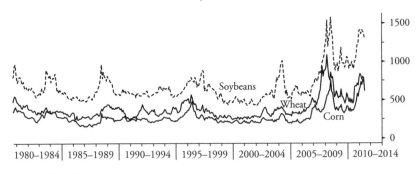

Source: Bloomberg.

and land-management lowers per-unit costs. The trend has allowed people in developed-world countries to spend less and less of their income on food. It doesn't make crops a particularly exciting area for investment.

That didn't mean commodities couldn't hold appeal for an investor. Stock-market prices didn't always go up, and when they didn't—usually when the economy struggled—commodities counterbalanced them by increasing in value as people sought the safety of investing in physical goods. In 1973 and 1974, when crop and oil prices were setting records, the Dow lost 40 percent of its value. Population growth added to the allure of crop investments. Every day the world has more people. More people need more food. More energy. More cotton fiber for clothes. More coffee to fuel the workday.

Commodities, in theory, can counter the ill effects of inflation on a portfolio. Stocks often suffer as prices rise, while physical goods may be better at keeping up with sudden increases. Often, they're the very reason why prices are going up. Research early in the 2000s found that commodities, including food, energy, and metals, offered favorable returns compared with stocks, bonds, and inflation. The concept became popular among commodities traders—and commodities-product marketers—to show why raw materials should be treated as a distinct asset class, an effective tool for financial management.[5]

Chicago crop contracts, so effective for managing risk, seemed to have potential as a long-term investment for all rather than as a short-term way for farmers to hedge against bad weather or for bakeries to make sure they have flour, corn, sugar, and soybeans. Buying and selling crops, and energy and metals for that matter, could do a lot more than feed people: It could help people save for their retirements, survive economic turmoil, and create greater wealth for all. Even a shopper paying more for bread would at least benefit from higher prices on the investment side, even if the consumer's pocketbook got hit when prices rose. Positive returns over the years would be practically guaranteed as demand increased. Big banks could provide the money, and electronic trading of futures anywhere, anyplace, anytime could provide the scale.

■ ■ ■

The pit had served Chicago, and Chicago had served the world. But the market wasn't yet truly available to everyone. That wasn't Greg O'Leary's role. It would be, for Goldman Sachs.

CHAPTER 3

Elephants in the Kiddie Pool

Various new financial products aided the 1980s stock boom, one being a new type of unregulated contract called a swap. Negotiated privately between two parties—called the over-the-counter market to differentiate from contracts cleared by an exchange—swaps offered financial mirrors of the contracts traded on the Chicago Board of Trade or other bourses. A key difference was that these contracts were unregulated, giving institutional investors and pensions a way to invest in raw materials without hitting the U.S. Commodity Futures Trading Commission's (CFTC's) limits.

The principle behind a swap is similar to the decision a homeowner makes when choosing an adjustable-rate mortgage or fixed-rate one. In a swap, if you had a mortgage you didn't want, you could exchange it with someone who has a mortgage you like better and who in turn wants yours. The middleman who brought you together takes a fee, everyone is happy, and markets are organized more efficiently. Swaps, like futures, are derivative products—called that because their value is derived from the price of an underlying entity rather than from the item itself. The first swap was engineered in 1981; by 2010, the notional value of all over-the-counter derivatives was valued at more than $600 trillion.[1] They've become essential for energy and food companies trying to manage difficult-to-predict price changes. Critics say the unregulated swaps markets have become so large that they can roil the regulated futures markets with which they interact, as one realm of trading is used to manage risk in the other. Three decades and trillions of dollars later, the tail is wagging the dog, they say.

The most common swaps are exchanges of interest rates, but they're also used for currencies, stocks, and other financial instruments. Most bets are mundane financial transactions, while some have gone massively wrong. Credit default swaps, insurance-policy-like agreements in which buyers receive a payout if a company goes bankrupt, cost taxpayers $180 billion in 2008, when the decisions of American International Group and others threatened at one point to take down the entire global financial system.

Swaps in commodities blurred the line between regulated and unregulated markets. The CFTC had long policed futures traded on a commodities exchange for manipulation, disruption, and excessive speculation. The new products didn't share that scrutiny. Commodities swaps brought new players into raw materials, as companies used them to lock in fixed oil prices and offer customers a different route to invest in physical goods. Swaps were a new way to manage risk and a new way for financial firms to profit. They created problems for regulators accustomed to clearly marked boundaries between commodity trades and other financial transactions.

■ ■ ■

Commodities swaps involved CFTC-regulated commodities, but swaps deals weren't taking place on the exchanges the CFTC regulated. They were taking place over-the-counter, as private, specially tailored deals that weren't standardized, publicized, or policed in the way that had kept the Chicago Board of Trade from becoming the Dojima Rice Exchange. Swaps activity potentially could spill over into regulated markets as swaps users bought actual commodity futures to manage their risk in the over-the-counter market. That opened the possibility that manipulation, or simply too much speculation, could push up food and energy prices for reasons having little to do with supply and demand for the actual goods. Free-market acolytes in Congress and the Reagan and George H. W. Bush administrations, including Bush CFTC chairwoman Wendy Lee Gramm, argued to keep over-the-counter, off-the-exchange trading exempt from agency regulation, which, done improperly, could make it harder to develop new financial-management tools. Congress and regulators loosened guidelines on who could speculate in commodities and how much raw-materials buying they could do. And in 1991, Goldman Sachs had an idea that changed commodity trading forever.[2]

J. Aron & Co., Goldman's commodities trader, wanted to enter into a swap with a pension fund that hoped to add commodities to its portfolio. Raw goods were looking attractive at the moment. Inflation had risen more than 6 percent the previous year, and the economy was in the recession that, in 1992, would elect Bill Clinton president. The pension fund wanted to buy into commodities to manage its financial risk, which Congress had said it could do. Goldman was willing to do the deal, but as a speculator that didn't rely on producing or using physical goods for its business, J. Aron could only do so much before it bumped up against CFTC limits on positions—the number of contracts bet that a price will either go up or down—that could be held by a speculator. Position limits, put in place to prevent market corners and manipulation, date to the Commodities Exchange Act of 1936.

The pension fund didn't want to invest in a single commodity—corn, or wheat, or natural gas have too many individual quirks—but it did want to benefit from commodities as an asset class, buying into oil, natural gas, corn, wheat, and other goods. So, Goldman created an index that would track prices of a predetermined selection of commodities, allowing index-fund buyers a way to speculate in physical goods. That let the pension fund manage its risk, often backing that index by buying up the actual futures of the foods, fuels, and metals the index covered. To make sure futures holdings matched the investment, Goldman asked the CFTC for an exemption from speculative limits on crop futures under a loophole Congress had opened in the 1980s. Gramm's CFTC granted the request.

Investment banks could buy crop contracts, just like a wheat merchant. Food no longer made for just a balanced diet. It balanced portfolios too, opening the doors for millions of investors to have a personal stake in food and energy markets beyond their groceries and gas tanks.

Goldman's innovation didn't instantly change trading. Shifts in political winds posed a danger to any bank getting overly involved in commodities. Bush's CFTC could give an exemption, but someone else's could take it away. The stock market was about to begin nine straight years of gains. Corn, thanks to the productivity of U.S. farmers and stable world markets, couldn't compete with that.

The year 2000 was a turning point. The Commodity Futures Modernization Act, passed by Congress as Clinton was leaving office, largely exempted over-the-counter derivatives from regulation. George W. Bush's election as president ensured that the CFTC would favor deregulation. For free-market advocates, the creative power of modern markets would be unleashed—just as crops, energy, and metals were about to look better than ever as an investment.

A quarter-century of stock-market triumph was ending. The Dow Jones Industrial Average reached 11,750 on January 14, 2000, more than 12 times its value 20 years earlier. Corn that day closed at $2.19 a bushel—down exactly 70.25 cents from where it stood at the end of the 1970s. The new decade wouldn't be like the previous two. The dot-com bubble burst, starting a recession that began before the September 11, 2001, terror attacks and lingered beyond it. Stock markets bottomed out in 2002 after the Dow lost 39 percent of its value. Real estate was the next bubble. The housing boom took markets to new heights—then, as prices collapsed, to another plunge and an even deeper recession, this time a 54 percent drop in the Dow from October 2007 to March 2009.

Investors accustomed to scarcely interrupted stock-market gains needed something that could restore a semblance of balance to their financial lives. Low interest rates made parking money in a bank account unattractive. Real estate that was supposed to rise forever, didn't. But everyone needs to eat. Investors wanted a safe haven from a stock-market boom gone bust.

Corn was ready for its close-up.

■ ■ ■

Greg O'Leary sits upstairs in his office in the Chicago Board of Trade building beneath a row of monitors that graph price trends. This is where most of the work gets done. Unlike dozens of his colleagues who fled the business or were forced out of trading as computer algorithms, ever-more-sophisticated technical analyses, and lightning-fast, high-frequency "cheetah" traders supplanted the relationships built on the floor, O'Leary has successfully made the switch. Big money now flows into and out of markets in less than a blink. He's learned to adjust, but he's uneasy with what trading has become. "It may take a generation" to learn how to trade in the new environment, he said.[3]

Unburdened by regulations and with a motivation to move money elsewhere, index funds created by Goldman, DeutscheBank, Pacific Investment Management Co. (PIMCO), Prudential Bache Commodities, and others began pouring money into energy, metal, food, and fiber. Assets handled by money management firms, hedge funds, or other financial services companies started the decade at $6 billion in value. They jumped to $10 billion in 2001, fell back with the recession, then started to rocket once the economy recovered: more than $25 billion in 2003, $54 billion in 2004, $143 billion by 2006. (See Figure 3.1.) Big banks managed their own risks by investing in commodities and sometimes by becoming commodities owners themselves. Goldman created a global network of aluminum warehouses. Morgan Stanley started chartering more tanker ships than Chevron. JPMorgan Chase hired a supertanker to store heating oil off Malta.[4] Yet market access alone wouldn't push prices up or down without something that would push traders into doing so. A desire for wheat futures required an appetite for real

FIGURE 3.1   Commodity Assets under Management and Commodity Index Swap Investment

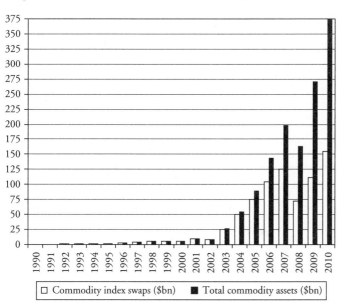

Source: Barclays Capital.

wheat—and just as the former became more readily available, the need for the latter rose as well. Food was gaining demand just as the ability to trade on that demand grew easier, pushed by events that expanded the world's appetite for consumption.

China entered the World Trade Organization (WTO) the year after commodities trading was deregulated, and brought a massive new market into global trade.

In the last half of the 1990s, just before joining the WTO, China's economy grew 49 percent to just over $1 trillion. By 2010 its economy was worth more than $5 trillion as Asia's most populous country vaulted past Japan to become the world's second-biggest economy. By 2011, one out of every four rows of U.S. soybeans was being shipped to China (see Figure 3.2); a third of the U.S. cotton crop was going there. Prices for both shattered records, and higher demand for those crops intensified competition for scarce American acres with corn, wheat and rice.

China's growth was repeated elsewhere. In the last half of the 2000s India rose from being the world's eighth-biggest to fourth-largest oil consumer, affecting commodity prices even as it remained largely self-sufficient in food

FIGURE 3.2   China's Soybean Production and Imports

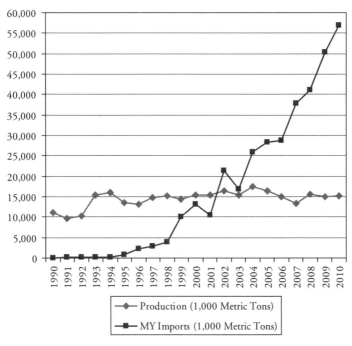

Source: USDA.

production. Russia, which at first contracted economically after the Soviet Union disintegrated, grew up to 8.5 percent a year for most of the decade. As a whole, the developing world outpaced rich-nation growth. In 2000, developing economies made up 40 percent of the world economy. In 2010, they accounted for nearly half.[5]

Rising prosperity also meant that food consumption was growing faster than population. From 2000 to 2010, world population grew 13 percent. Grain consumption increased 17 percent. Steadily increasing food demand alone couldn't explain why food prices would suddenly start rising mid-decade—or why they would suddenly plunge at the end of it. But needs were clearly going in only one direction, adding long-term, consistent pressure on nutrition costs.

Expensive energy uncoincidentally accompanied high food prices. Both are tied to higher demand, and rising transportation costs push the cost of food up as well. One 2011 study showed that Chinese soybean demand and corn used for ethanol were taking up about the same amount of U.S. acreage.

Together, the twin needs took up more than 46 million acres in 2010, nearly triple the need five years earlier and 29 percent of all land devoted to the two crops.[6] Up-and-down food costs increasingly mirrored energy swings. Farm commodities make up about 12 cents of a dollar spent for food in the United States, but transportation and energy take up another 10 cents.[7] Oil prices closely tracked the UN's World Food Price Index. The 2008 food peak roughly coincided with the 2008 oil peak, food prices after 2008 bottomed out two months after oil did, and when oil topped $100 a barrel again in 2011, food prices reached new records too (see Figure 3.3). Oil didn't only affect food consumption; it harmed production as well. Fertilizers that depend on natural gas for production became more expensive as energy rose, making it more expensive for farmers to invest in higher yields. Higher oil prices also made countries worry more about their dependence and desire alternatives. One of the most popular was ethanol.

Fuel made from food crops has been a potential renewable alternative to oil since the earliest days of the internal combustion engine. Henry Ford's Model T's could run on ethanol, which he called "the fuel of the future." Ethanol, however, never caught on because of the ready availability of cheap oil for gasoline. The first big political push for biofuels came in the 1970s, when Brazil and the United States both subsidized ethanol in response to that decade's oil shocks—in Brazil with sugar cane, in the United States with corn. Brazil became the early leader, requiring at least 20 percent ethanol content in its gasoline for most of the past 30 years. U.S. corn ethanol, less energy-efficient

FIGURE 3.3   Food and Oil

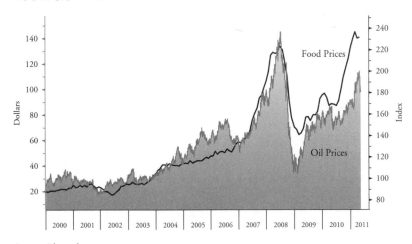

Source: Bloomberg.

than Brazilian sugar cane, developed more slowly. In 1980, corn-based production of ethanol, popularly known as gasahol, was at 175 million gallons,
a seemingly ineffective blind-alley response to the oil crisis. Farmers in the
U.S. Corn Belt didn't see it that way. In the 1980s, as U.S. farmers dealt with
a credit crunch that pushed the largest number of farms into foreclosure since
the Great Depression, ethanol provided a new market for growing U.S. grain
production and a way to keep prices from collapsing. Technical advances that
made production more efficient made it more competitive with oil. Tariffs and
tax incentives passed in Congress nurtured the industry.[8]

Ethanol production picked up dramatically as oil rose and government
support for biofuels increased. In 1990, U.S. ethanol production was 900
million gallons. By 2000, it was 1.63 billion gallons. Production doubled
again by 2004, then took off. The United States passed Brazil as the leading
producer in 2006, and plants produced 13.2 billion gallons of ethanol by
2010. (See Figure 3.4.) The federal production target is 15 billion gallons
by 2015. About two-fifths of the U.S. corn crop was devoted to gas tanks by
2011, driving up the price of everything from animal feed to other crops,
which now competed with highly profitable corn for land. U.S. corn prices
in 2009 were 21 percent higher than they would have been had ethanol been
kept at 2004 levels, and wheat and soybeans were 9 and 5 percent higher,
according to a 2011 study from Iowa State University. The main push for
biofuels, though, was no longer government subsidies; the thirst for oil meant
markets would support ethanol even if incentives went away.[9]

FIGURE 3.4   Historic U.S. Fuel Ethanol Production (Millions of Gallons)

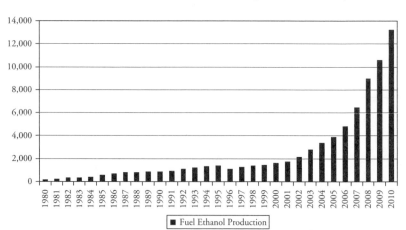

Source: The Renewable Fuels Association.

Other nations joined the biofuels bandwagon, although the United States and Brazil still accounted for nearly 90 percent of world output by 2009. The European Union, favoring biodiesel, produced a billion gallons from oilseeds. China and Thailand combined for another billion. Nearly all production competed with food for land and consumer use. And nearly all was subsidized—in the United States through government use mandates, tax credits, and tariffs, in Brazil through blend requirements and vehicle tax credits, and in the EU as a part of renewable-fuel targets meant to reduce greenhouse gas emissions.[10] That tightened food reserves already drawn down by policies and demand.[11]

■ ■ ■

Grain reserves are literally biblical. Joseph, he of the coat of many colors, got his career break as a commodities forecaster: By correctly interpreting the Pharaoh's dream of seven withered ears of grain that devoured seven fat ears as meaning that Egypt would have seven years of abundant crops followed by seven years of famine, he made Egypt the regional hub of grain trading when the lean years arrived. For his work, Joseph rose from slave to viceroy before age 30 and lived out his life as a wealthy man who never forgot his roots: When Moses ultimately took the Israelites out of Egypt, Joseph's bones came with them, per the grain trader's wishes. Joseph even engineered a rocky-but-successful reunion with the brothers who had earlier conspired to kill him—after they came to Egypt to buy his grain.[12]

Joseph, who also gets an entire chapter in the Koran, lived to be 110. The grain reserve concept survived him by centuries. Chinese dynasties maintained government supplies. Emperor Wu, a Han monarch in the second century BCE, used them to undersell private merchants and end speculation in grain markets. Today, China still maintains reserves well above world averages. Native Americans kept grain reserves in woven baskets within pits dug into soil. In the twentieth century, the European Common Agricultural Policy provided for "intervention stocks" to be released in years of poor harvest. East Asian nations have maintained an emergency reserve since the 1970s. Henry A. Wallace, President Franklin D. Roosevelt's agriculture secretary in the 1930s and later his vice president, called the idea that the government should maintain grain reserves to guard against supply shocks and smooth out price swings the "ever-normal granary," a reference to the Joseph story. From the Great Depression through the 1980s, the United States used surplus crops bought from farmers to maintain its own reserves, distributing some of it as emergency food aid to hunger-stricken countries.

Ever-normal was never cheap. Government grain reserves, like the Strategic Petroleum Reserve the U.S. government still maintains, are expensive to operate. Warehouses have to be climate-controlled and insect-free. Poorly managed reserves become wasted food—several African countries that started stockpiling after the 1970s food crisis abandoned them after they proved to be less effective in feeding people or stabilizing prices than they had envisioned. Releasing reserves becomes politically thorny, as governments have to decide when and where a supply intervention is justified. The impact of reserves on market prices—government manipulation of supply and demand—is unwelcome both to commodities traders and free-traders who would rather see a shortfall in one country met with someone else's surplus, which in the end should encourage bigger crops worldwide.

"There was a market overhang problem, a storage cost problem, and a competitiveness problem tied up to those higher inventories," said Keith Collins, the chief economist at the U.S. Department of Agriculture for 15 years until 2008, during which the United States largely dismantled its grain reserves. "It became pretty clear that if we were ever moving to a better marketing system in American agriculture we had to get away from those inventories."[13]

Tight inventories created some eye-popping stocks-to-use ratios by 2008. The ratio is a measure of scarcity that shows how much supply of a crop would be on hand if new supplies suddenly stopped coming. Traders watch it closely to decide whether the world has enough food to justify current prices. Early in 2011, corn stocks-to-use was seen at its lowest since 1974. In 2009, the United States at one point was forecast to have its lowest ratio for sugar since 1949. In 2008, wheat was its most scarce since 1947.

Lower inventories mean less room for error and more motivation to panic when something goes wrong. Poor information on what supplies actually are doesn't help. Nations such as China release less-than-detailed information on their grain inventories, which decreases the quality of data from organizations that try to release accurate estimates. That wasn't a big deal in the 1990s, when China was essentially living in its own food world and supplies were plentiful, according to Collins.

"I would literally exclude China from my analysis," Collins said. "Even if we were off 10 million or 20 million tons, it didn't really matter on world markets."

Now it does. In times of plenty, a few hundred thousand metric tons here or there doesn't worry markets. When inventories are tight, relying on informed guesses makes prices jump at the first sign a guess may be wrong.

■ ■ ■

Additional factors helped create the conditions for a commodities casino. A weaker dollar encouraged U.S. exports and higher relative prices for dollar-linked commodities. The first decade of the twenty-first century also was the hottest on record, encouraging more volatile weather such as the droughts and floods seen in Australia in 2008 and 2011 and in Brazil, Argentina, Russia, and Ukraine in 2010. Rising demand in emerging markets, competition for food acreage from energy, world inventories that had fallen by circumstance and by design, and bad weather all pointed to food prices that would face bumpy rides up and down, but more often up. The volatility could draw massive amounts of money to trading floors, adding more pressure and uncertainty.[14]

Diana Klemme, who helps grain elevators manage risk as the director of the grains division at Grain Service Corporation in Atlanta, spotted the trend early in the decade. Out of Purdue University in 1972, Klemme's first grain job was answering phones and taking dictation as a secretary for Continental Grain Co. The company later sold its grain marketing business to Cargill, long after Klemme had started rising in crop-industry ranks. Now in her sixties, she described Wall Street money attracted to tight food supplies—what she calls "the big money" as an elephant jumping into a backyard kiddie pool, inevitably changing the way food prices are set.

"It's not that the elephant is bad or that the kiddie pool is bad," she said. "It's just, when you put an elephant in it, it has to have an impact."[15]

Jim Zimmerman started at the Board of Trade in 1964. He left in 1965 to be a squad leader in Vietnam, came back from the war to trade again the next year, and never left. He's traded in every Chicago future that's been successful, as well as a few that failed—plywood futures, Ginnie Mae mortgages. He's seen attempted market corners fail, and he's seen out-of-whack markets correct themselves.

What he hadn't seen, until the past five years, were markets that seemed biased toward pushing prices up.

"With the index funds, you could drop the market a buck, they'll just buy more," he said. "Wheat simply shouldn't be what it costs today."[16]

Dale Durchholz is a senior market advisor for Agrivisor LLC, a crop-market analysis company in Bloomington, Illinois. The Illinois Farm Bureau started Agrivisor in 1973, when it offered a three-minute summary of commodity prices via recorded telephone message at the height of the 1970s price spike. Durchholz has been with the company since 1986. He's worked in commodities for more than 35 years.

Durchholz said he started following the dollars flowing into commodities from large investment banks—Goldman Sachs, DeutscheBank, Morgan

Stanley—around 2000. "In 2000 we had $6 billion in investment. Now we're at $340 billion. BILLION!"[17]

"We've got this massive flow of money that's been coming into the commodity market," he said. In the end, the fundamentals of supply and demand reassert themselves; in the short term, they accentuate the ups and downs of the market. "We have so much money in this market that basically positions itself on a trend-following system," he said. "For short periods of time they're getting further away from fundamental structure than people realize."

■ ■ ■

By mid-decade the trickle of money flowing into commodities funds was becoming a flood, tying financial portfolios ever closer to crop prices. Wheat futures rose seven out of eight years from 2000 to 2007. Corn and soybeans rose six years in the same period. But commodities weren't the hot investment—yet. Stocks peaked on October 11, 2007, and as the Federal Reserve furiously started cutting rates again to prop up the economy, investment money started to seek returns elsewhere.

The day the Dow set its record, corn cost $3.4375 a bushel.

The nerve center of America's Breadbasket for 150 years was starting to see changes. Good times had arrived for many traders, in part because larger volume gave them more money to work with and because the peculiarities of financialized commodities markets gave the people calling in the pits and flashing orders on screens new ways to make money.

On the floor of the Chicago Board of Trade, Scott Shellady, a manager at XFA Fixed Income, a Chicago-based derivatives trader, is walking the corn pit, wearing the distinct markings of a Holstein cow. His dad, also a pit trader, started the tradition as a way to remind Board of Trade visitors that "there still is a producer and an end-user" who are consuming the products, Shellady said.[18]

"It's not just funny money from Las Vegas trying to bet the market is going higher or lower today. There actually is somebody who buys the corn, and grows the corn, and somebody who eats it."

Shellady doesn't just trade corn anymore, as Chicago, Wall Street, London, Tokyo, and a globe of commodities markets become ever more linked. The connections have taught him to learn currencies, equities, treasury bonds, and their interaction with crop prices as dollars, yen, pounds, and euros seek the best return from any market in the world.

"I have a guy who's in the euro who also wants to do corn. So you don't say, 'I only do corn,' you say, 'I can do that for you sir,' with all the information at your fingertips.

"The fundamentals have a hard time keeping up" with billions of dollars hopping in and out of markets all over the globe, he said. The pain is greater, and the gain is greater," he said. "You have to be careful."

By 2006, commodity prices were going up, in some cases dramatically—wheat in Chicago rose 48 percent, the most in 15 years. World food prices went up 11 percent, the second-most since 1991. The market was bigger—and wealthier—than ever, and a boom in prices was about to put commodities at the center of world finance.

The world wasn't ready for what came next.

CHAPTER 4

A Recipe for Famine

Food distribution day doubles as a community gathering in Shala-Luka, the South Omo village to which Haylar Ayako has walked six miles to receive food. Farmers and pastoralist herders from outside the village start arriving hours before the 3 P.M. distribution begins. They dress in a mixture of foreign hand-me-downs and traditional garb. Ayako says tribal clothes are becoming more common again, as families have less money to buy the surplus T-shirts and skirts sent in bulk to Ethiopia, where, on this day in October 2008, more than 6 million people are at risk of starvation.

Older women gather around shade trees as some of the barefoot children, who are at varying levels of energy and health, play an impromptu soccer match with a weather-beaten ball. Leaning against trees or sitting cross-legged on the ground, men watch their children. Some have AK-47 rifles slung over their shoulders, which they carry to protect against animal predators or night-time thieves. Some children have swollen stomachs, a sign of malnutrition, and when I ask how old they are, I'm surprised by their answers; they're so much smaller than they should be. Many are tired from walking, and some simply sit and gaze. The air is hazy, and as I approach the warehouse, children press against me, holding out their hands and saying "birr, birr," the name of Ethiopia's currency.[1]

The food has been sitting in an otherwise empty shed since United Nations trucks brought it in the night before. Ayako stands near the shed, silently, arms folded, eyeing signs of the onslaught that will ensue when the door is unlocked. The bar is pulled, and villagers rush into the building of faded yellow paint and chipped concrete floors to pitch 50-kilogram bags of sorghum and peas, each marked with an American flag and the message "USAID From the American People" in English, over their shoulders. They throw them onto a pile outside the building. Once they're stacked, a knife is thrust into each bag as it is taken from the pile so the contents may be poured into the cotton, burlap, and polyethylene bags brought to be filled with rations. Coincidentally, it's October 16—World Food Day. None of the villagers know that.

Both women and men wait for food, which the United Nations delivers and Ethiopia's government insists must be distributed by its own officials. Some of the men and women are laughing as they compare bags and reconnect with acquaintances. Those who have been here before note that less food is available this time. The ration for each person this month has been cut to 10 kilograms of grains, 1 kilogram of pulses, and 300 grams of vegetable oil, a roughly one-third reduction. The UN World Food Programme (WFP) is caught in a supply shortfall by high food prices and has reduced the amount of food it can give South Omo. In Jinka, the hour-away town of 20,000 that's the nearest population center, food is sitting on grocery shelves, available for purchase for those who have the money. This is the problem. These are farmers caught in a drought that leaves them with no harvest or income. Their own food supplies are depleted, and they don't have any money for more.

The WFP aid is meant to provide the basis of a healthy diet for one month, until the next round of distribution begins. Over a 30-day period, the ration provides 1,315 calories per person per day, about one-third of what the average American consumes and about two-thirds of what the UN considers the minimum for a long-term healthy diet.

Ayako, who estimates his age to be in his late sixties, has outlived Ethiopia's life expectancy by more than a decade. He's one of the oldest recipients in line, and he's never before received food aid. He's also one of the area's wealthiest, most respected residents, and because of that he is pushed toward the front of the line, holding the coarse yellow sack that will contain the ration that will supplement the diet of his wives, his children, and his grandchildren before it becomes a part of his. Carefully holding the bag so the bottom lightly touches the ground, he receives a scoop of peas grown in North Dakota a year earlier and sold six months ago, before it began a long, complex journey on rail and ocean, through warehouses and bureaucracies to his village. He frowns, silent as the crowd crushes upon him, jostling toward the bags to get their own food.

■ ■ ■

The hunger that gripped Haylar Ayako's family had been increasing globally for more than a year as commodity prices kept nutrition out of reach for nearly one billion people. The food crisis that began in 2007 with wheat and rice crescendoed through 2008 with corn and soybeans, and was fueled throughout by oil, brought Ayako to a World Food Programme delivery point on the designated day for the world to remember hunger. It's described by traders, aid workers and government officials as the result of a "perfect storm"—a mix of supply shortages and increased demands connecting everything from drought in Australia to pork consumption in China to gas tanks in Houston to the commodities mania that took over Chicago.

The storm sent food prices to what were then record highs, prompted more than two dozen nations to restrict trade, and spurred riots worldwide.[2] It started with a drought, and wheat jumped first.

Low rainfall in Australia, Canada, Russia, and Ukraine, four of the world's top exporters, dropped global wheat supplies to levels not seen since the 1970s. U.S. extremes were even greater: In February 2008, at the height of the price spike, reserves in the world's biggest exporter were projected to reach their lowest since 1948. Short supplies meant panic buying. Countries and companies rushed in to make sure they could secure sufficient supplies to feed citizens and consumers. India upped its purchases in December 2007, then scrapped an order because prices were too high.[3] Pakistan in February asked Cargill, Glencore International, and the Canadian Wheat Board for extra supplies, bypassing normal buying procedures. "We have no time," the head of the state-run trading company said. "We've asked companies who won contracts last time if they could sell us more."[4] Pakistan had a bumper crop in 2007, but prices were reaching records as supplies were smuggled into neighboring Afghanistan. That same month, Bulgaria failed in its attempt to buy extra wheat from neighboring Ukraine, its biggest supplier, forcing it to go to U.S. and European Union sellers and driving up prices further.[5] The three major U.S. wheat exchanges, in Minneapolis, Kansas City, and Chicago, all began to see sharp run-ups in prices.

Chicago is the world's biggest wheat market, but it isn't the only one in the United States, and the variety it sells isn't the most important type for breadbaking or for global trade. The Minneapolis Grain Exchange, which started in 1881, has traded everything from oats, corn, and soybeans to sunflower seeds, rye, and shrimp, but its biggest, most important contract has always been for hard-red spring wheat, a high-gluten variety grown in the Dakotas and Minnesota used to make breads. It's the highest-quality wheat traded in the United States, and it's usually the most expensive. From its low of $4.64 a bushel on April 2, 2007, the most traded daily contract on the exchange rose to $19.81 a bushel on February 27, 2008—a 327 percent increase in less than 11 months. A futures contract traded less frequently topped $24.

The Kansas City Board of Trade, founded in 1856, has developed into the world's leading exchange for hard-red winter wheat, which is used for bread, rolls, and all-purpose flour. Hard-red winter is the most exported U.S. variety, and it also trades at a premium over Chicago. Its price in the same period rose 222 percent to $13.95.

In Chicago, where soft-red winter wheat is sold to makers of cookies and pastries, prices climbed during that time to $13.495 a bushel—up 228 percent.

In the Chicago wheat pit, contracts were smashing barriers that had been in place for years. Most commodities exchanges have price bands traders aren't allowed to exceed in a single day, a "limit" on price swings intended to forestall panic and keep volatility under control. When a market goes "limit up" or "limit down," something unusual is happening, and trading stops. After Chicago, Kansas City, and Minneapolis went limit up five sessions in a row, the three exchanges doubled their 30-cent-a-bushel ceiling to 60 cents. That lasted two weeks. In the space of a month, limit up went from 30 cents in a day to $1.35.[6]

The morning of February 27, 2008—the day wheat futures peaked in all three cities—Greg O'Leary took his spot in the Chicago wheat pit and lived through a day on the market that had no resemblance to any in his previous 28 years on the trading floor.

"The market is running half-dollars, quarters, dimes" as it climbed upward, he said. "I'm watching the news screen, and I was waiting to see the missile hit the White House. It was that crazy. I was expecting that kind of cataclysmic event."

Prices that day ranged from a low of $10.795 a bushel—which the previous year would have been a record—to $13.495, the all-time high. Within hours of the close, it became clear that what O'Leary was experiencing wasn't an attempted assassination. It was more of a page from the Board of Trade's history, a legacy of "Old Hutch." Evan Dooley, a then-40-year-old Memphis-based broker with MF Global Inc., a New York brokerage that trades commodities, equities, interest rates, fixed-income investments, and currencies, had snapped up commodities contracts on his personal account the previous night well beyond what he had the ability to cover in the event of a loss, according to charges later filed in Chicago to which Dooley pleaded not guilty. When the market moved against his bet, MF Global shut down his trading account and sold off his positions. The company's black eye drove its share price down 93 percent. The company fired Dooley, and as of 2011 was trying to collect insurance for its $141 million loss.[7]

In the end, only the farmers could calm the traders. U.S. spring planting began, and the Agriculture Department forecast that growers would respond to high prices by increasing wheat production 13 percent. In the meantime, "those weeks ended careers," O'Leary said. "You did not know what was going on."

The wheat supply shock directly fed into a rice panic.

The United States is the world's biggest wheat exporter, but it's not the biggest grower. It's number three, after China and India. Those nations try to be self-sufficient in the crop, with few imports or exports compared to what they grow. In 2007, India, since the mid-1990s a major exporter, was worried about its wheat stockpiles, which had been hit by droughts in two of the previous five years, and the political fallout from turning to imports. In October 2007 India moved to build up its wheat supplies, and keep consumer prices lower as lawmakers eyed re-election in 2008, by restricting rice shipments, keeping grain in the country for its own citizens, and cutting off buyers. Other countries followed India's lead, sending importers scrambling for supplies.[8] The Philippines, the world's biggest rice buyer, could only fill two-thirds of a request for grain in April. Every major Asian exporter except Thailand, the number-one shipper, either restricted flow outside its borders or simply withdrew from markets, their supplies sold out; Thailand was slow to sell government stockpiles, making markets nervous.[9] Rice trading in Chicago more than doubled from $10.71 per 100 pounds in August 2007 through April 24, 2008, when it peaked at a record $25.07.

Chicago rice futures don't set a genuine "world price" in the sense of other commodities because the product sees so little public trading and most rice is consumed near where it's grown. Only 5 to 7 percent of world rice ever crosses borders, and no open commodities market exists to encourage cross-border shipments. For rice, the main driver of higher prices was beggar-thy-neighbor policies by governments triggered by worries over shortages in other, more heavily traded foods. Export bans explained about 40 percent of the world rise in rice prices, according to a 2010 study.[10] As export restrictions sparked panic buying, prices kept rising until new harvests reassured buyers that supplies would improve. Japan, a country notoriously protective of rice, said it would ship government-owned inventories to the Philippines after first Indonesia, then the United States, encouraged it to do so.[11] In the end, Japan never shipped a grain. The signal that new supplies were available pricked the rice bubble, allowing panic to subside by midyear.

Corn came next.

Supply wasn't the problem with corn: U.S. farmers harvested a record amount of their biggest cash crop in 2007, and 2008 would be their second-biggest harvest up till then. Demand was the problem. Consumption of both corn and corn-fed livestock were rising along with developing-world incomes, and in the United States, more and more of the country's number-one grain was moving into gas tanks, thanks to government subsidies and mandates. Floods in Iowa, the biggest U.S. corn state, spooked markets further. On June 27, 2008, corn prices reached a then-record $7.9925 a bushel—more than doubling in less than a year.

Soybeans, grown in the same parts of the country as corn, peaked in price one week later. The U.S. soybean crop in 2007 was 16 percent smaller than it had been the year earlier, in part because farmers were moving acres to corn while exports climbed, mainly to China. When the price touched $16.3675 a bushel on July 3, it had more than doubled in the past 11 months.

Of all the commodities fueling the food-price jump, one of the most important was . . . fuel. From October 11, 2007 (the day the Dow peaked), to July 11, 2008, oil futures traded in New York, the price-setting exchange for that commodity, rose 81 percent, to a record $147.27 a barrel. U.S. consumers mainly focused their outrage at spending $4 a gallon to drive to the grocery store. But oil prices made their groceries more expensive too.

■ ■ ■

On Wall Street, the spike in commodities was working exactly as intended for investors. Portfolios damaged by falling stocks, declining home values, and a U.S. recession found a bright spot in raw materials, which kept attracting more money from hedge funds and the mom-and-pop investment vehicles created by deregulation. (See Figure 4.1.)

From the day the Dow Jones Industrials peaked to the day corn reached its record, the stock index fell 20 percent—a bear market for investors that commodity investments helped to balance, just as studies had predicted. The Federal Reserve cut its main interest rate six times from 4.75 percent to 2 percent, putting inflationary pressures on the economy—another good reason to invest in commodities that could serve as a safe haven. And while U.S. growth may have been sputtering, China, India, and other developing economies were still growing, keeping global demand high, even as richer nations throttled back their budgets. More people, more money, more food.

More profits.

Goldman Sachs, which had transformed commodities trading, beat the most optimistic estimate of any independent analyst on June 17, 2008, when its second-quarter profits dropped only 11 percent. Losses on investments on home mortgages were spreading to other debt, and inflation was expected

FIGURE 4.1 Dow versus Commodities

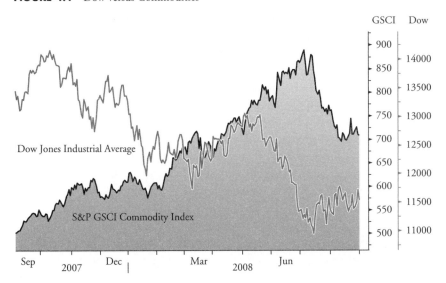

GSCI Dow

Dow Jones Industrial Average

S&P GSCI Commodity Index

900
850 — 14000
800 — 13500
750 — 13000
700 — 12500
650
600 — 12000
550 — 11500
500 — 11000

Sep 2007   Dec   Mar 2008   Jun

Source: Bloomberg data.

to increase. Higher returns in raw goods were shielding Goldman from the steeper losses suffered by peers such as Lehman Brothers.

"The magnitude of the beat is pretty astounding," Paul Sorrentino, a senior portfolio manager at Huntington Asset Advisors in Cincinnati, told Bloomberg Radio in an interview the day Goldman announced its results.[12] "For 20 years inflation was in the financial asset world, and so we had great bond returns in the 80s, great stock returns in the 90s," he said. "Now inflation is moved back into hard assets, it's gone out of real estate and it's into commodities."

Morgan Stanley, the other major commodities player on Wall Street, didn't fare as well, losing money on raw materials during the same time period by betting against rising energy prices. The company's traders "frankly got the timing wrong," Chief Financial Officer Colm Kelleher said.[13] Money was flowing into crops like never before. By April 15, 2008, index funds had almost doubled their agricultural-contract positions from the start of 2006.[14]

■ ■ ■

In Ethiopia that July, Haylar Ayako was burying his family. Dirt turns to dust in his hands as he squeezes the earth that stopped supplying enough food to feed his wives, his children, and his grandchildren.

His hollow face lined by decades of sun, he wears a safari vest he's owned for four years, the last time he had money to buy anything other than food. His dark green T-shirt hangs loosely over his frame, and he speaks animatedly as he runs dirt through his hands, leaving them with a yellowish tinge.

"We cannot plant," he says in his native tongue—most of the villagers don't speak Amharic, the language spoken in the capital of Addis Ababa. "Harvesting is not in the foreseeable future."

Family members are scattered about in his five fields, mending fences, tending animals and preparing the ground for the day when rain may come. The fields cover more than seven acres, qualifying him as a farmer of means in a country where more than four-fifths of all farms are smaller than five. He points at thatched grain bins, which offer little protection from the weather or insects. He says they have been empty this year, depleted of the corn, sorghum, and teff—a grain used to make *injera*, the spongy, yeast-risen flatbread central to Ethiopian meals—he raises on his land. The flat stretches of ground are broken up by trees and hills that rise into mountains and break up a cloudless horizon. They're cracking under the drought, leaving his animals to forage on weeds and wild grasses.

By summer, Ayako had been skipping meals and living on a dish made from coffee bean shells mixed with salt to preserve grain for his family. Some days, he chose which of his children and grandchildren would eat a meal. Since the spring of 2007, three of his adult children and seven grandchildren had died, all of illnesses complicated by a lack of nutrition.

Ayako had begun selling cattle, sheep, and goats to buy corn. Starting with hundreds of chickens, 40 goats, 30 sheep, and 15 head of cattle, he said, by the day he received food aid he was down to one chicken, one rooster, four goats, four sheep, and three head of cattle.

A goat wasn't buying much at the local market. A food-price shock was occurring in Ethiopia, which was importing grains at world prices to make up for poor crops at home. In Shala-Luka, a 100-kilogram bag of corn, enough to feed Ayako's family meals of porridge and thin pastes for a month, suddenly cost the equivalent of a cow and a goat; a few months earlier, the price had been one cow. Ethiopian consumer corn prices were 187 percent higher in April than a year earlier, according to the United Nations, putting normally safe urban diets at risk.[15] Inflation spiked when crops failed, forcing poor farmers to pay more for food just when they ran out of money. The numbers of hungry and malnourished people rose to 2.2 million people in April, up from the 860,000 estimated before the *belg* rainy season, the main period of moisture from March until June, began. In June it increased to 4.6 million. In October the government revised the number again, to 6.4 million.

Ayako said that long-established local trading networks are failing as people not secure in their ability to feed themselves hoard scarce supplies, driving food costs up further. And as trading ties frayed with the challenge of hunger, so did families.

■ ■ ■

One of the village's most competent farmers, the villagers said, is Banqe Geya, a woman in her mid-twenties. Banqe said she, her husband, and their four children for months have been living on cabbage and so-called "famine foods," which include plants and roots that can be toxic. With food aid she can add peas and sorghum to make a thin porridge. Her children, she said, will struggle to survive far into the next year without rain. Other farmers in the area have also devised temporary means to survive. Wado Isho, in his early thirties is one of the village's most educated farmers—he can speak, read, and write Amharic, a rare ability in his community. In good years, farmers can sell some of their extra grain for cash, perhaps another animal or fertilizer for their soil. A corn crop may be only four months away with proper moisture, he said. The previous month their field had received its first significant rain in three years, and additional water would ensure a harvest. None of the family's nine children have died during the drought—one had become sick from the famine foods but has survived. Until the next harvest, he said the family has enough livestock to sell that they can remain fed—selling their cattle will mean less wealth in the long-term.

He spoke more quietly. His wife, who is weeding a field as he talked, had been working extra hard, he said, because until two months earlier, she had been one of two wives. The other has left the farm for Jinka to seek work. He hasn't heard from her, and perhaps that is for the best, he said. The food she had been consuming was now available for others.

Etenesh Azmi also holds out Jinka as an option should crops fail. She has grown up near the town and has family in the city. Her four children, ages five to nine, are surviving, and for that she thanks God—as the only wife of a Christian husband, she had recently accepted Christ as her savior, she said. But with farm supplies depleted and with village food too expensive, the farmers could do little but wait—and pray—for rain.

Ayako said he hadn't seen such a failure in more than two decades.

"During other times of crisis in one village there would be plenty in the other, and we would go to the other village and barter for half a store amount of grain," Ayako said. "Now it's a whole village in crisis."

Ayako and his family had begun relying on *bedena,* a famine food, as a proper diet became impossible. "Because we are eating these grasses and cabbage, it makes you weak and kills you," Ayako said. "When you want cereals and what you get is meat, you cannot eat the meat. I have even tried to save some of the lives of the children by slaughtering the goat, but I am deeply so sad. They don't have the appetite to eat the meat" because of how malnutrition weakens the digestive system and steals the desire and ability to consume food.

Two more grandchildren, both of them infants, died in July 2008, when prices peaked.

■ ■ ■

Bizarre things were happening on grocery shelves, trading floors, and farms.

Asian governments weren't the only ones concerned about rice shortages. So were Costco and Walmart—the retailer's bargain-basement warehouse, Sam's Club—limited rice purchases, fearing consumer hoarding.[16]

In Long Island, New York, Richard Reinwald, owner of Reinwald's Bakery, a four-generation family business, laid off 5 of his 32 employees to offset more expensive flour and other rising ingredient prices. He didn't passively accept higher costs. The then-vice president of the Retail Bakers of America helped organize the March 2008 Band of Bakers March on Washington, possibly the first time bakery owners stormed the nation's capital as an organized force.

"A bag of bread flour that cost $17 in 2006 costs $52 today," Reinwald told the congressional Joint Economic Committee in a hearing that May. "Semolina flour was $21.00; today it is $72.50. Soy oil and eggs have doubled in the last year."

"In a matter of weeks, our cost of goods sold soared to an all-time high," he said. "Food prices, including baked goods, are reaching all-time highs at a time when the economy is already near its breaking point."[17]

In Grand Forks, North Dakota, the North Dakota State Mill and Elevator, the largest flour mill in the United States and the only one owned by a state government, lost $12 million in bad bets in a three-month period on the Minneapolis exchange in mid-2008, the largest quarterly loss since it was established amid a populist farmer uprising against speculators in 1922.[18] North Dakota taxpayers absorbed the loss.

In Auburn, Illinois, price swings were keeping markets from doing what they were originally meant to do—help producers manage their cash flows and risks. Growers were abandoning futures contracts as the chance of getting burned by them rose. Garry Niemeyer, a grain and oilseed farmer of

2,200 acres near Auburn, Illinois, said he was abandoning futures markets as a hedging option.

"It's the best of times for somebody speculating on grain prices, but it's not the best of times for farmers," he said. "The demand for futures exceeds the demand for cash grains."[19]

Farmers were less and less able to use Chicago prices as a way to manage their risk because cash prices for grain and the price of an expiring future—which for generations had "converged" near the expiration date as the future became the present—no longer lined up. Convergence is the tendency of a cash price—the price a farmer can get from selling a product immediately—to match a futures price the closer a sale is to the date a futures contract is set to expire. Intuitively, it makes sense—the closer the "future" gets to the "spot," the more likely the future is to resemble the present, and the less likely it is for anything ranging from storage costs to a hailstorm to disturb prices.

Something was throwing off convergence in Chicago. From 2000 through 2005, the average daily difference between the average cash and the futures price for Chicago wheat was about 25 cents. During the spike, the disparity topped $2; even after prices calmed somewhat, in the second half of 2008, the price of the nearest wheat futures contract on the Chicago exchange was $1.50 to $2.00 per bushel higher than the cash price.

"The fundamentals of supply and demand in the cash market alone cannot explain this unprecedented disparity in pricing between the futures and cash markets for the same commodity at the same time," wrote staffers for the Senate Permanent Subcommittee on Investigations in a report in 2009.[20] The ability of a future to lock in an accurate price for food producers and food users—the reason Chicago markets were created—was no longer working. U.S. farmers were being thrown back into the 1830s, growing crops without an effective means to secure their income stream.

Costs wound their way through the food chain as higher futures prices were passed on to consumers. Food inflation was rising its fastest since 1980. Eggs, dependent on corn-fed chickens, rose 14 percent in 2008. Baked goods were up 10 percent.[21] Members of Congress held hearings and looked for villains. Staff drafted bills. Presidential candidate Barack Obama said food prices were an immediate topic for his economic advisory group at its first meeting in July, calling costs a reason for falling consumer confidence.

"We have to give people some sense that they could absorb the rising costs in gas, food, and medical care," he said.[22]

Consumers stretched their budgets. Traders knew they were playing a high-risk game, but they hadn't thought they'd signed up for a casino. Everyone suffered the consequences, some more achingly than others.

Haylar Ayako says he doesn't discriminate among family members when he chooses which will eat each day. As the family elder, it's his task to keep as many of them alive as possible. It is only once he's dead that they divide his possessions and rule their own lives. His ties to land and family run generations, and when rain doesn't fall on his farm, the responsibilities toward his kinfolk fall on him.

He remembers previous famines they've survived. In the past, "some people survived eating the wastes of their cattle, some even the skins of their cattle," he says. "Sometimes we wonder if that time is going to repeat itself now."

He stands in his field, and his grain bins are empty, and markets half a world away mean nothing. His crops have failed, and he has failed his family—he believes.

"I am so sad," he says.

He stands motionless through a long, painful silence, punctuated only by the sounds of his family, working fallow fields and inseparable from the dust.

CHAPTER 5

The View from Rome

Josette Sheeran is in her office in Rome, where she really doesn't spend much time. It's late January in 2011, and she's about to leave for the World Economic Forum in Davos, where national leaders will express concern for the troubles arising in North Africa and the Middle East, including the role that food may have played in the crises. She attends G-20 and G-8 meetings, she speaks at humanitarian conferences, and she always carries a red cup, which she uses to remind people of those whose lives are ended, ruined, or stunted by hunger. She travels to villages, in Niger and Pakistan and El Salvador, investigating hunger's causes, monitoring successes in the fight against it, and figuring out how the agency she leads, the United Nations World Food Programme (WTF), can best solve one of the world's greatest (and, given its productivity, least necessary) problems: feeding those who don't have enough to eat.

In Sheeran's travels she encounters presidents, prime ministers, and despots; corporate plutocrats and long-suffering bureaucrats, technocrats, Republicans and Democrats; the planet's poorest farmers and some of its brightest scientists; the wide-ranging denizens of the nonprofit, government, business, and media worlds who make up the ever-moving caravan of humanitarian crisis response, its advice and its criticism; and its endless gauntlet of First and Third World hotels for conferences on global development and food security, where outrage and suffering is railed against in 90-minute panel segments, followed by coffee and pastries. It's a tangled and slow-moving world, but consensus must be built. With the right combination of moral suasion and hard-headed political and economic incentives, progress arrives, slowly. She gets high marks for her efforts.

Sheeran sits serenely in her spacious office, light streaming in through see-through white curtains. She wears a charcoal and white floral-print scarf

51

over a pantsuit and a charm necklace that could work at a hip import store or a meeting of the United Nations General Assembly. She pauses and waits with perfect posture as I struggle with the sound settings on my video camera. She expresses empathy: "Journalists are asked to do so much more these days," she says, "much more than when I was working as one."

Sheeran's career is a product of media, government, business, and nonprofits, and that may be why she's moved effectively in the hunger-fighting community during her five-year term at the WFP, set to end in 2012: As her old boss at the *Washington Times*, Arnaud de Borchgrave, says: "I don't think there's any job that she couldn't excel in."[1] She started in media in the 1970s, first in New York, then as a White House correspondent, and eventually as managing editor of the *Times*, founded as a conservative counterpart to the much larger *Washington Post*. Her business experience came after that, as managing director of Starpoint Solutions, a Wall Street technology firm that develops IT applications and places employees with Fortune 500 companies. She also served as president and CEO of Empower America, a Washington, DC, think tank. She worked in the U.S. government for six years before heading to the WFP. At the U.S. Trade Representative (USTR) office she handled trade negotiations in Asia and Africa and was a key force behind the African Growth and Opportunity Act, which was intended to aid sub-Saharan economies and improve ties between that region and the United States. After that she went to the State Department, serving as its undersecretary for Economic, Energy and Agricultural Affairs.

Her candidacy to become the executive director of the WFP came with controversy. For about 20 years, during her journalism career, Sheeran was associated with the Unification Church founded by the Reverend Sun Myung Moon, also founder of the *Washington Times*. She left the church at about the same time she left the newspaper, but the association was still made in news articles a decade later—the *London Times* referred to her as "a former Moonie" when writing about her expected appointment to head the WFP.[2] Nor was she the product of typical humanitarian channels. Empower America took a decidedly libertarian approach to public policy, featuring conservatives such as Reagan-era Education Secretary William Bennett, UN ambassador Jeane Kirkpatrick, another Reagan appointee, and Republican vice presidential candidate Jack Kemp, whom she lists as an intellectual inspiration, as directors. Empower America later merged with another free-market think tank, Citizens for a Sound Economy, into a new group called FreedomWorks, which, under its chairman, former U.S. House of Representatives Majority Leader Dick Armey, became a leading booster and organizer of the Tea Party movement that led the Republican takeover of the House in 2010. Her term at WFP ends in 2012, and she's hoping the agency's market-building orientation, a hallmark of her leadership, is sustained after that.

Former Senator and Ambassador George McGovern, the 1972 Democratic presidential candidate and antihunger legend who was the first head of the U.S. Food for Peace program in the 1960s and in the 1990s served as the U.S. ambassador to the UN WFP in Italy, joked at a State Department reception in 2010 about his great respect for Sheeran despite her status as a "registered Republican." McGovern got polite laughter for his remarks.[3] At the UN—an institution eyed warily by many American conservatives—the background she brings is unusual in global-aid circles.

"My goal here has been to help people help themselves and be able to feed themselves," she said.[4]

■ ■ ■

Since she took the job in April 2007, Sheeran's twin career interests—trade and markets—became twin headaches. The WFP, as the world's largest food-aid agency, is prominent in sub-Saharan Africa. UN-marked Land Rovers with satellite antennas may be the only vehicles encountered on a pitted gravel road for hours, and its workers have become very good at getting where few others can go. Food-aid distribution is often a logistical nightmare. It involves getting bulk goods as quickly as possible to places torn apart by war, in areas where road and telephone access are nearly nonexistent, and where governments tend toward obstruction and corruption. Donkeys, camels, and helicopters all play into the ad hoc solutions forged in crisis. The WFP has more than four decades of experience in dealing with this. Its role in delivering aid increased significantly as it took over the efforts of individual governments, depoliticizing a process shaped too often by Cold War rivalries. Most countries consider the WFP an honest broker, and its deliveries are usually respected, yet danger is part of the job. Five employees were killed in a 2009 attack on a WFP office in Islamabad, and employees have been targeted and killed in other world hot spots.

The agency handles its figurative and literal roadblocks by trying to anticipate where needs are likely to occur and by directing donations toward those spots. Its Famine Early Warning Systems Network, commonly called FEWSNET, uses weather forecasts, crop-production data, and public-policy analysis to predict where hunger is most likely to rise at least six months in advance. From that, they can start gathering food—often from the United States, which provides as much as half of the WFP's donations—and shipping it to wherever it's needed around the world. Food aid is procured in two ways. For decades, countries donated surplus commodities, often bought from farmers to support domestic prices, then sent to poor countries for assistance. The conveyor belt of food aid from rich nations fed the needy while doing little to encourage those regions to grow more of their own food—sometimes it actually discouraged that production, when cheap goods from overseas flooded local markets and made it impossible for an area's own farmers to compete. In the past decade, most countries have switched to donating cash to the WFP, which then buys the food closer to the source of hunger, trying to support local markets that then, in theory, will be encouraged to grow more food themselves and stop needing assistance. The United States still primarily donates surplus food.

The system has saved millions, perhaps tens of millions, of lives. Its greatest success may be that it's helped make famine in the popular sense of the word—widespread starvation—much less common. Hunger and malnutrition that stunt children's growth and increase the risk of disease are the challenges of today's famine-fighters, as are rapidly rising prices that wreck family food budgets and topple governments.

That's what Sheeran faced as she settled into her job. Her agency's efforts to meet global needs were being suddenly and unexpectedly threatened by price shocks that ruined people's ability to feed themselves. The global food market was failing, with tragic results, as high food prices and hunger fears fueled the new era's first unrest.

In Mexico, 75,000 protesters took to the streets to oppose rapid spikes in the price of tortillas, the staple food of the country's poorest families, one of the first signs that something was awry with the world food system. The so-called tortilla riots led to an agreement between the government and the tortilla industry to keep prices stable, followed by a decision to buy more U.S. corn.[5]

In China, the world's biggest grain producer, the government marked New Year's Day of 2008 by issuing export permits that curbed shipments of wheat, corn, and rice.[6]

In Cameroon, large-scale riots against high food and fuel prices that erupted over three days in late February 2008 killed at least 40 people, most around the port city of Douala. The government promised to lower import taxes to reduce prices.[7]

In Egypt, where rice exports had been banned in January, three people, including a boy who took a gunshot to the head, were killed in riots centered around the northern textile town of Mahalla El-Kobra in early April, evoking memories of riots in 1977 when the government had tried to lift subsidies on bread. President Hosni Mubarak called for a 30 percent wage increase for government workers and expanding subsidized bread and cooking oil for the poor. The protests subsided, and the threat to the Mubarak government ebbed.[8]

In India, protesters blocked trains and roads in Andhra Pradesh and West Bengal. The government ratcheted up interest rates to break the hold of inflation that had accelerated to its fastest pace in more than a decade.[9]

At least five people were killed in food riots in Haiti, one of more than 30 countries where such disturbances occurred in the first half of 2008. A Haitian presidential plan to slash rice prices failed to quell demonstrations; the government fell shortly thereafter.[10] Thousands rioted in Bangladesh, smashing vehicles, attacking factories and clashing with police while demanding higher wages to buy bread.[11] Eventually, at least 115 million additional people were chronically hungry since before prices began rising.[12]

Higher prices didn't only affect whether people who spent 70 or 80 percent of their meager incomes on groceries could afford to buy food. It affected whether food was available at all, especially in countries dependent on imports (see Table 5.1). At the height of the rice-price crisis, long-time customers in Africa could no longer buy Thai rice, said Kiattisak Kanlayasirivat, a director at the Bangkok office of Novel Commodities, which trades about $600 million of the grain each year.

"They were priced out of the market," he said. "Nations that were willing to pay a higher price drove the price higher to acquire their own supplies, and I couldn't sell to other nations."[13]

The WFP was running out of money, too.

"Two things happened," Sheeran said. "One, we lost half our food in six months because the prices doubled. So in six months, we had half as much food. And because the price had doubled for people, they needed twice as much food from us.

"We could not buy palm oil in Africa," she said. "There was a shortage of tradable food on the markets," leading to ration cuts and triage solutions as malnutrition spread.[14]

"I realized very quickly here that hunger is very connected to how markets function or don't function," she said.[15] "There was not a lot of understanding of how we could have what I called at the time a global humanitarian tsunami, affecting virtually every village at the same time."

FEWSNET predicted natural disasters, not human-produced ones. It had never needed to predict a sudden, worldwide explosion in crop prices in which everything became worse everywhere, all at once, without much

TABLE 5.1 Imports as Share of Food, 2008

Rank	Export Destination	Share
1	Djibouti	75.25%
2	Somalia	65.37%
3	Kiribati	59.79%
4	Afghanistan	49.51%
5	Guinea-Bissau	41.92%
6	Benin	39.90%
7	Sierra Leone	39.50%
8	Timor-Leste	38.27%
9	Haiti	34.78%
10	Gambia	34.50%
11	Comoros	30.45%
12	Senegal	27.47%
13	Mauritania	27.17%
14	Liberia	26.72%
15	Yemen	24.88%
16	Libya	24.77%
17	Sao Tome and Principe	24.49%
18	Cape Verde	23.52%
19	Tonga	23.31%
20	Saint Vincent & the Grenadines	22.69%

Source: United Nations Food and Agriculture Organization.

warning. The food-aid conveyor belt snapped. By April 2008 the WFP found itself needing $755 million more in funds—about one-third of its annual budget—than it had originally anticipated.

The agency scrambled to cover a widening disaster that was cutting into supplies. Sheeran searched for answers, traveling to grain markets in Ethiopia to figure out why prices were going berserk, everywhere, all at once.

"I talked to one of the grain marketers in his stall. He had donkeys, bags of food, no electricity. It was a very rudimentary market. And the teff and wheat were both twice as much as six months ago.

"I asked him how he set his prices. He said it's easy. I go on the Internet every morning, I go to the Chicago Board of Trade, I discount 10 percent because we're a poor nation, and I set the price. And I thought, wow. We are seeing a real connection between these markets, even if it doesn't look obvious as to why they'd be connected."

The world responded. Saudi Arabia kicked in $500 million in response to the WFP's call for help.[16] The U.S. Congress passed an extra $770 million for food assistance in June 2008, including a record amount of U.S. cash aid, and $590 million of that for emergency response. By the end of that year the WFP had served 102 million people in 78 countries, up from 86 million the previous year. Nearly 84 million of them were women and children. The amount of aid distributed rose to 3.9 million metric tons from 3.3 million in 2007. Contributions to the agency rose to just over $5 billion, compared to $2.7 billion the year before.[17]

Money wasn't the only outpouring in the wake of the food crisis. The world was galvanized around what was now being called food security in a way not seen in decades. The High-Level Conference on World Food Security in June 2008 led to a declaration signed by 181 nations saying that "the international community needs to take urgent and coordinated action to combat the negative impacts of soaring food prices on the world's most vulnerable countries and populations."[18] The first of several global meetings that generated larger commitments to helping the hungry called for more aid, more cooperation, and more attention to be brought to the world's poorest.

In July 2009, the Group of Eight nations representing the world's wealthiest economies pledged $20 billion in food-security assistance over three years, a number that grew to $22 billion.[19] The United States, announcing its Feed the Future initiative in April 2010 to encourage agricultural development, said it would pledge $3.5 billion in hopes of leveraging an additional $18.5 billion in commitments from other donors—a way to jump-start the $22 billion commitment.[20]

Countries committed money while others soul-searched. The World Bank, which had allowed its lending for farm projects to drop from an inflation-adjusted $7.7 billion in 1980 to $2 billion in 2004, pledged to recommit itself to agricultural development to boost the world's ability to feed itself.[21] The Bill and Melinda Gates Foundation, which had devoted little attention to agriculture before 2006, pledged to increase its spending on farming projects by 50 percent, to $240 million, for developing agriculture in poor nations.[22] Former president Bill Clinton, speaking to the UN on World Food Day 2008, said it was time for rich nations and global financial institutions to admit that they had neglected farming for too long.

"We need the World Bank, the IMF, all the big foundations, all the governments to admit that, for 30 years, we all blew it, including me when I was president," he said. "We were wrong to believe that food was like some other product in international trade, and we all have to go back to a more responsible and sustainable form of agriculture."[23]

It took a 42 percent gain in world food costs, dozens of riots in dozens of countries, and 115 million more hungry people, but finally, the world was paying attention. Yet by the fall of 2008, efforts to cut the number of the world's hungry people in half, support poor farmers, and reduce food-price pendulums had already lost something crucial:

The spotlight.

■ ■ ■

General David Petraeus, newly appointed head of the U.S. Central Command, said on September 15, 2008, that trends had been going in the "wrong direction" in Afghanistan and that force alone wouldn't bring a resolution to hostilities. Republican presidential candidate John McCain was holding a narrow lead over Democrat Barack Obama in two national polls. Democratic strategists, always unnamed in press accounts, said the Illinois senator needed to stop focusing so much on McCain's running mate, Sarah Palin, who had somehow tangled Obama up in a debate over lipstick and pigs. And Lehman Brothers filed the biggest bankruptcy in U.S. history, triggering a financial crisis that pushed the world financial system to the brink of collapse, plunged the planet into its first global decline in economic output since World War II, and diverted attention from poor nations and hunger even as the problem grew worse.

The global economy had already been teetering before Lehman, and commodity prices had ceased serving as a counterweight. Corn on September 12, the Friday before Lehman, was trading at $5.6325 a bushel. A year earlier that would have qualified for a record, but in the casino world of commodities it was already down 30 percent from June. Same with oil—down 31 percent from July. Soybeans, 27 percent less than July. Wheat had tumbled 47 percent from February. The monthly UN index of world food prices, which had peaked at the end of June, had fallen 8 percent. Panic had subsided, governments had stepped in to meet food needs, and investment money everywhere had fled to safer havens.

Lehman was only an early chapter of the financial crisis. Global lending ground to a halt as banks took inventory of toxic assets. The Dow, which fell 4.4 percent on September 15, fell another 7 percent on September 29 and kept dropping. Unemployment skyrocketed, as did government bailouts and debt. McCain was criticized for fumbling his response to the Lehman collapse; Obama regained his footing in the polls and won the White House. The Dow bottomed out at 6469.95 in March 2009, down 54 percent from the record. Corn fell 62 percent, to $3.02 a bushel in September 2009, an 11 percent gain from . . . 30 years earlier.

Oil at one point had lost 78 percent of its value. Money started flowing out of crops and energy, reversing the mania of a few months before. By October, UBS AG, the Swiss Bank that had bought Enron's energy unit after that company collapsed, said it planned to exit the area altogether.[24] About 15 percent of the investors in billionaire energy trader T. Boone Pickens' BP Capital hedge fund asked for the option of getting their money back after they'd lost more than $1 billion.[25] After five years of steady gains, the amount of commodities money managed by index funds fell 17 percent in 2008 to $164 billion. World food prices kept dropping, reaching their lowest in February 2009, down 35 percent from their peak. But even as richer nations turned their worries to their own bank accounts, hunger never went away. Nutrition costs were still higher than any time before 2007. The declines brought enough relief to urban areas to stop the riots—and thus televised images of unrest. Lower prices did nothing to lessen malnourishment as government safety nets for the hungry frayed and joblessness depleted incomes.

"When you're one of the bottom billion, your investments are limited to food," Sheeran said. "Just as the price started easing up and they got a little of that food back, their incomes started shrinking."

Because prices were fluctuating, rather than staying high or low, farmers in the countries struggling most weren't willing to boost harvests even if they could afford it. Price swings just made that too risky.

Kanayo Nwanze is the president of the International Fund for Agricultural Development, which works to reduce poverty in rural areas. The Nigerian is a former director of the Africa Rice Center, where he helped introduce and promote a drought- and pest-resistant strain of rice specifically suited to African climates and farm practices. He also holds a PhD in agricultural entomology from Kansas State University in Manhattan, Kansas, which he received in 1975 before embarking on the career that led to his IFAD appointment in 2009. In his Rome office he shows a collection of commemorative plates marking the first African Rice Congress, a gift from the Consultative Group on International Agricultural Research—a consortium of agricultural research institutes rooted in the Green Revolution era of the 1960s—and a token from Chengdu in China's Sichuan province.

African farmers are in a perpetual struggle to make planting decisions and obtain financing for each year's crops, he said. Unlike rich-world farmers who can fall back on subsidies if costs get too high or prices get too low, swinging prices bring chaos to a farmer's ability to expand beyond a subsistence level.

"If you look at the volatility of prices from 2007 on, the up and down and up and down and up and down—are the farmers at the mercy of the speculators? Of the governments putting bans on exports? Or weather? If farmers can predict the price of maize is going to be high, then they can predict that summer," he says. "But when the price just goes down like a yo-yo, it is difficult for them to manage that risk. When the choice is to plant a new variety or send a sick child to the hospital, they can't manage it."[26]

The consequences of volatility rise further up the food chain. In Long Island, Richard Reinwald raised his cookie and cupcake prices as sudden spikes in raw-materials costs had to be permanently baked-in to his retail prices, he said. In 2008 it was wheat; in 2009 it was sugar. The cost of ingredients had normally been 22 percent of his costs; with volatility, it now averaged 28 percent; to make up for higher commodity prices, he laid off staff.

"You try and budget to make money, but that's becoming impossible to predict," he said. "We budget the best we can and almost take a wait-and-see attitude toward profit."[27]

In Kenya, Sheeran asked farmers whether higher prices meant good news and new development. The answer was no.

"The farmers had been planting half as much as the year before, and I asked why. It was because their inputs had doubled in price. And even if they could afford it, which they couldn't because they couldn't get credit, they didn't trust that they'll get that high food price at the end," she said. "They can't invest in the inputs because they're afraid the price will crash."

Plunging prices hurt farmers, but they alleviated pressure on urban consumers and reduced the urgency for government attention. Not that governments had ever been fully on the same page to begin with. Even during the Rome conference in 2008, strains showed under its carefully worded declaration. Argentina held up the meeting's closing session for hours, arguing against the inclusion of the word "restrictive" in a clause discussing the need "to minimize the use of restrictive measures that could increase the volatility of international prices"—also known as export bans and tariffs. Argentina, which had restricted grain exports in December, lost. The United States, the world's biggest subsidizer and producer of corn-based ethanol, successfully fought off strong antibiofuels language in the declaration, instead accepting calls for "in-depth studies" and "international dialogue on biofuels."[28] Commodities speculation, the subject of condemnation in European media and congressional hearings in the United States, wasn't mentioned. The meeting, billed in part as a chance to discuss climate-change impacts on agriculture, actually said very little about climate change.

The foreign minister of the host, Italy, called the whole exercise "disappointing" and said that the text had been "watered down."[29]

While global organizations were deciding how to combat food security, other countries and investors were taking matters into their own hands. Lack of trust in the world's ability to feed everyone spurred an increase in what media reports call land grab, the acquisition of African farmland by outside countries or investors for their own development.

The 2008 crisis made richer investors in food-importing nations more interested in securing food supplies by gaining land rights in farmland elsewhere. Sub-Saharan Africa is the biggest target for foreign land takeover, with 48 percent of all land deals made worldwide from October 2008 to August 2009 involving that region, according to the World Bank.[30] Land-grab data is hard to come by because property law is skeletal in many poor countries, and many deals fall through—the World Bank study found that only 16 of 46 projects in the Amhara region of Ethiopia were actually followed through as intended.

As the estimated area of acquisition worldwide has risen to nearly 200 million acres, about 125 million in Africa—more than the combined farmland of Great Britain, France, Germany, and Italy—few jobs seem to have been created and little development has occurred as a result of the projects.[31]

Land grab touches nerves, with its echoes of rich outsiders carving up Africa to exploit its resources and residents. In March 2009, protesters overthrew Madagascar's government after then-President Marc Ravalomanana agreed to lease 3.2 million acres, about half of the country's arable land, to Daewoo Logistics Corp., descendant of the now-defunct South Korean conglomerate. Daewoo's plan was to grow palm oil and corn in Madagascar to replace U.S. and South American imports. Two months of protests and at least 100 deaths pressured Ravalomanana to flee the country. His successor promptly cancelled the deal.[32]

Brazil placed severe restrictions on all new foreign farmland buys in 2010 and tightened its restrictions in 2011.[33] Argentina's president, Cristina Fernandez de Kirchner, also signaled her concern, backing her own plan to limit foreign land ownership.[34] Nations with less-developed legal structures remain open for investment. South Korea's government successfully secured 1.7 million acres for wheat in Sudan even as Daewoo failed in Madagascar. Chinese firm ZTE gained 7 million acres in the Democratic Republic of Congo to grow palm oil for biofuels. And Saudi Star Agricultural Development PLC, owned by Sheikh Mohammed al-Amoudi, whose mother is Ethiopian, said in early 2011 it planned to develop nearly 25 million acres of Ethiopian land for rice, part of the nation's plan to lease an area about the size of Belgium to foreign investors. A separate al-Amoudi venture leased 600,000 tons of Ethiopian land in 2009.[35]

Some observers prefer the tamer term *foreign direct investment* to land grab, touting its potential benefits for development and the benign nature of many of the projects. Ethiopia, where resistance to colonialism is central to the national narrative, is a hub of outside land acquisition. Its government defends the practice, saying the long-term leases (Ethiopia doesn't have private land ownership) it offers to companies bring in money that helps it build infrastructure the government can't afford.[36] Daewoo estimated that its Madagascar project would have brought $2 billion in infrastructure investment and 45,000 jobs to the country, benefiting Madagascar's own production as well as the potential Korean exports.

"It would be wrong to characterize them as all good or all bad," said Bill Gates, whose foundation works on health care and agricultural development in the same countries where the buying takes place. "There's potential for some of those deals to be quite good," he said. "Usually, when you invest in a country, if you build roads, you build processing factories, the benefits flow greatly to the place where that land is.

"Capital has to flow to Africa," he said. "We ought to look at, are there some of these deals that could be done that are beneficial?"[37]

The troubling part of land grab lies in the unequal relationships between nations, acquirers, and citizens, Howard Buffett told Bloomberg News.

"Having agricultural investment where there's good land available with good infrastructure and they can farm it reasonably well, that's not such a bad thing," he said. "It's really when they go in and there's very poor governance and resources get abused is where the big problem's going to be."[38]

Buffett is the son of billionaire investor Warren Buffett and head of the Howard G. Buffett Foundation, an organization stated to be dedicated to improving the quality of life for the world's most marginalized people. The foundation has made land grab a priority in its study of development. The world, not sure what to do about it, has so far done little. Nongovernment organizations that advocate for small farmers have blasted the World Bank and its private-sector arm, the International Finance Corporation, for aiding investors that buy massive quantities of farmland in countries where land-ownership codes are vulnerable to abuse. The United Nations in October 2010 failed to endorse a foreign-land-investment code of conduct that outlined seven principles for "responsible agricultural investments" developed by the World Bank and the UN, simply stating that existing land rights should be respected.[39]

Still, even as some nations and investors decided it was everyone for themselves, other countries were pledging aid, and food security was being addressed—and that was a start, Sheeran said. The issue was fading from the headlines, but the WFP director stays upbeat, saying the crisis had at least brought order to what had at first been a disorganized response.

In the early days of 07, "I remember thinking, Who do you call to discuss this?" she said. "It wasn't on the agenda of the G-8. It wasn't on the broader agenda for the international institutions in the world. Today that is not true."

Others were less charitable: Economist Jeffrey Sachs described the global response with one word: "Nothing."[40] Broader world attention lagged without visuals of riots or sticker-shock egg prices. The number of global hungry declined to 925 million in 2010. That would have been a record before the food crisis, yet was an improvement from the year before. The perfect storm had seemingly passed. Perhaps it had been an aberration.

Advocates for more action were worried that structural causes behind the previous price spike hadn't been addressed. By October 2010, former UN Secretary-General Kofi Annan was lamenting that the aggressive response needed to make sure that food prices and hunger didn't spike again had faltered, creating a "lost opportunity" for the world.[41] Gawain Kripke, the policy director for Oxfam America, the U.S. arm of the global humanitarian nongovernmental organization, predicted danger ahead:

"The dip in the number of hungry people has more to do with luck and a weak economy than action," he said. "A new global food crisis could explode at any time unless governments tackle the underlying causes of hunger."[42]

The will for that was lacking. A global food summit held by the UN on November 2009 drew a higher-profile cast than its 2008 predecessor: Pope Benedict XVI, Brazilian President Luiz Inacio Lula da Silva, and a bevy of African leaders including Zimbabwean strongman Robert Mugabe, who used his time on the food-summit stage to urge western nations to drop sanctions against him for human rights violations. The G-8 countries—those behind the pledges—sent noticeably lower-profile delegations. Oxfam rated the effectiveness of the meeting as a 2 on a scale of 1 to 10. Reported Bloomberg:

> The delegates did take advantage of their time in Rome. Via del Corso, a boulevard that cuts through the city's central shopping district, was at times choked with official summit cars, with delegates and their escorts milling around shops from the Disney Store to Gucci. Libyan leader Muammar Qaddafi was spotted at a café in Piazza San Lorenzo in Lucina. He also

hosted two parties that young women were paid to attend. The Libyan leader tried to convince them to convert to Islam and gave them a copy of the Koran, Italian media including news agency Ansa reported.[43]

Sheeran, in her Rome office, stressed that discussions supported the long-term agricultural development and better coordination of global responses she said can end global hunger in our lifetimes. Food security remains tenuous in many places until those changes occur, she said. For now, the biggest determinant of whether a person could eat or not—the price and availability of food—is still the domain of highly volatile, spiking-and-falling markets that are as predictable as the weather.

And the weather was getting hotter.

CHAPTER 6

Hot Air

Mohamed Bouazizi's self-immolation in December 2010 alerted the world that a new crisis, fueled by food, had begun. It had first flared in June, as a hot summer across Russia burst into flames that extended into Mozambique— and ultimately, Cairo.

World food prices had stabilized in the first half of 2010. Economies were expanding again, and so were fields. Russia and its neighbors in the former Soviet Union were crucial new sources of production. Wheat crops in 2009 in countries that had been part of the USSR were 76 percent larger than a decade earlier. The Russian harvest alone rivaled its Cold War competitor, the United States. Together with Kazakhstan, Ukraine, and others of what agricultural analysts call the "Former Soviet Union-12" nations, they surpassed the United States.

Russia's comeback is a return to power lost a century ago. Before the U.S. Midwest became the world's breadbasket, the Russian Empire was the world's major wheat exporter. The *chernozem* black-earth belt, stretching from the Romanian border through Ukraine, Russia, the Urals, and southwest Siberia, was and remains some of the world's most productive farmland, almost effortlessly yielding high-quality crops. The Czar's wheat was hedged in nineteenth-century Chicago. On the eve of World War I the Empire accounted for more than a third of the world's exports, even as upstart American farmers were getting yields from their land that were five times that of their less-mechanized counterparts across the Atlantic, many of whom were only a generation away from serfdom.[1]

Little did those Russian farmers realize they were on the road back to it.

Communism dramatically reversed Russia's role in global grain markets. Josef Stalin's forced starvation of 7 million Ukrainians in the 1930s destroyed the *kulak* landowner class that had provided leadership and expertise and forced those who remained into inefficient collectives. Food was shipped at gunpoint to Moscow until none was left, bringing independence-minded Ukraine to heel in service of Mother Russia. Political persecution continued after the famine, interrupted only in 1941, when Hitler sent troops into Russia for ideology, *lebensraum* (living space), and a food supply.[2] Postwar farm production sputtered. Soviet leaders, including Nikita Khrushchev, the grandson of a serf, shifted agriculture from grain-growing toward expensive livestock production, buying wheat from the West to support a nation that, under saner circumstances, should have been a leading seller. By 1972 the Soviets needed to make massive purchases from the Midwest to offset a poor crop, secretly buying entire boatloads of grain as their food situation became more desperate. What came to be called "The Great Grain Robbery" because of the secrecy of the sales involved a massive fleecing of U.S. taxpayers, when a U.S. government subsidy for grain exports made Americans foot much of the Soviet bill. The unexpected export surge helped raise U.S. food prices 18 percent in 1973—three times its jump in 2008—while Soviets fed themselves with the subsidized wheat of their Cold War rivals.

The Soviet Union's demise brought another contraction in agriculture as regional economies collapsed. The Russian breadbasket is re-emerging, championed by large corporate farms that succeeded the collectives. The FSU-12 became a net exporter for the first time in a quarter-century in 1998 (see Figure 6.1). Russia's 2009 crop accounted for 14 percent of the world's exports, even though yields were still at levels similar to those of U.S. farmers of the 1930s. The June 2010 issue of *Amber Waves*, the in-house food-trends magazine of the U.S. Department of Agriculture (USDA), predicted that by the end of the 2010s, Russia will overtake the United States as the world's top wheat exporter as yields improve and U.S. farmers continue to plant more profitable corn and soybeans on land formerly cultivated with wheat. By 2019, the FSU-12 may more than double U.S. shipments, according to the article.

The *Amber Waves* piece concludes with a warning:

> The region's climate is characterized by variable temperature and rainfall, with severe drought possible in any year. These conditions can produce major fluctuations in annual grain output and exports. This effect can be exacerbated if the countries react with policies that restrict exports.

On June 9, as the article was distributed, wheat prices in Chicago fell to $4.255 a bushel, their lowest in three years, as the USDA predicted the highest

FIGURE 6.1   Net Wheat Exports of United States and the Former Soviet Union
(Metric Tons)

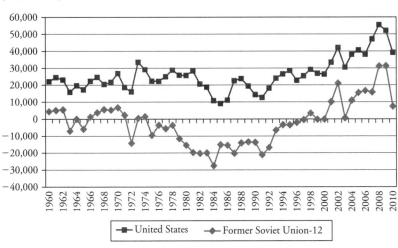

Source: USDA.

global inventories since 2002. In Russia, the weather was turning warmer, much warmer than usual. By mid-month, high temperatures in Asian regions were routinely hitting the upper 90s Fahrenheit, 10 to 12 degrees above normal for much of the country.

The fires began in July.

■ ■ ■

Mozambique's government had announced that, as of September 1, 2010, it was raising water and electricity prices by 30 percent. On September 6, bread would increase 25 percent.[3]

The country's leaders were facing a budget crunch brought about by lower exports of aluminum, the mineral mainstay of what for decades has been a basket-case economy. The country that lies just northeast of South Africa, east of Zimbabwe, and south of Tanzania, has been one of the world's poorest countries since it gained independence from Portugal in 1975. A civil war from 1977 to 1992 destroyed what little infrastructure the country had, but Mozambique has grown quickly in recent years as its government has become more stable. Four-fifths of Mozambique's population farms, and agricultural productivity and income lag from lack of investment. The population relies heavily on imports to meet nutrition needs. To this day, more than half of Mozambique's federal budget comes from foreign aid.

The Russia-driven wheat spike soon reverberated 5,500 miles to the south, where the price of a 50-kilogram sack of flour sold outside Mozambique's capital of Maputo rose 50 percent in a month.[4] The country's government explained the need for the price hikes as the unfortunate result of its weakening currency compared to the U.S. dollar and the rand of South Africa, from which it buys one-third of its imports, including most of its wheat.[5] Disgruntled consumers across Mozambique sent text messages urging a general strike in Maputo the day the increases went into effect. The protests began, followed by arrests—more than 300; injuries—more than 400; and deaths—at least 14 in Maputo and in Chimoio, 475 miles to the north. The government within days reversed its bread-price hike, instead scrounging its treasury for money to subsidize food in a move to stay in power.

■ ■ ■

On June 25, 2010, the temperature at Belogorsk, Amur Oblast, a far-eastern Russian province bordered by China to the south, exceeded 108 degrees Fahrenheit. The weather pattern moved west, settling over the Black Earth belt for a long, hot July.

Peat bogs drained for farming near Moscow in the 1960s, a legacy of Soviet agricultural planning, caught fire later that month while the heat wave killed hundreds in cities each day. By the first week of August, an 1,850-mile-wide cloud of smoke covered western Russia, as Moscow residents wore masks to work and embassies closed because of health risks.[6] Beaten by relentless heat and going for weeks without rain, the wheat crop fell by a third from the previous year's level—and markets responded. Russia's hottest July in 130 years prompted the biggest jump in wheat prices since 1973, except this time the problem wasn't a sudden Soviet need to buy grain from world markets. It was because Russia wouldn't sell to customers who needed its food. Buyers were now dependent on a Russia that couldn't, or wouldn't, deliver.

On August 5, Prime Minister Vladimir Putin, responding to domestic concerns about higher bread prices, pulled Russia off the world market, announcing an end to wheat, barley, rye, corn, and flour exports in 2010, then extending the ban into 2011. Putin called the move "appropriate" given local grain needs, saying that "we must prevent domestic prices from rising." Kirill Podolsky, the chief executive officer of Valars Group, the country's third-biggest grain trader, called the ban "a catastrophe for farmers and exporters alike."[7] Wheat in Chicago that day touched $8.155 a bushel, the highest price since August 2008. The grain's price had already risen 92 percent in less than two months.

The Russian ban was intended to reassure consumers that supplies would be secure. It achieved the opposite. The Soviet-conditioned population hoarded flour, convinced that nothing more clearly foretold disaster than political leaders telling them everything was okay. The ban succeeded in stabilizing domestic supplies, ensured that no images of Russian wheat leaving the country while grocery shelves were bare would be shown on television, and allowed Russia's grain-sellers to declare *force majeure* on contracts, a legal clause that allows a company to cancel a shipment because of circumstances beyond its control.

Force majeure, Podolsky explained, would allow Russia to cancel 600,000 tons of contracts, about four-and-a-half days of its annual consumption, to the world's biggest wheat importer—a country the USDA estimated needs more than 9 million tons annually to feed its citizens. That country now would be forced to scramble to buy wheat from other suppliers, who would be charging higher prices now that Russia was off the market.

"We would have hoped that the Russian side would have given a longer notice period so that the trading companies could have had time to reorganize," the vice chairman of that country's state-run grain buyer said the day the ban was announced. "No doubt this will affect the agreements," he said.[8]

Russia was protecting its citizens. Egypt would have to fend for itself.

■ ■ ■

To say that Egypt and Tunisia's governments fell because of food prices, or that Algeria would have remained stable or Syria would have avoided protests or Yemen's president wouldn't have been wounded in an attack or Libya would not have plunged into civil war had only it rained in Russia for a few days in July 2010, would distort history. The Egyptians who gathered in Tahrir Square were angry about much more than the price of bread, just as a poor wheat crop in France was not the main reason citizens stormed the Bastille in 1789. Perhaps high prices were a necessary part of a push toward a better government and a brighter future.

It's worth noting that on July 13, 1789—the eve of the original Bastille Day—a Parisian mob seized wagons of wheat held at a convent and distributed it to the public. Bread costs were a preoccupation of protests against the *Ancién Regime*—the attribution of "let them eat cake" to Marie Antoinette underscored the callousness the Bourbons were seen to have toward bread prices, a symbol of people's basic necessities. It's also worth noting that Egypt is the only country where the word for bread, *aish*, is also the word that means life, and that food riots had destabilized the country before, in 1977 and in 2008. The country made up for lost Russian supplies by buying 12 times as much U.S. wheat from October 2010 through January 2011 than it had during the same period a year earlier[9]—but more-expensive grain fed inflation. Egyptian food prices outpaced general inflation throughout 2010, with their most dramatic spike the month Russia's export ban was announced (see Figure 6.2). After a decline in the last three months of the year, they were back on the rise when 2011 began. Fast-moving nutrition costs can create a volatile political situation in the right set of circumstances, a lesson of 2008— and of 1789—that the world had forgotten, only to relearn as 2011 began.

Mozambique's riots prompted the United Nations Food and Agriculture Organization (FAO) to call a special meeting on food prices within a month. The delegates said they were worried about recent increases in global costs— the FAO's monthly index had risen for three consecutive months and had returned to where it had been exactly two years earlier—while explicitly stating the world was not seeing a repeat of 2008.[10] Adequate rains in much of Africa had aided crops on that continent, at least until the next growing season, and world inventories, in spite of Russia, were still in better shape than they had been late in 2007. Wheat markets calmed down. On October 4, 2010, two months after Russia's announcement and one month after Mozambique, Chicago wheat fell to $6.435 a bushel, 26 percent below its August 6 peak. U.S. growers picked up much of Russia's lost business, and

FIGURE 6.2 Egypt on the Rise

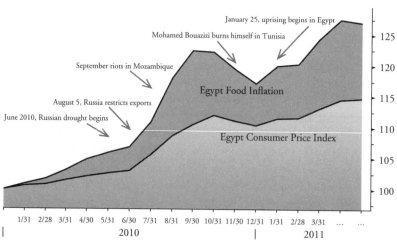

Source: Bloomberg.

rice and corn inventories remained high enough to offset concerns about cereals supplies.

As it turned out, a 2008-style "perfect storm" wasn't needed to cause unrest; near-perfect would do. Ukraine followed with its own limits on wheat, corn, and barley shipments in October, further tightening supplies and pressuring markets.[11] Weather kept roiling crops, hurting wheat further and turning expected gains into losses: Drought damaged yields in Argentina; cyclones and torrential rains hit Australia; Saskatchewan downpours kept Canadian farmers from planting 10 million acres of wheat. U.S. and European grain and soybean harvests were coming in smaller than forecast as the northern heat wave cut starch content in kernels and stunted soy pods. A drought in China further alarmed grain markets, and by February 2011 wheat was topping $9 a bushel again as traders watched weather reports from the North China Plain. Wheat, corn, and soybean futures were all at three-year highs.[12]

Investors were pouring money back into food futures. Commodities assets under fund management rose to $412 billion at the end of March 2011, a 9.6 percent rise from the end of the previous year. Agriculture was the biggest contributor to the gain, with $7.1 billion going into corn, wheat, soybeans, and other farm goods.[13] Wide price swings came in with the new money, reigniting the debate over whether food prices were driving investors or whether it was the other way around. Rice became the saving grace of world food markets. Vietnam and Thailand had ample supplies to make up for shortfalls, and Japan and China began selling from state reserves to relieve price pressures on both foreign and domestic markets. In Japan's case, the sales came even as it cut plantings in a struggle to ease panic over food safety after an earthquake and tsunami led to a nuclear meltdown at the Fukushima Dai-Ichi power plant.[14] Global rice production was expected to surpass the previous year's, and trade was expected to increase. Sugar led world price gains early in 2011. That was unwelcome to consumers, but high sweetener costs posed less of a famine threat, since poorer people rely more on grains for their diets. Staple-foods prices were up, but not at records.

High food prices created outcomes from the tragic to the comic. A vegetable-bandit theft ring in Florida stole $300,000 worth of tomatoes, cucumbers, and frozen meat from unsuspecting growers: The thieves "were just sitting and waiting, watching the produce because they knew it was climbing" in price, the owner of a transportation firm victimized by the gang said. "It was like a snake in the grass, and they struck."[15]

More ominous to the UN was the rise of annual food imports to more than $1 trillion,[16] once again for the first time since 2008, and higher energy prices. When those costs started to rise, governments like Mozambique's, which, like many countries after the financial crisis, had less money to spend, had little ability to cushion the blows against their citizens—leading to the possibility that upset citizens could come to blows against them.

■ ■ ■

The blows came to Algeria the first week of the year. At least five people died in rioting. Hundreds were injured and more than a thousand jailed when food prices jumped up to 30 percent as the year began.[17] The same week the UN said grocery costs had reached a record, Algeria's government pledged to subsidize basic foods and cut taxes on sugar and cooking oils.[18] It also stepped up wheat purchases to relieve pressure on food prices. The riots receded, only to be followed by a round of self-immolations beginning mid-month, mostly by unemployed youth following the example of Mohamed Bouazizi. Protests continued into the spring and summer, with outrage over food, energy, and housing costs, unemployment, and political repression all feeding the outrage that flourished in the weeks and months after Bouazizi's death in Tunisia.

"The Arab soul is broken by poverty, unemployment and general recession," Arab League Secretary-General Amr Moussa warned at an economic summit in Egypt on January 19, 2011. "The Tunisian revolution is not far from us."[19] Street protests over politics and the cost of living had already begun in Libya, Jordan, Mauritania, Sudan, Oman, and Yemen. Arab leaders committed to $2 billion in economic aid to poorer members. Saudi Arabia and Kuwait kicked in the first billion.

Egyptian president Hosni Mubarak made no reference to the Tunisian protests at the summit. Muammar Qaddafi, known to pitch his tent wherever regional leaders gathered, was staying at home.[20]

In Egypt, an average of 40 percent of household income is spent on food and beverages (see Table 6.1). In Tunisia, it's 37 percent. In Jordan and Algeria, it's more than 45 percent. In Bahrain, the percentage is only 15 percent. In Kuwait, it's 16 percent. For the poorest citizens, the proportion is much higher. Countries where people spend more of their incomes on food were more likely to see their governments topple in 2011 than countries where food spending wasn't a dominant part of household budgets. World Bank President Robert Zoellick called food prices an "aggravating factor" in Middle East violence as Egypt's government fell.[21] The only hope for food prices to fall was better crops in 2011. The message from the United States was mixed—larger crops, but only so much more land could be plowed as productivity in the rich world was nearly maxed out on acreage. In Russia, where the turmoil began, the wheat crop was expected to be 53 million tons

TABLE 6.1 Portion of Household Income Spent on Food in Selected Countries

| Country/Territory | Share of Consumption Spending | | Total Household Final Consumption Spending[b] | Spending per Capita on Food[b] |
	Food[a]	Alcoholic Beverages and Tobacco		
	Percent		*U.S. Dollars per Person*	
United States	6.2	1.9	32,051	1,979
Ireland	7.2	5.4	23,879	1,727
United Arab Emirates	8.7	0.4	22,845	1,994
United Kingdom	8.8	3.7	21,788	1,928
Canada	9.1	3.9	23,088	2,091
Australia	10.5	4.0	25,510	2,685
Germany	11.4	3.6	22,812	2,596
Sweden	11.5	3.7	20,415	2,353
Spain	13.2	3.1	18,505	2,448
France	13.5	3.1	24,271	3,268
Greece	14.0	4.8	22,150	3,098
Malaysia	14.0	1.3	3,371	472
Japan	14.2	3.2	22,909	3,260
Kuwait	14.5	1.6	12,203	1,770
Bahrain	14.5	0.4	6,413	932
South Korea	15.1	2.6	8,865	1,341
Czech Republic	15.6	7.7	9,346	1,455
Israel	17.7	1.6	14,693	2,597
Ecuador	19.0	1.9	2,551	484
South Africa	19.8	4.6	3,440	680
Argentina	20.3	3.3	4,347	881
Poland	20.3	6.6	6,910	1,405
Lithuania	21.8	6.6	7,430	1,622
Saudi Arabia	23.7	1.3	5,206	1,236
Brazil	24.7	2.0	5,118	1,265
Thailand	24.8	5.6	2,266	563

(*continued*)

TABLE 6.1 (*Continued*)

Country/Territory	Food[a]	Share of Consumption Spending — Alcoholic Beverages and Tobacco	Total Household Final Consumption Spending[b]	Spending per Capita on Food[b]
		Percent	*U.S. Dollars per Person*	
Iran	25.9	0.7	2,522	653
Colombia	27.6	4.7	3,155	872
Russia	28.0	2.7	4,572	1,280
Bolivia	28.2	2.2	1,154	326
Venezuela	29.1	3.1	7,293	2,119
Dominican Republic	29.2	3.0	3,507	1,025
China	32.9	2.9	1,257	414
Romania	34.3	5.0	4,649	1,593
Kazakhstan	34.9	3.7	3,097	1,080
India	35.4	3.2	620	219
Guatemala	35.5	1.7	2,227	791
Tunisia	35.7	1.0	2,330	831
Philippines	36.7	1.7	1,278	469
Vietnam	38.1	2.8	749	285
Egypt	38.1	2.3	2,111	805
Nigeria	39.9	2.5	631	252
Jordan	40.7	4.8	3,073	1,250
Ukraine	42.1	6.4	1,665	701
Indonesia	43.0	6.3	1,357	583
Belarus	43.2	6.0	2,942	1,271
Algeria	43.8	2.0	1,305	571
Kenya	44.9	3.0	541	243
Pakistan	45.5	2.5	681	309
Azerbaijan	46.9	2.4	2,033	954

Source: USDA, EUROMONITOR data, July 2010. Compiled by the USDA Economic Research Service.

[a]Includes nonalcoholic beverages.
[b]Household expenditures for goods and services.

in mid-2011, 14 percent less than the year before the drought.[22] The export ban, which had lowered domestic prices, also made growers less likely to plant grain.[23]

Export restrictions remained a popular way to keep populations calm and prices under control. Trade barriers made farmers less efficient and less able to feed the globe even as new obstacles were erected that increased prices. In early 2011, India's ban on rice exports, first triggered by a wheat-price shock that hadn't existed for three years, remained in place. At the end of 2010 and into the first months of 2011 India also banned onions, for which it was the world's second-biggest exporter.

In China, where food prices rose about 7 percent in 2010, the government released emergency reserves and put restrictions on wheat and other crop sales to keep consumer prices from higher gains.[24]

In Kenya, the nation's Red Cross began to report deaths from hunger in a region struck by its worst drought in 60 years. Corn was becoming scarce, and what grain was available was too expensive to buy. The government cut taxes on corn and wheat imports to lower prices.[25]

Sri Lanka, where the local diet heavily relies on coconuts, banned shipments after a poor harvest.[26] Ivory Coast, the world's leading cocoa producer, barred its beans from leaving the country in January after president Laurent Gbagbo refused to step down after losing an election, sending prices to their highest in more than three decades until the new government finally took power after a brief civil war.[27] Myanmar banned rice exports in March.[28]

■ ■ ■

In Nicaragua, the second-poorest country in the Western Hemisphere, the government banned the export of beans, the staple of Nicaraguan diets. The official reason was concern that the country's bean crop was not of high enough quality to meet international standards and that the government wanted to maintain the country's reputation; leaders also said the domestic crop was too small to be allowed on export markets when local consumers needed it.[29]

The government led by President Daniel Ortega, who is best known globally as the youthful leader of Nicaragua's Sandinista government in the 1980s, was gearing itself up for re-election, its first as the incumbent party after Ortega's Sandinista National Liberation Front regained power in the 2006 elections. The Sandinistas have tempered their earlier ways of land redistribution and state management of the economy while still stating socialism as the party's ultimate goal. Capitalism, he has said, is in its "death throes," and the 2008 financial crisis, he has said, was punishment from God against the United States for oppressing the world's poor.[30]

The country's economy is primarily agricultural, with farming a major source of income for a labor force in which one-half of the workers are unemployed or underemployed. Ortega has promised prosperity, but had been constitutionally banned from seeking re-election until 2009, when his country's highest court ruled he could seek office again. In 2011, Ortega was ready to run in the vote slated for November. With food-price riots emerging in other countries—and not being kind to the leaders of those countries—an artificial increase in red and black bean supplies could stabilize prices for urban consumers, even as the rural poor, the traditional Sandinista base, suffered from the loss of markets for their food. For Rosa Benavides, president of the board of directors of a new bean plant built with the help of the U.S. Agency for International Development for $800,000 near Sebaco, the largest city in Nicaragua's most fertile valley, the ban was complicating the new crop-processor's chances of success. Growers were counting on the plant to create new markets for their burgeoning bean production.

"When the beans stay in the country that lowers the price for the consumers, but it's not good for the growers," Benavides said. "It's removed their incentive and motivation to produce more.

"Our vision of more production and more services for our growers, it has not become able to reach reality," she said.[31] The plant, which at full production employs 120 people (mostly young women who sort through the beans and separate them for quality) by May 2011 was down to 22. Limited bean shipments resumed in the summer, with the government keeping a lid on exports until it could judge the next harvest.

■ ■ ■

Export bans, price controls, and other short-term measures governing everything from cooking oil in Bangladesh to beer in Ethiopia distorted prices domestically and, in the end, drove them higher in other places and for other goods. The restrictions were allowable under international trade rules. The World Trade Organization (WTO) requires members to eliminate restrictions and prohibitions on exports—except for those imposed "temporarily" to prevent and alleviate food shortages as well as those intended to allow time for the application of regulations such as classification and grading. It also doesn't restrict members from imposing duties, taxes, or other charges on exports, another way to discourage shipments. In January 2011, WTO chief

Pascal Lamy said the temptation to impose bans could be lessened were a conclusion brought to the Doha Round of WTO negotiations, soon to celebrate their tenth anniversary. A new treaty would cut agricultural subsidies and trade barriers in general.[32] Export bans added fuel to the food-inflation fire internationally even if they calmed prices at home, he told a meeting of agriculture ministers discussing the cause of food-price increases, "Restrictions lead to panic," he said.

Or worse.

■ ■ ■

Unrest showed how the mix of instability in the global nutrition system along with political instability carried impacts far beyond who did and didn't eat. That much was clear.

The problem was what to do about it.

Commodities prices were at their highest levels since before the financial crisis. Algeria, Tunisia, Egypt, and countries across the Middle East and North Africa had all seen riots over living costs, and Uganda saw the first food protests of sub-Saharan Africa in April as inflation rose 14 percent, led by food costs that had risen by an annual rate of nearly one-third.[33]

Governments were wary to take on sensitive issues, like regulating the commodities casino or repealing benefits for industries that were raising prices, even as the environment for food-price crises only grew hotter: literally, as in Russia and its drought, and figuratively, as in riots. The quick fixes resorted to by many leaders—subsidies, export bans, and price controls—exacerbated the problem while obscuring, and sometimes working against, the longer-term need for higher production. Foreign aid to assist impoverished populations, meanwhile, was becoming a tougher sell after a record global flow of $129 billion in 2010 ran into the worldwide debt worries of 2011. While poor nations witnessed high prices and dry weather, richer ones were drowning in debt. Many nations, especially in Europe, were not making their stated commitments to aiding agricultural development, the Organisation for Economic Co-operation and Development (OECD) said in April 2011.[34] The United Kingdom, Japan, and the United States all announced cuts in assistance in 2011, even while they pledged to focus spending on the neediest people in the neediest countries.[35] A promise to boost African aid by $25 billion fell $14 billion short.[36] In 2010, only 63 percent of UN emergency food-aid appeals were funded,[37] and with governments eyeing foreign-aid budgets as part of fiscal austerity, reliability seemed more likely to decrease rather than improve.

French President Nicolas Sarkozy pledged to purge speculators from crop-trading, saying he would make commodities regulation a centerpiece of his country's presidency of the Group of 20 nations. Speaking to African Union members in Addis Ababa in January 2011, he said that speculation in agricultural commodities was "simply extortion" and "pillaging" of food markets in "a veritable scandal" of profiteering at the expense of the poor.[38] Efforts to rein in traders received limited political support, as well as serious skepticism about how well new regulations would work, or even whether speculators were a major contributor to the problem.

Oil, meanwhile, stayed near $100 a barrel, ensuring high transportation costs as U.S. drivers settled into a summer of higher gasoline costs. Global trade talks were stagnant. International efforts to arrest climate change remained muted. The world kept growing wealthier, and hungrier. Left as is, the global food market was destined to fail everyone, and its poorest people most—and not just in the short term. Tight food supplies would take years to overcome, with weather shocks continually threatening to set back attempts to rebuild inventories.[39]

One approach to meeting the endless appetites remained simple: connecting the farmers in places most harmed by hunger to the markets that can end it. Growing food more efficiently in more places creates more sources of food to replace lost production elsewhere. Growing it sustainably conserves scarce water and land. Growing it profitably ends poverty. Growing it for everyone ends unrest. The details involved in a seemingly simple solution can be staggering. Hundreds of millions of farmers could provide the answers. As Abebech Toga said, "A farmer needs a market."

The world needs them too.

CHAPTER 7

Promise

By the summer of 2004, the farmers and villagers of Angata Barakoi had had enough of thieves from rival groups who would raid their cattle. So when bandits arrived one afternoon, Christina Chebi Ngogi's husband stood firm, refusing to surrender his 10 head of livestock.

Then the guns came out.

Christina didn't see her husband die. Most of the villagers were fleeing the bullets. Her brother-in-law watched helplessly as the thieves stole first the cattle, then her husband's life as he died of a gunshot to the head, as did others who resisted. The village wailed as children whose parents had seen them off to school came home as orphans. Christina was left with a family to raise and a farm to watch against thieves in a dangerous Kenyan village.

Ngogi's story may sound like another harrowing tale from lawless, helpless Africa, a continent of unstable governments, endless wars, and hopeless poverty. That was true in the recent past, and remains so in some places today. In many countries it's becoming an inaccurate stereotype that's holding back a continent just when it will be needed to help feed the world. And it's only part of the story of Christina Chebi Ngogi, a grieving widow, struggling mother, prosperous businesswoman, and community leader who helped organize her fellow widows, some who had lost their husbands to violence, some to HIV, into an economic unit that's sending grain to hunger-stricken parts of Kenya. Christina Chebi Ngogi considers herself fortunate. She survived for a better future, one that gives hope that farmers like her can help banish hunger from their homelands.

Six of the world's 20 fastest-growing economies, as ranked by the International Monetary Fund, are in Africa. Debt burdens in many of the continent's 54 countries are lower than those in the developed world, thanks in part to loan cancellations by the World Bank, International Monetary Fund (IMF), and African Development Bank made in return for meeting economic goals. Chinese demand for minerals is fueling the continent's traditional export strength—China is now Africa's biggest trading partner, to the discomfort of its rich-world rivals—even as service, manufacturing, and agriculture are growing, as is foreign investment.[1] As a whole, Africa is both freer and more important to global growth than ever before. Obstacles remain daunting in many places—along with 6 of the fastest growing nations, 6 of the world's 10 most corrupt countries are in Africa.[2] Poverty remains, climate change threatens crops, and political stability remains elusive in many places, as anyone in Ivory Coast, Nigeria, or across North Africa in 2011 could attest.

For Africa's promise to be met, more change must occur. Still, as Christina says, "This isn't the place it was before.

"Now we can spend our time growing our crops instead of protecting our land."[3]

■ ■ ■

One paradox of hunger today is that the world can produce enough food to feed everyone. The second is that places where food is most desperately needed are often near where it could be grown, sold, and used to fight malnutrition, with a properly functioning market.

The world is already seeing a shift toward relying on more places to meet global food needs. The former Soviet Union is equaling or surpassing traditional exporters in wheat. Brazil ships more than five times as many soybeans as it did two decades ago. South Africa has more than doubled its corn shipments in the same period. Vietnam and Cambodia are becoming rice leaders. These are countries that a generation ago included communist dictatorships, a military junta, a government based on racial segregation, and a killing field. Countries do change—and relatively quickly when the proper conditions are in place.

Sub-Saharan Africa, the world's most famine-prone region, also includes some of its most fertile lands. Nearly every country has some potential to fill a market need—from the tropical fruits of Uganda and Kenya to Nigeria's cassava—if a market is available and developed. Growth could come quickly because Africa's late to the game—as a late adapter of agriculture's innovations, it ideally can learn from other positive experiences while avoiding the pitfalls.

In West Africa, the partnerships are often quite direct, with countries receiving aid and advice from their South American latitudinal cousin, Brazil, possibly the world's biggest farm success story of the past 40 years, and a major source of additional food production. Brazil's soybean output has tripled since 1990 under the guidance of the Brazilian Agricultural Research Corporation, with the Portuguese acronym EMBRAPA, which was set up in 1973 by the country's military government during the food-price spikes of that era. EMBRAPA invested in reducing soil acidity and developing strains of crops that could grow effectively in tropical climates. The result was a vast new productive area in its *cerrado* region, far from the Amazon rainforest and with ample access to water, which helped reduce the percentage of underfed Brazilians from 11 percent to 6 percent of the population by 2007. The joke that Brazil was the next global power—and always would be—is no longer true. Its day is already here.

The *cerrado* has been characterized by massive-sized farms that rely on heavy equipment. That leads some environmentalists and poverty advocates to worry that Brazil's poorest aren't benefiting from farm expansion and that deforestation and more intensive agriculture will contribute to climate change. In reality, Brazil contains two agricultural systems, with export-based megafarms and a smallholder culture that serves local populations, noted Olivier de Schutter, the United Nations Special Rapporteur on the right to food. It's a crucial distinction, he said, because more exports doesn't equal food-security: The farmers themselves have to benefit, and environmental damage has to be considered when evaluating a system's success.[4] As such, the Brazilian model may be difficult to translate to Africa's smallholders. Still, Brazil's model holds lessons in parts of Africa where the climate and land are appropriate, and its previous experience means lessons can sorted out quickly. "Africa is changing," said Silvio Crestana, a former head of EMBRAPA, in 2010. "Perhaps it won't take them so long. We'll see."[5]

The Black Sea region, where the soil's rich color matches the name, has emerged from the wreckage of the former USSR. Here, Soviet collective farms were privatized, updated, and made more efficient. The region, which also includes parts of Turkey, is now an exporter to oil-rich, water-poor nations of the Middle East and North Africa, with the caveat that, as the 2010 drought showed, it can't be relied upon as a consistent source of nutrition. The region also has political challenges, as countries with varying levels of democracy, stability, and economic development are inevitably intertwined with its nearby Middle East and Iraq-Iran-Afghanistan neighborhoods, not the most tranquil place to do business.

That turbulence creates opportunity, said Oleg Bakhmatyuk, a Ukrainian farm and poultry entrepreneur who aspires to be the leading top source of egg powder to North Africa and the Middle East. The billionaire in his mid-thirties makes food security part of his market pitch as he travels the world looking for partnerships and investments, saying that Black Sea food can reduce the consumer frustration that spawns violence in the nations next door—and by extension the rest of the world when it's forced to intervene.

In the political centers of Washington, Brussels, and Beijing, "food supplies are a top concern," he said. Black Seas farmers can be leaders in addressing this, he said.[6]

Brazil and the Black Sea—and Argentina, and Asian nations, and South Africa, and other countries with specific strengths in specific crops—have already enriched the sources and production of food worldwide over the past generation. Sub-Saharan Africa is the biggest piece of solving the food-security puzzle. The key comes in connecting farmers to markets, where producers plugged into their own local, regional, and global food grids can grow incomes along with crops, reduce poverty, and supply their neighbors when bad weather or high prices create shortages.

"Once a farmer is connected to a market, it lowers the price of everything—seeds, fertilizers, transportation—which automatically makes everyone better off," said Steve Radelet, the chief economist for the U.S. Agency for International Development and a former senior fellow at the Center for Global Development in Washington.[7]

■ ■ ■

The thought of Africa, farming powerhouse, may sound utopian. Headlines from sub-Saharan Africa in Western media tend to revolve around natural disasters, revolutions, famines, or human rights violations. Both cynics and idealists can be complicit in what becomes a hopeless, self-defeating image—cynics because bad news is what they're looking for, and idealists because a tug at heartstrings gets people to open their wallets. For many in the middle, the net reaction is a numbing of concern. "For less than the price of a cup of coffee," a famous phrase associated with Africa-aid fund-raising in the 1980s, is true—small donations can make a difference. The phrase is also mocked, as trillions of dollars spent on foreign aid over the past half-century seemingly haven't made much difference. The annual Christmastime call to help a hopeless person in a hopeless, a mainstay of charitable organization budgets,[8] may be accompanied by a nagging thought that nothing will really improve. The letter goes into the trash.

For about two decades, from the mid-1970s to the mid-1990s, that wasn't an unreasonable assumption. The Big Man era that ranged from Mobuto Sese Seko of Congo to Samuel Doe in Liberia to Idi Amin in Uganda, who was rumored to keep the severed heads of his opponents in a refrigerator, was marked by kleptocracy, post-colonial violence, and Cold War rivalry that reduced assistance to a sideshow in the global U.S.-Soviet standoff. Political turbulence and misguided policy meant farming lagged while other nations struggled to feed the planet. World food production has increased 145 percent in the past 40 years while African food production has fallen by 10 percent since 1960, turning what once was a crop exporter into a continent that imports more than $30 billion of food annually, on top of the roughly $3 billion it receives in food aid each year.[9]

Times are changing. Continent-wide growth has been steady in the past decade. From 2000 to 2009, African GDP as a whole grew 4.5 percent annually, according to World Bank data. In comparison, the United States grew 1.8 percent a year and the European Union grew 1.5 percent. China gained 10.3 percent. Aggregate growth masks greater success stories in specific countries. Mozambique, still one of Africa's poorest nations, has seen its per capita income double from 15 years ago. It's more than two-thirds higher in countries including Botswana, Cameroon, and Tanzania. Much of the expansion is unrelated to mineral extraction, the continent's stereotypical source of wealth. Uganda's growth has been driven by services and farming, while mining comprises less than 1 percent of the economy, though that may soon change with the development of oil deposits. Mauritius was ranked 20 out of 183 countries on the planet as a place to do business in 2010 as it emphasizes development of its financial and real estate sectors. South Africa at 34, Botswana at 52, and Rwanda at 58 are in the top third, with Ghana just outside, according to the World Bank and the International Finance Corporation.[10]

Ease of doing business is connected to stable government, another area of improvement. Beginning with Namibia, a former German colony that held free elections in 1989 days before the Berlin Wall fell, and the end of apartheid in South Africa, sub-Saharan Africa has embraced a slow, halting march toward democracy and better governments.

Big Men still rule many African countries, including Robert Mugabe of Zimbabwe, Omar Hassan Al-Bashir of Sudan, Isaias Afwerki of Eritrea, and Meles Zenawi of Ethiopia, all members of the top 10 in the Foreign Policy/Fund for Peace's 2010 list of world's worst despots.[11] Yet the number of African countries rated "free" or "partly free" in Freedom House's annual ratings in 2010 rose to 27 from 22 in 2000. Ghana, Kenya, Senegal, Sierra Leone, and Zambia all made transitions to democracy around the turn of the century. Liberia elected Africa's first woman head of state with Ellen Johnson Sirleaf in 2005. Violence and war in many nations are also ebbing—battlefield deaths have been at post-colonial lows since 2002, in contrast from the last quarter of the twentieth century, when sub-Saharan Africa was often the planet's bloodiest region. (See Figure 7.1.)

The transition has occurred because of increasing prosperity in some countries and the sorting-out of post-colonial baggage in others. As Hartmann, the single-named director of the International Institute of Tropical Agriculture, based in Ibadan, Nigeria, jokes, you can tell the health of an African democracy by where its former presidents live. Those whose presidents are exiled to wealthy estates—assuming they aren't killed while in power—are not places to do business, he said. When more of them retire in their own countries, investors know the coast is clear.

"If you can see a former president on the street, in a market, you know you have stability," he said.

Relative peace has also meant slow improvements to infrastructure, the most basic part of linking a farmer to a market. China is playing a major role in African road and infrastructure developments, financing projects from Angola to Zambia and boosting ties in everything from energy projects to funding scholarships for African students to study in China.[12] By the end of 2009, China had helped construct more than 500 African infrastructure projects, and from 2001 to 2010, trade volume between China and the continent rose from $10 billion to $130 billion, according to Li Changchun, a member of the Chinese Communist Party Standing Committee.[13] The country's government in 2007 launched an equity fund to encourage Chinese companies to invest in Africa, with starting capital of $1 billion. Less than two years later, the fund reportedly had reached $2 billion.[14]

In 2009 and 2010 China lent more money to poor countries, mainly in Africa, than the World Bank.[15] Western companies noting China's inroads are

FIGURE 7.1   Number of Battle-Related Deaths in Sub-Saharan Africa and the World

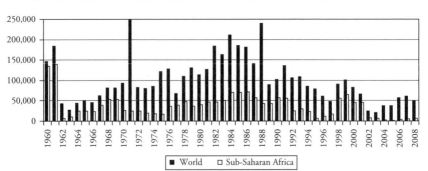

Source: World Development Indicator.

Tringo Negaso sells corn by the cup in an outdoor market near Soddo, Ethiopia, January 2011.

A trader signals orders in the corn options pit at the Chicago Board of Trade shortly after the U.S. Department of Agriculture (USDA) released a crop report in March 2008.
Source: Frank Polich, Bloomberg News.

A man sells tea to customers from a street stall in Tahrir Square, Cairo, Egypt, in 2011. Egyptian President Hosni Mubarak left power after pro-democracy protests fueled by outrage over consumer prices.
Source: Andrew Burton, Bloomberg News.

Hugo Alejandro, Nicaraguan tomato farmer. The veteran of the country's civil wars of the 1980s now sells tomatoes to a subsidiary of Walmart.

A butcher chops up a pig carcass at a meat wholesale and distribution center in Shanghai, China, March 2011.
Source: Qilai Shen, Bloomberg News.

Longshoremen unload U.S. food aid at the Port of Djibouti in Djibouti, East Africa, in August 2008. The aid, consisting of dried green peas and vegetable oil, was bound for Ethiopia.
Source: Jason McLure, Bloomberg News.

Haylar Ayako stands outside empty grain bins at the edge of his field near Shala-Luka in Ethiopia's South Omo region on October 16, 2008. Ayako received a ration that included peas from the August Djibouti shipment.

Wado Isho (left), Ethiopian farmer. Wado, one of the few literate men in his town, sold cattle to feed his family during the 2008 food crisis. His nine children survived.

Josette Sheeran, executive director of the United Nations World Food Programme, speaks during a hearing of the Senate Foreign Relations Committee in Washington, DC, May 2008. *Source:* Brendan Smialowski, Bloomberg News.

Eleni Gabre-Madhin, CEO of the Ethiopia Commodity Exchange. The leader of the commodity trading floor, established in 2008, has promoted transparent trading of grains in Addis Ababa as coffee and sesame have become the dominant crops traded.

Monsanto Co. insect-protected Genuity Roundup Ready 2 Yield soybean plants grow in a research field near Pirassununga, Brazil, in February, 2011. Monsanto, the world's largest seed company, is testing these genetically engineered soybeans to tolerate the company's Roundup herbicide and further boost Brazilian yields.
Source: Paulo Fridman, Bloomberg News.

Tissue-culture bananas in a jar at the Kenya Agricultural Research Institute in Thika. Mass cloning of bananas in a lab protects the pathogen-prone plants from an early death, even while climate change threatens necessary water supplies.

Rebecca Wairimu Njoroge, standing, at the Sabasaba banana-weighing station. The agribusiness center, one hour from Nairobi, gives farmers a chance to collect and store tropical fruit and increase the number of potential buyers.

Wilfredo Meneses, a potato farmer in Nicaragua, is experimenting with organic cabbage, which commands a higher price from urban buyers.

Rice buyers in Thailand. Traders have tried to revive rice markets even as political parties promised to isolate farmers from the forces of supply and demand.

stepping up their own involvement, with everything from Harley-Davidson dealers in Botswana to General Electric opening its first aircraft-leasing office in Ghana.[16] China's exports to the continent were $54 billion in 2010, compared to $5.6 billion in 2000. U.S. shipments rose to $21 billion from $7.6 billion in the same period.

Greater trade and better governance give countries more opportunities when they work together. The African Union's establishment of the Comprehensive Africa Agriculture Development Programme (CAADP) in 2003 is a continental effort to increase public investment in agriculture to 10 percent of national budgets annually and to coordinate approaches to land and water management, access to markets, and agricultural research. Robust agricultural extension services that teach better farming in the countryside, crucial to boosting production around the world, are key to creating a framework for growth. By 2015, the effort is aiming for 6 percent annual agricultural production growth across the continent, which would also help nations reach national Millennium Development Goals set at the century's start. African countries need to better connect farmers to better seeds, fertilizers, and equipment so they can grow more and higher quality food for growing urban markets, according to Josue Dione, food security director for the Economic Commission for Africa.

African agriculture needs to go "beyond the narrow confines of the farm stage to embrace the agro-industry and agribusiness stages that connect farmers to markets," he said in Addis Ababa in January 2011.[17]

More cooperation among better-governed countries in turn generates more investment from more sources. Foreign direct inflows to sub-Saharan Africa rose from $6.8 billion in 2000 to $30.7 billion in 2009, according to World Bank data. The amount needs to be put in context—world direct investment in all countries in 2009 was $1.2 trillion, and foreign investment in the United States, the leading destination of global dollars, was $134.7 billion, down from $328.3 billion the year before because of the financial crisis. Still, the trend points to Africa's increased interest from the private companies it needs to connect with the global market.

With world food prices rising and more food needed from more places to satisfy the planet's growing appetites, that couldn't come at a better time.

■ ■ ■

A. Namanga Ngongi was a retired career agronomist in Cameroon when the Bill and Melinda Gates Foundation asked him to lead their new initiative to transform African agriculture, the Alliance for a Green Revolution in Africa (AGRA), started in 2006 with funding from the Rockefeller Foundation and the Gates Foundation. Running his finger over a large map of the continent in his Nairobi office, he gives a primer on the continent's farming challenges, breaking down their complexities and offering a set of solutions that, while admittedly easier said than done, frame a comprehensive vision of what the continent could become.

The first change needs to be in the traditional mindset of many African farmers, he said.[18]

"Agriculture today in Africa is seen as a way of life more than as a business," he said. His job at AGRA, he said, is to put in place lasting agricultural networks rather than simply dole out money on development projects that may have short-term gains but not much of a recipe for long-term success. Better seeds, efficient water use, more fertilizer, more research, more training—all are necessary to improve productivity, feed hungry populations, and integrate farmers into the global marketplace, he said.

"The systems will be self-sustaining," he said. "Once they begin to benefit, it won't require anything more from us. They will be linked to the market."

Agricultural development is at least twice as effective in reducing poverty in the poorest half of a country's population as growth from nonfarm sectors, according to World Bank estimates.[19] There's room to grow. Africa has nine times the land area of India and fewer mouths to feed. Even with a tripling of population by 2100, its population density would remain less than much of the world today. If farmers brought more land into use, raised crop yields to 80 percent of the world's average, and focused on higher-value crops, African farmers would nearly double their wealth to $500 billion in the next decade, according to one study.[20] That would encourage further investment, make rural and urban populations less vulnerable to price shocks, and create new food sources that countries could turn to when their own supplies were disrupted.

The time frame for when this happens varies from country to country. South Africa joined the BRIC (Brazil, Russia, India, and China) bloc of emerging-nation powers for a summit in April 2011, coining the acronym BRICS. The same year it planned to launch its own development aid agency, positioning itself to help the rest of the continent.[21] Gains in Ghana and Malawi are encouraging self-sufficiency in their own regions. The continent is not a monolith, and chances are a revolution or civil war will be occurring somewhere at some time, and chances are good that's what will receive the most daily attention on other continents. Elsewhere there is progress, the updated narrative.

An Africa that feeds itself, and others, seems ambitious, but it's been done elsewhere. The story of Asia's Green Revolution is practically a catechism in food-security circles, a model for how famine-afflicted parts of the world can make themselves more productive. From the 1940s to the 1970s, a steady series of agricultural innovations, including hybrid seeds, extensive irrigation, synthetic fertilizers, and pesticides, dramatically improved crop yields in Asia and Latin America. The gains upended expectations that crops couldn't keep up with population growth.

Norman Borlaug, a plant scientist from Minnesota who refused to accept that assumption, led the way toward increased food production in some of the world's poorest regions, first with hybrid-seed projects in Latin America, then in India in the 1960s. Miracle rice fed populations previously considered impossible to sustain, and better wheat varieties boosted yields. The Green Revolution not only helped countries feed themselves, it set the stage for manufacturing and services growth, raising prosperity throughout the region.

Borlaug won the Nobel Peace Prize in 1970 for his efforts, and until his death in 2009 at age 95 he touted the necessity of ever-more-sophisticated science in agriculture, saying that genetically modified crops were the only way to feed a growing population. His attempts to bring the Green Revolution to Africa largely failed. Reasons ranged from political turmoil to technical challenges: African nations rely on staple foods ranging from cassava, corn, sorghum, and millet to bananas, wheat, and teff, making a solution based on one or two crops impractical. The revolution also included government interventions such as price supports, an approach frowned upon by rich-world development institutions at the end of the twentieth century but more tolerated today.

Better conditions and the need for new food sources may make the Greening of Africa more successful this time. Ghana, Mali, Mozambique, Tanzania, Zambia, Malawi may be (literally) low-hanging fruit, with Uganda, South Sudan, and the Horn of Africa nations of Ethiopia and Kenya not far behind. The continent's breadbaskets could become an engine for food security and growth for their neighbors, connected more closely by trade ties and better prepared to ship surpluses to the world. Food security would become global security, as the world marketplace develops new sources to meet its needs.

The challenges are daunting. Road and electricity access are up, but still not comparable with Latin America or South Asia and seemingly not on the same planet as other regions. Governments still deteriorate rapidly for reasons unfathomable to outsiders, making stable law and contract enforcement dicey. Trade and subsidy rules bedevil relationships both within and outside the continent. Permeating everything are difficult questions about how hotter weather and higher populations will be handled.

But in Angata Barakoi, Christina Chebi Ngogi has hope as she prepares her maize for market.

■ ■ ■

Her upbringing was typical of her time and place. She did not attend school, working instead on the family farm. At age 16, a man three decades her senior, a friend of her father's, visited the family home. She said they struck up a friendship, and the family found him an acceptable husband for her. She became his third wife. The first of her 13 children was born when she was 18. Three died shortly after birth, and 10 are still alive.

After the massacre the village was in chaos. Many of its leaders were dead. Still wary of bandits, more than 80 widows banded together into a self-help group, a less formal type of farmer cooperative in which growers with a common interest combine to sell their crops together. Her husband's other two wives, both older, are also cooperative members. Running the co-op's operations, with financing from AGRA and sales to the WFP and local buyers, along with her own farm is challenging, she said; when older members are sick, they ask her to assist in delivering grain when she has her own to harvest.

These are small concerns compared to the days when bandits kept her village in fear.

■ ■ ■

The village's potential is seeing its first glimmers of being reached.[22] Sub-Saharan Africa has a long way to go. Much of the region remains poorly connected, ill-supported in development, and even bandit-prone. As a Council on Foreign Relations paper put it in 2008, the typical sub-Saharan African farmer is someone who resembles Ngogi half a decade earlier: "a woman with no fertilizer, no high-yield seeds, no irrigation, and no medication for her animals."

And a lot of children.

The world's population, long expected to stabilize at 9 billion around 2050, will more likely keep rising to about 10.1 billion people by 2100.[23] Africa is the hub of high fertility, with its population potentially rising from 1 billion to 3.6 billion by century's end. Farm production already has badly lagged population growth, turning sub-Saharan countries into food importers rather than exporters. The combination of import dependence and subsistence farming practically ensures poverty. When import costs spike and farmers aren't connected to food markets, city dwellers receive all of the pain of higher costs without the consolation of farmers getting more income for their goods. Subsistence farmers aren't selling a surplus—in fact, if they don't grow enough for themselves, they'll actually become poorer, since they rely on imports, too. Poorer farmers have little incentive, or income, to invest in fertilizers or chemicals that may give them better crops if they can't first get to the level of selling extra food to local markets. And without finance for new seeds and fertilizers, roads to get their crops to market, or storage bins to hold their surplus for a better price, the food market works for no one.

The woman with no fertilizer, no high-yield seeds, no irrigation, and no medication for her animals also usually lacks access to education, which has an inverse relationship to family size. In many countries, she isn't allowed to own or lease land, depriving her of one possible route to financial security; only 3 percent of Kenyan women have title deeds, and in Tanzania, only 1 percent own land.[24] Simply providing women farmers with the same access to resources as men could boost yields by 20 to 30 percent, according to one study.[25] Education of girls has seen slow, steady progress over the past decade. (See Figure 7.2.) As women gain skills and more life options, birth rates decline, which is necessary to keep population gains from cancelling out bigger crops. Integrating educated women into commodity markets and food

FIGURE 7.2 Sub-Saharan Africa Ratio of Girls to Boys in Primary and Secondary Education (%)

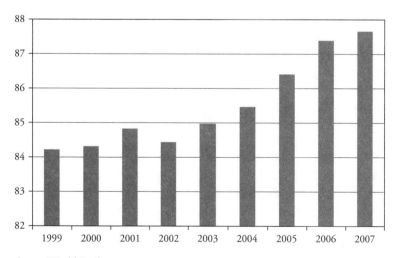

Source: World Bank.

production is tricky in places where the rights of women may be equivalent to, or somewhat below, those of their livestock. Without women who control their own farming and have the training to be better at it, African agriculture will grow more slowly while populations rise faster.

Political unrest still harms investment. An Ivory Coast election where the losing president refused to step down threw cocoa exports into chaos in early 2011. Wars have killed any hope of nonmineral growth in the Darfur region, the Niger Delta, the Central African Republic, and Chad for the foreseeable future. Two-thirds of the world's HIV/AIDS cases are in sub-Saharan Africa, combining with other diseases to drive down life expectancies. Zimbabwe, potentially one of the continent's most fertile regions, has seen its average lifespan fall to 47 for women and 48 for men. In 1990 it was 60. Robert Mugabe, Zimbabwe's leader since 1980, is closing in on 90.

South Sudan, Africa's newest nation, is a stark example of the continent's challenges. With vast arable lands and plentiful rainfall, the region is a potential breadbasket, yet when it became independent in July 2011, was dependent on food aid for its citizens. Border warfare, internal rebellion, and the worst poverty rate in Africa persist, with only 100 miles of paved roads in the country, an adult illiteracy rate of 85 percent, half of its population living on less than $1 a day and 98 percent of its national budget coming from oil revenue. On top of that, weak legal codes make it a prime target for foreign land-buyers, who held up to 9 percent of some of the nation's best farmland the day of independence. Euphoria quickly fades in such a setting.[26]

Lack of finance remains a major growth constraint, even after generations of development plans and well-meaning loans that yielded few tangible results. At the local level, microfinance, pioneered by Nobel Prize Winner Muhammad Yunus and Grameen Bank in Bangladesh, has helped start small, community-oriented projects that build markets. Mainstream African and international banks, the ones with resources to make a major difference, remain hesitant to extend credit to cash-poor, weather-dependent farmers, and farmer cooperatives, an alternate means for agriculture financing, often remain without enough capital to be an effective growth engine. African farm investment remains caught in a paradox in which finance is needed to build prosperity, but prosperity is what attracts finance. And because progress in many places requires a larger dose of patience than many investors require elsewhere, capital remains difficult to attract.

"Bankers like to have security and collateral, and farming is very risky," with price swings making it riskier, said Lars Thunell, chief executive officer of the International Finance Corporation, a member of the World Bank Group. High prices can also create opportunity, he said. "There is more money to share now, and where you have the potential for a profitable investment, you can do it. The entrepreneurs will find solutions."[27]

Ngozi Okonjo-Iweala was the first woman to be either finance minister or foreign minister of Nigeria, to which she returned in 2011 after serving as the managing director of the World Bank. Financial shortcomings plague efforts to boost farm investment throughout Africa, she said. "Moving into a market requires finance," she said. "If you can sell a product and create savings, then you can create more credit in rural areas," which in turn motivates investment and production.[28]

Once production rises, it has to go somewhere—otherwise, surpluses drive down prices and destroy any reason to grow more food in the first place. Trade barriers within Africa, apart from the ones that limit their access to richer regions, still pose problems for the continent's farmers. Even if African farmers did have access to credit, roads, storage, and free trade, the incentive to invest in productivity is dampened by the lack of the insurance protection and subsidies that keep rich-country farmers in business in years when rain doesn't fall. Even when a price signal is calling for more food, poor farmers don't necessarily heed the message.

Those are problems of the present. In some ways, the future will be more difficult.

All that available farmland isn't just sitting there, waiting for a tractor. Coexisting with fertile lands are soils depleted from overplanting and overgrazing, making a brown revolution to improve soil quality more important than new seeds and fertilizers, according to Howard Buffett.[29] Soil quality, like air or water quality, is necessary to provide the structure and nutrients necessary for sustainable crop growth.

A warming planet poses the danger of lower yields that will make it even more difficult to feed a growing population. World demand for cereals—corn, wheat, rice, and less-common grains—is expected to rise about 1 percent a year through 2050. Sub-Saharan Africa's demand is expected to double that, rising almost 2.5 percent a year. Yield gains may not match the need, in part because its warming is expected to be above the global average and bigger crops may not keep pace with population.[30]

The end result would be greater dependence on more expensive imports, a step backward in the fight for more food. Eastern Africa would see food imports rise an additional 15 percent as more volatile weather damages corn yields.[31] Tighter food supplies will push local prices in sub-Saharan Africa even higher than they would have been without worse weather—corn, rice, and wheat prices at 4, 7, and 15 percent higher than they otherwise would have been, while important local crops such as cassava will rise 20 percent, lowering calorie intake and increasing child malnutrition.[32] By 2030, nearly 1 million additional children in sub-Saharan Africa will be malnourished because of climate change, according to one study.

Africa, especially famine-prone East Africa, where Ngogi lives, features the most rainfall-dependent farming in the world, with only 6 percent of its cultivated land under irrigation. About two-thirds of that area is in Egypt, Madagascar, Morocco, South Africa, and Sudan. That area produces 38 percent of Africa's crop value. Well-deployed irrigation systems could boost production and mitigate the effects of climate change. But irrigation requires investment, and it often requires a desire for regional cooperation that' may still be lacking; for example, Egypt's revolution has complicated negotiations for a new water-sharing agreement on the Nile River, crucial to developing East African irrigation and electricity. Even with adequate soil and water, crop disease looms as a continual threat, with scientists racing against time to combat pathogens such as aflotoxins and the Ug99 stem rust fungus, which originated in Uganda and is devastating wheat crops in East Africa's highlands. New wheat strains bred for resistance hold promise in fighting the scourge, but mobile populations and ever-changing strains will perpetually threaten yields.[33]

Unstable governance, high birth rates, lack of finance, trade barriers, climate change, human diseases from HIV to malaria and more, oppression of women, suppression of political freedom and free speech—all these issues, and more, threaten to stymie development of the breadbasket the world needs. A world trying to satisfy its appetites doesn't really have much choice but to bet that such a breadbasket may develop, a reality increasingly recognized by the world's philanthropists and policymakers as they call for more foreign aid.

■ ■ ■

Assistance alone won't be the answer.

In 2009, the signers of the L'Aquila Joint Statement on Global Food Security wrote they were "deeply concerned about global food security, the impact of the global financial and economic crisis and last year's spike in food prices on the countries least able to respond to increased hunger and poverty." The statement also called for $20 billion over three years for a "coordinated, comprehensive strategy focused on sustainable development."

The call for action echoes decades of global declarations on the need to end hunger.[34] That is not to condemn foreign aid or international declarations, from which tangible progress can occur.[35] Talk is, indeed, cheap—pledges don't always follow. Two years after L'Aquila, donors had not come anywhere near meeting the $22 billion pledged for aid.[36] Even that number was paltry by some estimates of what's needed—while L'Aquila was driving toward $22 billion over three years, the UN Food and Agriculture Organization was saying developing-world farmers needed $83 billion annually to feed the world.[37] Lowering enthusiasm for aid is the sentiment that money doesn't always help. The more than $2 trillion of official development assistance given to Africa in the past half-century—not to mention the billions contributed by individuals giving less than the price of a cup of coffee—hasn't pulled many nations out of poverty. In fact, it may have made some situations worse, as assistance distorted local markets and bred government corruption (see Figure 7.3). The dreaded "Dutch disease," in which an abundance of natural resources crowds out other forms of economic wealth, may also be applied to an over-allocation of aid, some experts argue.[38]

"The fact is, agricultural development efforts over the past 20 years have failed miserably in many developing countries, especially in Africa," said Howard Buffett. "With standard development projects, at some point the project ends and the money stops. If done poorly, these projects can even create a dependency."[39]

Buffett tries to avoid past failures by focusing on efforts that develop farming skills and connect farmers to markets, giving them a way to succeed

FIGURE 7.3   Net Official Development Assistance Received per Capita (2010 US$)

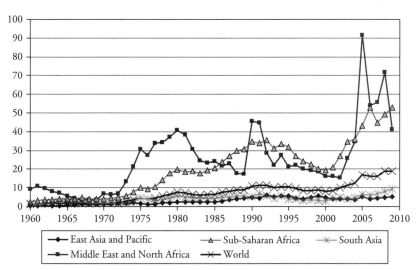

Source: World Bank.

after the money is gone. The World Food Programme's (WPF's) Purchase for Progress (P4P) initiative, a five-year pilot project that started in 2008, is targeted for 21 countries and 500,000 smallholder farmers—using the WFP's purchasing power to develop local markets for their goods. Working with partners ranging from local government extension services to other humanitarian groups, the program is meant to introduce modern warehouses, grading practices, and contracts that will allow growers to become part of the world food chain. It receives most of its donations from the governments of Canada and Belgium along with the Buffett and Gates foundations, as well as partnerships with dozens of other groups.

P4P takes different approaches to connecting farmers to markets in different countries. In Ethiopia and Zambia it buys food through commodity exchanges, putting small-farmer products on national trading platforms. In Uganda and Tanzania, it's developing warehouse receipt systems where farmers can deposit their produce and get immediate financial credit while storing for a better price later. The WFP buys much of the food through cooperative unions of farmers, allowing small-scale production to be aggregated to levels meaningful to a buyer. Throughout, farmers learn how to grow higher-quality food that will be more competitive on markets, gain access to better storage techniques, and learn how to use credit to finance improved production.

In Kenya's transmara region, the shift is evident in David Leposo's jacket and pants—the neatly pressed outfit he wears while going everywhere with his walking stick and his knife, two essential accessories of a Maasai tribesman. The governments of Kenya and Tanzania have encouraged the pastoralist Maasai to embrace farming, an approach that some aid groups have criticized as short-sighted, saying that climate change will make their ability to farm in deserts more necessary for survival.[40] Many Maasai continue to herd in the vast ranges near East Africa's game parks, but as their populations have increased, farming has provided income and a way to stay fed as cattle herds dwindle.

Leposo started farming on a two-acre plot he got from his parents when he was 16. Now in his early twenties, he farms 20 acres and rents a tractor to help cultivate his corn and beans. He gets a better price for his goods at a WFP warehouse, where his beans can be stored while he waits for a more advantageous time to sell, rather than be dependent on private buyers who visit his farm.

Leposo, a lanky young man who turns from jovial to earnest when asked about how he can serve the Maasai, is saving his extra income for college in Kisii, where he wants to study business. After that, he'll have enough money saved to seek out a wife and enough education to make a difference in his village, with the knowledge of how to sell their goods. "For my people not to buy their food from outside, from other countries, that is my aim," he said. "And then, when the drought comes, or when the other people, they are in pain, I can be their star."[41]

The key difference between the new WFP approach and previous aid, Buffett said, is the emphasis on transitioning farmers toward self-sufficiency. "Success is when these farmers sell to commercial buyers, not WFP. WFP is simply the catalyst that allows the program to be initiated," he said. The idea is to put tools in place for farming to expand and connect growers with the businesses that can both be stable partners and providers of some of the investment the UN says is needed, but which governments and aid agencies will never—and probably shouldn't—provide.

The initiative doesn't promise to be transformative, or even universally successful—one of its goals is simply figuring out how market building may work in a world of difficult-to-connect small farmers.[42] Once the pilot is complete, the WFP hopes the farmers will become viable sellers to local hospitals, universities, and retailers that can take advantage of the inexpensive, nearby production. The WFP, meanwhile, would use the lessons learned from its efforts to expand its purchases from smallholder farmers.

The market mantra easily predates P4P and has been a part of the aid landscape for years, with groups such as TechnoServe, ACDI/VOCA, Food for the Hungry, World Vision, Catholic Relief Services, and CARE all working to build farmer capacity. AGRA's market focus includes creating seed-seller networks, leveraging loan guarantees into financing in Tanzania, Mozambique, Ghana, Uganda, and Kenya. Market-building aid isn't the magic-bullet solution to all that ails African agriculture. It's becoming more central to development as the food economy becomes more globalized and government budget cuts make aid flows less certain.

The U.S. Agency for International Development's Feed the Future initiative, led by agency chief and former Gates agricultural development program director Rajiv Shah, fits this framework. Feed the Future shares more with Purchase for Progress than catchy alliteration; it also aims to target investment toward building the abilities of small-scale farmers and agribusinesses along with support for agriculture research. It also tries to be more hands-off in top-down requirements for nations that receive the aid, listing "supporting country ownership" as a goal. Donors are better at recognizing at what they can and can't do, said Radelet.

"Poor people don't need handouts," said Kanayo Nwanze of IFAD. "They are looking for economic opportunity like you and I," he said. "They want their children to go to school. Infrastructure, electricity, social services, clinics. It's going to happen."[43]

For Christina Chebi Ngogi, what's happened is a better life.

Tensions with neighboring groups haven't disappeared, but a government security station near the village has reduced the threat of violence, as has a peace agreement that has kept warring factions at bay. Angata Barakoi's farmers can now focus their worries on weather, yields, and market prices—the same things that worry farmers everywhere—with bandits a thing of the past.

Her family has also done well since the massacre. Most of her children have found good jobs in town, and during tough times they have the farm to fall back on, although one son—who failed his final school exams in the weeks after his father died—continues to struggle.

Ngogi lives in a Christian area of Kenya. She says faith has helped her survive, and grow, in her transformation from grieving widow to cooperative leader. She believes in heaven, and she believes her husband knows of the family's success. He would be very proud of her and her children, she said. "They've grown up well.

"And none of them will ever steal anything."

Farmers like her will be increasingly important to feeding Africa, and Africa will become increasingly important to feeding the world. To get there, business investment, intelligently applied aid, stable governments, and leadership from the countries themselves will all be necessary, Radelet said. The developed world may not always agree with what developing nations do, and actions may have unintended consequences. The approach—letting markets evolve, with a little help from aid and acceptance of trial-and-error, will ultimately create food-security solutions that stick.

And that may change the price of a cup of coffee.

CHAPTER 8

The Price of a Cup of Coffee

The 3 P.M. coffee trade is about to begin in Addis Ababa, and buyers and sellers are putting on their jackets as they take their places in the single pit of the Ethiopia Commodity Exchange (ECX). The jackets come in two colors: Tan denotes a coffee buyer; green indicates a seller.

About 50 traders fill the floor of the terraced pit. A green, red, and yellow display flashes reference prices—coffee from New York; wheat and corn from Chicago; sesame from Nigeria, India, and Sudan. The tan jackets stand with their backs to the walls, waiting for the green jackets to make an offer. Most of the traders are men, though a sprinkling of women including two in hijab, are scribbling on their notepads and waiting for trades.

Dinku Sileshi is a seller. The general manager of Chefa Dira General Business has been supplying coffee from Ethiopia's Oromia region to the country's exporters for 17 years. Working the trading floor, he punctuates his bids with high-fives, signifying a deal has been made. ("It's like spitting on your hands before shaking them in your country," he says.) He calls the ECX a "seismic change" for traders such as himself.

Before the exchange, "we had to chase the exporters to get our check. Now we can buy and get the money tomorrow," he said.[1] Farmers also benefit from the more transparent market, he said. The ECX gives them a national reference price they use to negotiate with buyers, ensuring that they know what varieties they should grow for national and international markets.

Separate sessions for coffee, sesame, white pea beans, and maize are held throughout the day on the trading floor that opened in 2008, just as the world's most famine-prone region was poised for another. The exchange, says its chief executive officer, Eleni Gabre-Madhin, is meant to bring the benefits of sophisticated commodities trading—what made Chicago great—to Addis Ababa. The entire agricultural production chain, from farmers to consumers, can benefit, she said. In 2011, the exchange was taking "baby steps," not yet offering Chicago-style futures contracts. Anecdotal evidence suggests that transparent trading was helping farmers who have received roughly 30 percent of the price paid for exported coffee now get more than 60 percent, additional income that's crucial to improving Ethiopia's food security, she said.

In Victoria, British Columbia, family-owned Discovery Coffee boasts two cafes, its own roaster, and coffee-tasting classes for its clientele. It prides itself on bringing the world's best coffee to its customers, and its owner, John Riopka, is disappointed. Discovery's menu boasts beans from Central and South America and Indonesia, bought through brokers who buy directly from farmers through relationships that take years to cultivate. Seldom on the menu are beans from the beverage's self-proclaimed birthplace. Ethiopia can't be trusted, he says.

"We don't buy coffee from Ethiopia anymore," said Riopka, whose company had been buying from the Yirgacheffe and Harrar regions before the Ethiopia Commodity Exchange made it more difficult for him to buy coffee that had "traceability," the ability to follow a bean back to the farmers who grew it. Discovery's purchases now go to places where it's easier to know where the coffee came from and farmers are more directly connected to buyers in the specialty coffee market, a fast-growing segment of the $70 billion global industry, he said.

"The risk for me is if we cannot be assured the quality of the coffee, we're not going to buy it," he said.[2]

Ethiopia, in many years the world's biggest recipient of food aid, is trying to end that, in part by becoming Africa's most innovative nation in using a trading floor to help feed its people. Its founders hope the exchange will evolve with and improve Ethiopia's rapidly growing economy. Chicago is an inspiration, but the ECX is meant to be a commodities exchange with African characteristics, adapted to the smallholder farmer. After its first three years, it has shown just how complex food security can be when government, foreign and domestic businesses, and attempts to link farmers to markets intersect. Trading is growing, as is the country. Whether it will be central to solving Ethiopia's daunting food-security needs is still to be seen.

"The jury is out on Ethiopia," said Nicholas Sitko, a Michigan State University researcher on food security and commodity exchanges in Africa.

■ ■ ■

Gabre-Madhin is leaning forward in her office chair at a desk laden with family photos, a multi-colored cross, and a deer-shaped paperweight. Dr. Eleni, as she's commonly called, is in her mid-forties and speaks of her exchange, and the challenge of feeding Ethiopia, with the enthusiasm and earnestness of a teenager energized to change the world. She returned to Ethiopia in 2004 after nearly 30 years of absence, living in more than half a dozen countries and learning three languages after her family fled Ethiopia's Marxist regime, the Derg. Her mother was from Harar, an eastern Ethiopian city famous for its coffee, and her father, a senior United Nations official, was born in the Southern Nations region.[3] She earned a bachelor's degree in economics from Cornell University in New York, a master's from Michigan State, and a doctorate in applied economics from Stanford University. She's worked at the World Bank, the United Nations, and the International Food Policy Research Institute, which returned her to Ethiopia to improve the country's agricultural markets and policies. Her credibility in finance and development garners attention for the exchange as she travels abroad to evangelize how modern markets may bring food security to Ethiopia. And she's media savvy. When I let slip that ECX security took away my camera after I told them I wanted to shoot the exchange floor, she sends someone to get it back so I can chronicle the day's coffee trade.

From her office overlooking the trading floor, she explains her vision for the ECX. Like Chicago, it's located at the hub of its region's road, telecommunications, and commercial networks, giving Ethiopia's traders a central place to set prices that then can be broadcast nation- and worldwide. Like Chicago in the 1800s, it's intended to raise the quality of the nation's food, centralize a warehouse system where farmers can store their crops until they find a good time to sell, and communicate prices that tell farmers and consumers the true value of the food they're buying and selling: answering "What's it worth?" in the Horn of Africa.

Ethiopia is far from the first African country to attempt a commodities exchange, though it may be the most ambitious in what it's trying to achieve. Malawi, Zambia, and Nigeria have all started exchanges in the past decade, following South Africa, Kenya, and others. South Africa, an outlier in African agriculture in many ways, has the biggest farm-derivatives exchange; others provide limited services, such as regulating warehouses in Uganda and helping World Food Programme procurement in Malawi. Some succeed in niche roles, others fade away. They tend to suffer from similar problems: Funding withers after initial donations from aid agencies; the countries the exchanges serve often aren't large enough to sustain the volume needed to maintain efficient trading; and governments that are more than happy to give markets a chance change their minds when prices don't go the way they want them to. Their intervention tends to kill trading, because buyers and sellers begin to wonder whether the market is being manipulated.

A test of success for the ECX is whether it can connect farmers with surpluses to areas that are hungry, Gabre-Madhin said. Hunger in Ethiopia, like famines everywhere, is often a matter of food distribution rather than availability—in the famines of the 1980s, surpluses in one region coexisted with shortages in others. An exchange that gives buyers and sellers a platform to buy and sell encourages the trust needed to get goods moving—again, a concept that would have been familiar to Iowans and New Yorkers of the 1850s. The exchange will help Ethiopia feed itself as roads and communication improve, she said. Ultimately, it will help expand Ethiopia's food production and give its citizens more money to feed themselves. The distribution challenge in Ethiopia is a microcosm of the world at large, said Wyn Morgan, a professor at the University of Nottingham in the United Kingdom who researches food prices and volatility. "What they're trying to do is support that movement, that flow of resource, driven by clear and believable prices," he said. "This is about providing confidence to traders, both buyers and sellers, in the price information they've got."

If Ethiopia can adapt modern trading to its own needs, Gabre-Madhin continued, grain farmers in one area could relieve another when rains fail and famine spreads. Ethiopia's food processors could hedge their risks on the market, smoothing out supply and demand. Famine, the ever-lurking national nightmare, would fade.

Understanding famine is essential to understanding why the exchange was created.

■ ■ ■

Subsistence agriculture has dominated Africa's second-most-populous country for centuries. Farming accounts for more than 45 percent of the country's Gross Domestic Product and more than four-fifths of its exports and workforce, populated by Haylar Ayako and millions of farmers like him who plant and cultivate their land as their families have for generations. As in much of sub-Saharan Africa, Ethiopia's poor roads, those that are barren and those lined with boys selling fruit, trinkets, or khat, a stimulant banned in many nations, make it difficult to get crops to market. Inadequate storage keeps surpluses from being held over from one year to the next. Food insecurity is a cause and an effect of poverty: In 2010 about 10 million Ethiopians, roughly 11 percent of the population, received food aid. The total was second only to Pakistan, which had experienced devastating floods. Only one-fifth of the landlocked country's roads are paved, and the country has one railroad line, which extends from Addis Ababa to Djibouti, an independent city-state that serves as Ethiopia's port.[4]

The lack of infrastructure has bedeviled Ethiopia for decades, creating famines that were as tragic as they were unnecessary.

Historically, poor farmers had little reason to manage surpluses. Extra food was a privilege of the aristocracy, who seized it when they needed it. Farmers' inability to ride out lean harvests inevitably led to starvation. Famine in the 1970s brought down the government of Emperor Haile Selassie and ushered in the Derg, a Soviet-aligned state that drained Ethiopia's economy, treasury, and brainpower. Farm productivity worsened under the leadership of the Derg's dictator, Mengistu Haile Mariam, who after his ouster was found guilty of genocide for ignoring hunger and killing thousands of his political opponents.[5] The mid-1980s famines spurred an outpouring of assistance that included the Live Aid concert organized by Irish singer Bob Geldof, "We Are the World," co-written by Michael Jackson and Stevie Wonder, and the beginning of the era in which rock stars became players in Africa's development. It also undid the Derg, who by 1991 were completely ousted by the Ethiopian People's Revolutionary Democratic Front, whose leader, Prime Minister Meles Zenawi, has ruled the country to this day.

According to the 2010 Ibrahim Index (an attempt by the foundation founded by Sudanese telecom billionaire Mo Ibrahim to statistically measure government quality in Africa), Ethiopia's governance was ranked 35th out of 53 African nations; 17th in environmental and rural policy, 16th in public management, and 40th in human rights.[6] It's also rated 40th out of 48 African countries in press freedom, according to Freedom House.[7] Regions near conflict- and famine-ridden Somalia are closed off to foreign press, and the government is suspicious of journalists with cameras.

Ethiopia's legal structures are weak, and private land ownership doesn't exist, making it a prime destination for foreign land acquisition. Yet, Addis Ababa is being taken over by construction cranes as Ethiopia experiences a period of relative peace. The *Economist* magazine predicted that Ethiopia will follow only China and India in growth to be the third-fastest-growing economy in the world from 2011–2015, and the fastest in sub-Saharan Africa.[8]

Ethiopia in 2010 adopted a five-year growth plan to expand the country's road network to 90,720 miles from 49,000, build a 1,200-mile rail network, and increase electricity coverage to 75 percent of the population from 41 percent. The country also plans to lease 7.4 million acres of land for large-scale farming.[9] Agricultural income and trade are key elements to funding the expansion.

■ ■ ■

The changes will enable Ethiopia to feed its own population and have a surplus for export, Zenawi said upon the growth plan's approval by parliament. The country is seeking outside investors to help maintain its double-digit growth, although reminders of the country's violent heritage persist: Zenawi was quoted in the *Ethiopian Herald*, a government-run English-language newspaper, in February 2011 as saying that "investors are not criminals and enemies; they are our development partners. Our focus should be to correct them, not behead them."[10]

While higher production is a national policy, bigger crops can be a disaster without a place to sell them. Early in the 2000s, plentiful Ethiopian harvests perversely caused a hunger crisis, when farmers with no desirable place to store, ship, or sell surpluses saw crops rot in the field as prices plunged. Because it cost more to grow food than what they received for selling it, farmers cut back their next plantings. When drought arrived, the surplus ran out and the new harvest wasn't enough to feed rural and urban populations as nutrition ran out and prices spiked over the next year. The result was 13 million Ethiopians at famine risk.[11]

The idea of a commodity exchange to connect the nation's crop markets gathered steam. Gabre-Madhin emerged as the key voice behind the creation of what became the ECX.[12] After more than a year of meetings by a government-appointed task force that she led, the ECX was established by government proclamation in September 2007 "to ensure that the marketing system is fair, transparent and efficient to protect the interests of the different actors of the system and the public at large."[13] The exchange opened in April 2008. The dream, Zenawi said at its opening, would be to "revolutionize the country's backward and inefficient marketing system."[14]

The dream was accompanied by money: $31.6 million in aid from the United States, European Union, Canada, the World Bank, and the United Nations.[15] (In comparison, the Malawi-based Agricultural Commodity Exchange for Africa has received $1.2 million.)[16] The exchange is being watched by other countries contemplating or implementing their own

exchanges. And coffee—a crop vital to the incomes and food security of Ethiopian farmers—became a crucial test of the exchange's early
development.

■ ■ ■

The legend of Ethiopian coffee begins with the story of Kaldi, a first-
millennium goatherd who noticed that animals eating the berries of a certain
tree grew so frisky they could not sleep at night. Kaldi told a local monk of his
discovery. The cleric examined the berries and made them into a drink that
kept him awake for evening prayers. He shared it with other monks, and soon
word of the great-tasting stimulant spread to the Arabian peninsula and its
trade routes, sending coffee around the world.[17]

It's a fun creation myth, an homage to coffee's actual East African
origins and its Ethiopian importance. The story also indicates Ethiopia's
potential as a market for coffee aficionados and their premium-price purchases of single-origin specialty coffee, beans bought from a specific source
with unique characteristics. Coffee is Ethiopia's most lucrative crop; worldwide, about 25 million farmers rely on it for income. Many see only a
fraction of the money a consumer pays for a drink in a coffee shop—one
study showed that Ugandan coffee farmers received just 2.5 percent of
the retail price of coffee sold in the United Kingdom.[18] Price pressures from
buyers push down payments to farmers, as growers have a short window of
freshness during which to sell their coffee and limited access to the buyers
who visit their villages. Companies such as Discovery; Portland, Oregon-
based Stumptown Coffee Roasters; Our Mission Coffee near Nashville,
Tennessee; or Royal Coffee Company in the San Francisco Bay area attempt
to increase farmer income by buying directly from them and speeding up
coffee exports, creating a higher-quality, higher-value, more profitable
product. Their buys are increasingly important to coffee sales; single-origin
sales rose in 2009 even as other parts of the industry struggled with the
recession, according to the Specialty Coffee Association of America, a Long
Beach, California, trade group.[19]

Elite coffees are a drop in the industry ocean—in 2008, less than 4 percent of Ethiopia's exports were specialty varieties, Gabre-Madhin estimates.
But their influence and market potential is outsized: "It's like the $500
bottle of wine. It sets the standard, and it pulls up the price of everything
else," she said.[20] Ethiopia may have the richest specialty-coffee potential of
any country in the world, with hundreds of different varieties grown on tiny
farms in a dazzling array of microclimates, according to Sarah Kluth, quality

manager for Intelligentsia Coffee and Tea, a Chicago-based purveyor of top-notch brews. Niche coffees, properly developed, ultimately could provide 80 percent of Ethiopia's coffee income, boosting revenues by a third, according to a study done for the exchange in 2010.[21] That would be a significant boon to Ethiopia and its farmers, which in 2008 sold $562 million of coffee, with buys led by Germany, Saudi Arabia, and the United States. (See Figure 8.1.) In total, Ethiopia's coffee shipments annually are by far the biggest in export value among the country's 20 most-exported crops, according to the United Nations.

In Chicago, 7,500 miles from Addis, Kluth prepares to "break the crust" of a cup of coffee she's testing for quality. She holds the cup gently, making sure the grounds are fully saturated as she prepares her special cupping spoon to puncture the crust of coffee grounds accumulated at the top of the brew, all while inhaling the warm aromatics wafting onto her face. The 20-something quality director has a singular passion for coffee that escalates when she speaks of Ethiopia, where Intelligentsia sends tasters to seek out the world's next spectacular cup.

"Ethiopia is in its own class," she said.[22]

Intelligentsia invests in projects from agricultural training to schools in the towns where it buys coffee, she said. Seekers of fine brews have evolved a complex system of certifications that focus on everything from tree canopies and production practices to social conditions and bird habitats to encourage

FIGURE 8.1   Top Ten Destination Countries of Ethiopia's Coffee Export (% share)

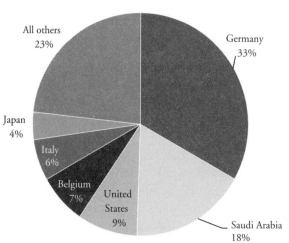

Source: Access Capital Research.

both sustainable agriculture and high-quality coffee that puts extra income in the hands of some of the world's poorest farmers.

Kluth is a trained cupper, someone who tastes coffee and grades it according to accepted industry standards. Cupping is similar to wine-tasting in that a highly developed palate can differentiate among regions, climates, soil type, and farming practices. With her close-cropped red hair, oval wire lenses, violent-green fingernails, and thorough knowledge of the distinct coffee qualities of each world region, she embodies the knowing barista at an upscale coffee shop—which is exactly how she started out.

Cuppers don't drink most of the coffee they taste, though they may swallow some to evaluate its finish and aftertaste. At Intelligentsia's main Chicago roasting facility, in a nondescript 25,000-square-foot warehouse on West Fulton Street, Kluth inhales, then sips some of the world's finest coffee with a distinctive SLURRRP!! sound.

■ ■ ■

SLURRRP!!

Medhin Tamiru pauses for a moment, contemplates the cup he just sampled, and makes note of it before moving to the next. Five cuppers will taste from each bag, so that the coffee can be assigned the proper grade for storage at the ECX's warehouse in Hawassa, four hours south of the trading floor in Addis Ababa.

Tamiru, the same age as Kluth, is the eldest of five children from a coffee-growing family. After he received his degree in plant science at Jimma University, more than 100 miles northwest of Hawassa, he worked in Ethiopia's agriculture ministry before being trained as a cupper in Addis Ababa. Most Ethiopian cuppers have university degrees, many in plant science. Tamiru said his goal is to learn the coffee industry thoroughly, then return to coffee-growing, fully educated in what foreign buyers want and in the best production practices.

If he creates a proper business plan, "the government has money for investors," he said. His work at the ECX will help him advance Ethiopia's food chain—and in the meantime, he's developing an incredible palate for quality coffee.

Tamiru is one of 200 people who work at the Hawassa warehouse. He wears an apron that says Specialty Coffee Association of America, which took a keen interest in the ECX, working with the exchange after association members complained that the country's coffee law, intended to create the trading volume necessary for the exchange to prosper, was strangling the discovery and purchase of what could be one of the most lucrative cash crops Ethiopian farmers could possibly grow—the single-origin coffee they prize.

■ ■ ■

Ethiopia may be the birthplace of coffee and a darling of its most discerning buyers, with trademarked regional names and a reputation for pungent, wine-like tastes and an acidity that's bracing to consumers used to weaker coffees, but it's a second-tier exporter, trailing South American shippers like Brazil and Colombia and Asian powers like Vietnam and Indonesia.[23] Just as the exchange was opening in 2008, the country's profile threatened to slip further.

Japan, then the third-biggest buyer of Ethiopian coffee, banned the East African beans in 2008 after customs officials seized shipments deemed to contain "abnormally high" pesticide levels linked to contaminated bags. Total shipments fell to their lowest since 2001. That August, amid accusations that high-quality coffees were being switched with lower-grade ones by unscrupulous traders, Ethiopia's parliament passed a law assigning the country's coffee grading and quality control system to the ECX, ending the traditional auctions that had taken place.

"Ethiopia loses a significant premium on international markets because of its inability to meet certain standards," Gabre-Madhin said. "Ethiopia's domestic market is trying to clean up its act."[24]

The move, which the government had decided would happen before the ECX had opened, created instant volume for the exchange, which by the end of 2008 had traded only 935 tons of corn and 90 tons of wheat in a country that can produce as much as 9 million tons of the two crops in a year.[25] By 2010, volume had increased to nearly 222,000 tons, though 99 percent of it was coffee.[26] The new law had teeth: jail terms of three to five years and fines of almost $5,000 for persons convicted of rigging coffee quality. In March 2009, the government shut down the warehouses and suspended the licenses of six private exporters, accusing them of stockpiling coffee and selling export-grade beans on domestic markets, adding that it had taken unspecified "similar measures" against 88 domestic suppliers.[27] Zenawi said he would "cut off the hands" of any exporter who tried to undermine Ethiopia's modernizing coffee industry.[28] The businesses were later reinstated.

The ECX increased government control over the foreign exchange brought in by the coffee trade as well as tax revenue linked to transactions, boosting state revenues. The exchange graded coffee by quality and region, but not to the specificity wanted by direct-trade coffee buyers who demanded traceability—an important part of the premium they paid. Those buyers were suspicious of the new bourse, which disrupted their supply chains and complicated their attempts to market what was to them a precious part of Ethiopian coffee equality: its story.

"One of the key principles in the specialty coffee trade is that coffee is not a commodity," said Geoff Watts, a buyer for Intelligentsia, which has responded by spending more time in Ethiopia to find top-notch brews. "It's not like wheat, and it's not like corn, and it's not like rice.[29]

"The biggest impact that the ECX has had is it's made it more difficult for that segment of the market to find the coffee that it needs."

The timing of the move, which pushed coffee trading to the exchange before a traceability system could be put in place, was made so the exchange could handle a coffee harvest that soon would be underway, Gabre-Madhin said. In the context of the overall market, she said it was a logical choice, even though she knew complaints would be inevitable and some purchases would be lost; bulk grades and less-traceable specialty coffees dwarf elite-coffeehouse buys and benefit more farmers, she said. Many coffeehouses, from illycaffe of Trieste, Italy to Blue Bottle Coffee of the San Francisco Bay area, feature Ethiopian coffee to this day. The coffee controversy was an early hit to the ECX reputation, but that recovered, as did sales, as buyers adapted and the ECX evolved, she said.

■ ■ ■

Small mud homes dot trek in a Toyota Land Cruiser up back-bending red-dirt roads from the city of Dilla to Dama, a town of 3,000 more than a mile above sea level. Children run alongside the vehicle and are easily able to keep up with it, calling "YUYUYUYUYUYU" as the cruiser lurches past rocks and avoids ditches, except when the ditch is more passable than the road, which is often. Dama farmers sell single-origin coffee to foreign retailers, including Intelligentsia, and the sight of a white man in a Land Rover who may be a buyer draws a crowd. The farmers are at first excited to see me; when they learn I'm a journalist, many melt away.

These are some of the world's best coffee farmers, and they know it. They don't always know how the ECX relates to them. Kasu Gebre Kidan, a farmer in his late sixties, grows more than six acres of coffee, avocados, corn, and *ensete*, commonly called "false banana" because of its close resemblance to the domesticated banana plant. It's the most important root crop in Ethiopia because of its drought tolerance and edible roots; the banana-looking fruit itself is inedible. He is a member of the Yirgacheffe Coffee Farmers Cooperative Union, one of the organizations charged with selling direct-trade coffee to foreign buyers. The coffee law still allows direct sales to coffee companies that want to bypass the exchange via farmer cooperatives. But private buyers dominate coffee purchasing and processing, controlling hundreds of small washing stations that process the raw coffee cherry, removing the skin and pulp, fermenting the beans, and cleaning them. The cooperatives also are notoriously underfinanced, which often makes them slower to pay farmers. All this makes cooperatives less able to compete with private buyers who sell through the ECX.

Poor farmers living from day to day "prefer to get their money quickly, so they go through private buyers," said Kidan. The father of eight says he sells through his cooperative, which dries the coffee beans he picks for eight hours a day during harvest. "We get money from the union, but it comes too late in the season" to help expand his production. He knows nothing detailed about the ECX.[30] The inability of cooperatives to compete with private buyers is a weakness of Ethiopia's current farm development, one Gabre-Madhin characterizes as "transitional." Wondirad Mandefro, Ethiopia's state minister of agriculture, acknowledged that finance is a problem among farmer co-ops, for which the government offers assistance through its expanding network of agricultural extension agents who advise farmers throughout the countryside. He also said both private companies and the cooperatives can access the same banking system. "It's a free market," he said.

Because the cooperative is often not a viable buyer, growers don't get the income they otherwise would, said Berhane Irbaye, a Dama coffee farmer in his mid-thirties. "We are told that there is no money to purchase our produce," Irbaye said. "Peasants, since they cannot go elsewhere and seek buyers, are forced to sell at the price set by businesses and suffer." Ethiopia's government needs to take "the realities on the ground" into consideration when deciding policies, he said.

"I say additional support should be given to the peasants."

■ ■ ■

Dr. Eleni keeps two books on her office coffee table—a history of the Chicago Board of Trade and a history of the Minneapolis Grain Exchange. On top of them sits a small bag of Starbucks seized from a hotel in Washington, DC, where she was speaking at a development conference in 2009, when direct-trade coffee concerns were at their peak. Dr. Eleni grows even more animated when talking about the world's biggest coffee chain and its at-times strained relationship with Ethiopia: Starbucks settled a dispute with the country in

2007 after being accused of trying to block Ethiopia's efforts to trademark its premium coffee varieties.

At the conference, the ECX, the coffee law, and whether it helps farmers was discussed. The CEOs, most of whom led companies not connected to the coffee industry, were asking why the exchange was disrupting coffee trading. She pulled out her Starbucks bag. "And I said, well here's the main reason. It's because I'm looking at the label this morning on my way to come to this panel at this conference, and this label for this 'Africa Kitamu,' it says—this coffee, it has this map that has Ethiopia in it—and it talks about this 'flavorful interplay of exotic citrus and floral notes.'

"That's the value added—the citrus and the floral notes. But if I went to a farmer in Ethiopia and asked them, 'Did you know that we have coffee that has a citrus note?' They'd be clueless! And we have been trading of millions of bags of coffee, and we have no idea what's in it that the market wants.

"And that's what the ECX is all about. A value chain should not be a one-way street. Farmers need a third party that can collect data, communicate information, and help them better understand the market and benefit from it. That's the whole purpose of setting up an exchange."

Since the ECX began, the exchange has worked with specialty-coffee buyers to address traceability. In February 2010 the ECX opened a bidding session designed to bring farmers and large commercial coffee growers together with international buyers in what's referred to as the Direct Specialty Trade (DST). Along with the DST, the exchange developed a grading system with the Specialty Coffee Association of America that allows for certification of coffee as organic, fair trade, and rainforest Arabica.

Starbucks—by far the world's specialty-coffee giant—and the ECX have worked on creating a bar-code system to make sure that even coffee traded through the exchange can be traced to a farmer. The plan in mid-2011was in testing stages, with no implementation date, Gabre-Madhin said in a separate interview in Washington, DC—at a Starbucks.[31] The exchange has been adjusting its practices to meet customer needs, but she stressed it would put Ethiopia's interests first.

"Any producing country should have its first priority as creating a system that enhances value to its own producers. That's our responsibility as a country."[32]

When asked about Ethiopian coffee and traceability, Starbucks said they continue to work with the nation's smallholder farmers to increase Ethiopia's coffee potential and have featured small batches of the country's specialty coffees to its consumers. "As a longtime purchaser of Ethiopian coffees, we believe we have been able to provide the ECX with our business perspective as a specialty coffee buyer."[33]

■ ■ ■

The government continues to steer business to the exchange as the coffee controversy has quieted. In April 2011 it again threatened to ban exporters and producers caught hoarding beans. Such merchants were "stopping the country from getting the foreign exchange it could earn, making foreign buyers lose trust, and spoiling the country's image," Yakob Yala, the state trade minister, said. The regulation was "drafted by someone who does not know anything about the coffee industry," and doesn't understand supply and demand, said Fekade Mamo, owner of coffee exporter Mochaland Import and Export and a board member of the ECX.[34]

Ethiopia's government, deeming the coffee experiment a success, has required other crops (specifically sesame and white pea beans, for which the country is a major exporter) to move to the exchange. The result is even more volume; for the year ending midway through 2011, the exchange traded 504,000 tons of crops, more than double the previous year. About 238,000 tons were of coffee, but 225,000 tons of sesame and 41,000 tons of beans diversified the ECX product line: "We are no longer a coffee exchange," Gabre-Madhin said with pride.[35]

In February 2011, as the government placed controls on food prices that shaped the price of beer and bread, throwing supply and demand out of balance, the ECX celebrated a milestone: 1,000 days (and no defaults—equal to Chicago, although Chicago has a 160-year head start) and 1 billion U.S. dollars in trading.

The volume, and the reliability, shows the exchange is on the right path, Dr. Eleni said. But the vision of food security still contains a glaring omission: Trading in grains, the staples of food security, still doesn't generate significant volume. About 5,000 tons were traded in the 2010–2011 fiscal year, most of it to the World Food Programme. The ECX isn't even the most active staple-foods market in Addis Ababa. That distinction belongs to the nearby Merkato, Ethiopia's traditional sales bazaar, where grain-sellers vie with Isuzu trucks, donkeys, and wandering peddlers for attention, selling goods to local supermarkets and restaurants in sales warehouses as they have for generations. Merchants of grain stack their wares toward the rafters of open-air sheds, haggling with buyers and catching up on stories from fellow sellers who have worked there for decades. The only time I see anyone get upset is when I start taking video of the market, at which point a vendor tells me to put away my camera, lest it be taken away.

"Merkato is the center of all business. It's where you start, and where you end," said Mitiku Birega, a seller of corn and wheat in Merkato for the past 30 years.

At the sprawling Merkato, where price discovery can be chaotic and the best way to evade a speeding truck is to hope a goat lies in front of it, buying and selling is a well-trod path. The vision of the surplus farmer selling to people in need has a long way to go. The theory behind the exchange may make sense, but in practice it takes much more time to become real; in the end, a commodities exchange isn't one of the most important ways to combat hunger in a poor country, said Sitko, the Michigan State economist.

African exchanges, with the exception of South Africa, all share a crucial difference with Chicago, Minneapolis, or numerous exchanges created in richer countries: a top-down evolution that doesn't necessarily reflect what a country needs, said Peter Robbins, a consultant to the United Nations on African issues, a former adviser to the African National Congress against apartheid in the 1980s, a writer of books on tropical crops, and for three decades a commodities trader in London.

"All markets in history have been created in a kind of evolutionary way," which isn't the case with donor-driven bourses. "There are much cheaper, tried and tested, better ways of helping the entire agricultural community." Commodities exchanges attract aid "because it looks like something modern," he said. "Spending a couple of million dollars on an exchange where people are shouting and there are flashing lights is very sexy compared to the humdrum job of teaching somebody to produce a different crop in the countryside."[36]

And as long as Ethiopia maintains an autocratic government, trust in trading will be difficult to build, he said.

"You have to take into account the government is a very scary thing in Ethiopia," he said. "Democracy would help a lot."

Gabre-Madhin said she remains convinced the exchange will broaden its appeal in other crops and further Ethiopia's farm development. The government, she said, is a Catch-22. Its involvement in the exchange will make some observers and potential participants skeptical, but without it, the ECX probably wouldn't have happened, she said. When it came time to set up warehouses and extend phone lines, the government could get things done. The link between transparent pricing and farmer income needs more study, she said: Meanwhile, farmers like Gashaw Kinfe Desta, who employs up to 250 workers during harvest in southwest Ethiopia, say the exchange has encouraged higher-priced, higher-quality coffee.[37]

Grain buyers and sellers in far-flung regions of Ethiopia don't have an obvious reason to trade their grain in Addis Ababa on a trading floor that doesn't yet offer forward or futures contracts that lock in prices and help manage risk, which is how the ECX will differentiate itself from local markets. The exchange's tax requirements, which aren't part of the Merkato economy, are also keeping them away at the present time, she said. Once larger buyers understand the exchange's benefits, they will migrate, free of government intervention, she predicted.

"It took Chicago about 15 years to have standardized futures contracts. It will take us three years," she said.

"If there's anything we have shown in the last couple years, it's our willingness to listen and adapt.

"We've never shied away from criticism."

CHAPTER 9

A Better Banana

"During this stage you don't talk! There are microbes!"[1]

Susan Muli's admonishment is followed by 15 minutes of careful cutting as she silently slices the two-foot foundation of a banana plant into a portion of stem tissue the diameter of a silver dollar, pruning away layers of the plant with surgical knives that she sterilizes with a solution of 70 percent ethanol soaked in cotton and wearing a surgical mask to keep pesky contaminating microbes in check. She then separates the tissue further, into tiny bits the size of a fingernail, and places them in a pint jar containing a milky liquid with the consistency of a thin paste. The liquid contains all the nutrients a banana plant needs to thrive. The jar is marked by date and variety—Chinese Cavendish, Uganda Green, Ngombe—then placed in a climate-controlled, 15- by 20-foot side room next to the lab, 30 miles northeast of Nairobi. The room holds seven shelves of pint jars that, when full, hold the beginnings of 100,000 banana trees, enough to cover about 200 football fields and support nearly as many smallholder farms seeking a lucrative, year-round cash crop.

The room is timed to simulate daylight for 16 hours and darkness for 8, heated near 82 degrees—a perfect day for bananas, every day. The tiny piece of plant tissue multiplies from one shoot to 10 within five weeks. The tender green shoots grow strong in a sterile environment that avoids the pathogens and nematodes that stunt and kill bananas grown naturally and have traditionally devastated African harvests. After five months on the shelves, with short breaks for more milky nutrition and separation of new shoots from older ones as clones multiply exponentially, the plants will be transferred to an outdoor greenhouse, where the Kenya Agricultural Research Institute outside the town of Thika will sell them to farmers from across the country, who will raise them into fully grown banana trees ready to bear fruit sold to the prospering buyers of Nairobi and Kenya's growing cities.

The "tissue-culture" bananas are the products of simple plant science—it's biotechnology, but there's no gene modification. The tried-and-true methods common in Asia and Latin America are only beginning to take root in much of Africa, where one-third of the world's bananas are consumed. In Kenya, only about 5 percent of banana acreage was under tissue-culture cultivation in 2006, a number at that time projected to expand to as much as 40 percent by 2016, according to Africa Harvest Biotech Foundation International, which promotes the technology.[2]

Building a better banana, and a better banana market, can improve income for farmers as well as food security for Kenyans, and eventually, the world—a hope Muli shares with DuPont Co., the Bill and Melinda Gates Foundation, and the Rockefeller Foundation, all of whom have funded tissue-culture banana projects in Kenya. It also buys goodwill for foreign agribusinesses in the nation's fractured political arena, where Kenya accepted the cultivation and trade of controversial genetically modified (GM) crops in 2011. A better banana isn't only about improved fruit production. It's about helping poorer farmers in poorer countries connect with local, regional, and international markets. Together they can grow and prosper. As is the case with cultivating bananas, there are bruises along the way.

Interest in African minerals goes back centuries, while farming has always been a more mundane investment. Diamond and gold mines attract outsize investment because they offer rewards that make the high-risk gamble of an unstable region worthwhile. An agricultural investment that doesn't offer the same returns will be passed over. Put bluntly, morally detestable "blood diamonds" can make money for the unscrupulous investor. The world may need more food sources, but as of yet, "blood bananas" still seems over the top. There's just not enough money in it.

High food prices and lower risks in Africa may change that. A patchwork of projects spanning the continent—with investors ranging from large multinationals to mid-size shippers and processors to small- and medium-size local enterprises—is moving to boost the region's farming possibilities as markets emerge, said Simon Winter, senior vice president for development at TechnoServe and former director of its African operations.[3] Even successful growth creates a new round of questions. Are the right crops being grown? Is the financing, and the soil and water, sustainable? If the crop grown well, will it have a market? Will the weather ruin everything?

And who are the investors helping?

Corporate support for African farms often involves contracts for export crops or "outgrower schemes" in which a company ensures a supply of crops in return for financing and assurance of a buyer. For products like coffee or cocoa that are attractive to rich-world consumers, such an approach is a way for an outside business to support farm development. Unilever, Cargill, Olam International, and various breweries use this approach.

Also common are public-private partnerships, in which DuPont, Monsanto, PepsiCo, Nestlé, Coca-Cola and other companies work with foundations and nongovernmental organizations—themselves often corporate-funded—along with governments on projects that help farmers. Still another is the "cluster" approach, where a group of companies partner with nongovernmental organizations to build a promising region. The Southern Agricultural Growth Corridor of Tanzania that's intended to increase that area's agricultural productivity, launched in 2010, is an example of that approach. Members of that group include Unilever, Yara International, DuPont, Monsanto, SAB Miller, Diageo, Syngenta, General Mills, the UN, the U.S. and Norwegian governments, the Alliance for a Green Africa (AGRA), Tanzanian groups, and banks.

Multinationals investing in Africa include Monsanto and DuPont, which sell seeds and develop new varieties, and Mars Inc., which is studying how to improve cocoa-farmer incomes in West Africa. Pepsi and Nestlé are examining ways to lower water use; Jain Irrigation Systems, an Indian company that has dealt with water shortages for decades, is planning to open a plant in Africa, responding to a need for drip-irrigation systems.[4] Deere & Co. is developing equipment built for African plots of land. Unilever, the world's biggest seller of tea, is planning to expand the number of smallholder farmers in its supply network to 500,000 in 2020, up from 100,000 now. Cargill is training 60,000 cotton growers in Zimbabwe on how to rise above subsistence-level incomes.[5]

Farm development is also tied to urban growth.[6] Prospering cities developing near impoverished rural areas give poorer producers a local market that can raise their incomes as well. Companies like Coca-Cola, which has the continent's most sophisticated distribution network, take advantage of the connections. Africa is an undertapped market for Coke, even though, with more than 65,000 people and more than 160 plants, it's the continent's largest employer. In Kenya, per capita consumption of the beverage is 39 servings compared to the world's leader, Mexico, where people drink an average of 665 Cokes a year.

About 59 million African households earn at least $5,000, the point when families begin spending more than half their incomes on nonfood items. A McKinsey & Co. study suggests that number could reach 106 million by 2014—with that in mind, Coke plans to double its spending to $12 billion during the next 10 years.[7]

Better communications technology, such as the explosion of cell phones over the past decade (see Figure 9.1), has made companies more confident in operating in Africa on their own, Winter said. Still, the collaborative approach makes sense as companies leave their comfort zones and enter less-understood parts of the world, he said.

The danger of such efforts, critics say, is that the outside efforts can trump local business, tempting cash-strapped governments with weak legal codes to listen to western cash more than their own citizens. And memories of exploitation die hard. Slavery, both colonial and modern-day, abhorrent conditions in some mining operations, and below-poverty wages create skepticism of corporate motives. Those concerns will need to be addressed and worked through as countries across the continent emerge. And emerge they will: Africa's future business development is clearly going in a positive direction said Paul Schickler, president of Pioneer Hi-Bred, the Iowa-based seed division of DuPont, which has put more than $3 million into Kenya tissue-culture banana projects.

FIGURE 9.1 Mobile Cellular Subscriptions (per 100 people)

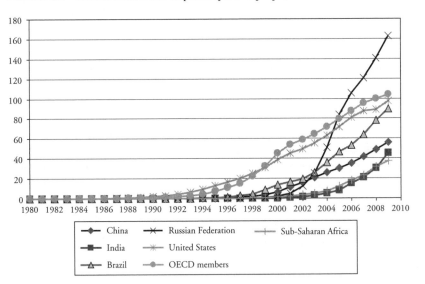

Source: World Bank.

"I am convinced that 10 years from now, sub-Saharan Africa will be where Eastern Europe is today," as a new major source of food exports. "But you need to do the work today to take advantage."[8]

■ ■ ■

Kenya, Ethiopia's equator-straddling southern neighbor, is both wealthier and more democratic. It faces no shortage of turbulence.

Farming is the second-biggest part of Kenya's economy after its tourism-dominated services sector, but it's still the dominant employer, involving three-quarters of the country's workforce. Per-capita income is $1,600 annually, compared to $1,000 in Ethiopia.[9] Kenya has other advantages in integrating with the world compared with its northern neighbor. Kenya's roads are the region's best developed, and the country isn't landlocked, a problem that bedevils many African nations. And while Ethiopians are proud to say they were never colonized (the brief period of Italian administration is termed an occupation), Kenya's time under British rule left it with English and Swahili as dual official languages—a less proud, perhaps more practical heritage.

The Nairobi Stock Exchange is Africa's fourth largest, making it East Africa's financial hub. Its commodities exchange, Kenya Agricultural Commodity Exchange Ltd. in Nairobi, is a lower-budget, limited-function counterpart to its Ethiopian neighbor. It operates a network of spot-trading markets and provides price data to subscribers across Kenya, and is probably best known for *Soko Hewani, The Supermarket on Air,* a national radio show in which buyers and sellers of farm goods make bids and offers for goats, honey, or even houses while listeners call, e-mail, and text responses. It's a raucous form of price-setting, but the show and the exchange help raise farmer income.[10]

Kenya's rough-and-tumble politics have intensified. Kenya gained its independence in 1963, after the British colonizers and Kenyan supporters had put down the Mau Mau anticolonial rebellion. Until his death in 1978 the country was led by Jomo Kenyatta, a founding father who guided one of the early economic leaders of postcolonial Africa, backed by the United States for its anticommunist stance. Kenyatta's successor, Daniel arap Moi, known as "Nyayo" (Swahili for "footsteps," as in "footsteps of Jomo Kenyatta") is less highly regarded. Unresolved tribal rivalries of the Kenyatta era continued to fester beneath the surface of one-party government. The end of secret balloting in 1988 and accusations of corruption and meddling with the judiciary marred his rule. The International Monetary Fund, which suspended Kenyan aid in 1997 because the government failed to curb corruption, resumed the loans in 2000 to help Kenya through a drought, then stopped again in 2001 when the government didn't adopt further anticorruption measures. Growth sagged. Cities stagnated.

Western donors also wearied of supporting the arap Moi government. Still, he won reelection twice in multiparty contests in the 1990s, and in 2002, when he was constitutionally barred from running again and his hand-picked successor, the son of Jomo Kenyatta, was defeated, he turned over power peacefully, a landmark in any democracy's development.

Subsequent governance has been troubled. Graft scandals again slowed the flow of loans. A tightly contested election in 2007 led to violence that killed almost 1,000 people and displaced hundreds of thousands. The two main rivals in that election, Mwai Kabaki and Raila Odinga, continued feuding even as a new constitution was adopted in 2010. Tribal rivalries distort political decision-making and stand behind much of the turbulence. As Kenyan Nobel Peace Prize winner Wangari Maathai wrote in 2009, "Our politicians govern the country by mutilating and manipulating the constitution" and by "playing divisive tribal politics."[11] Bloodshed in future elections is expected.

Yet elections and power transfers do occur, and most battles are fought in the press, not on the streets. Ranked 18th (tied with the Republic of the Congo, Senegal, and Uganda) out of 48 sub-Saharan African countries, Kenya was rated "partly free" by Freedom House in its 2011 press freedom survey.[12] Kenyans, despite the turmoil, are among Africa's happiest people—80 percent of them say they're satisfied with their lives, according to a survey done by Coca-Cola's Open Happiness campaign, intended to help market Coke in the country.[13]

Donkeys may disrupt traffic, the lights may go out erratically in many cities, and the government may be uncertain of itself. Road-building is booming. New bypasses heavily financed by the Chinese are being built around Nairobi, and other projects across the country are meant to improve infrastructure to Kenyans who are becoming more connected to one another and to the outside world.[14] Along a highway on a 90-degree February morning, lined with businesses with signs almost entirely in English—except the ones for Coca-Cola, with the slogan "Barudika na Coke" (Refresh With Coke) showing the soda's global street cred—a teenage boy walks toward a village wearing a T-shirt emblazoned with the single word, "YU."

It's the name of a local telecom.

■ ■ ■

Two men struggle to push a wagon laden with deep-green bananas up the final hill to the Sabasaba Agribusiness Centre as the wagon's alleged leader, a recalcitrant donkey, stares downhill at them in immobile mockery of their intentions. The men try one angle, then another, to get the wagon to move ahead—but if the donkey refuses to move, there isn't much they can do to get their cargo to the weighing station.

The men angle, grunt, and heave their way ahead, cajoling their donkey while two other men approach on motorcycles, which also carry loads of bananas. The motorcyclists weave around the men, the wagon and their donkey, up the hill and to the station, where they kickstand their bikes, remove their bananas and queue for weighing. They look down the hill in bemusement on the battle of man vs. beast. Machine's victory over muscle is obvious to all.

The Sabasaba Agribusiness Centre, 90 minutes north of Nairobi, was started in September 2010 by AGRA, the Rockefeller Foundation, and TechnoServe to connect small growers of a tropical staple crop with national, and ultimately, global markets for the fruit that's most consumed in the United States and third-most-consumed in the world. The center, built on 1.5 acres of land for about $14,000, gives buyers and sellers a place to weigh, grade, and set prices for the bananas, reducing transaction costs and making villagers more knowledgeable about pricing. Eventually, the farmers hope to build a cooling facility to make longer-term storage possible, further helping their bananas gain access to new customers and getting higher prices for their bunches.

Such a facility already exists near Meru, an eastern Kenyan city on the slopes of Mount Kenya, one-half mile south of the equator, where Rosemary Muthomi and her husband, Gerald, have built two businesses, Meru Greens Horticulture and Mt. Kenya Gardens, that have become leading suppliers of bananas to Nairobi's prospering shoppers—and soon, the Muthomis hope, the world.

In the cold-storage shed they built, with plastic crates coated in charcoal to absorb the equatorial heat and keep their fruit from bruising, they can keep ripening bananas fresh longer than they could outdoors. From the world's standpoint, a better Kenyan banana couldn't come at a better time.

Global exports of the Cavendish variety, responsible for 99 percent of the world's shipments, are threatened by a pest called Tropical Race Four that has wiped out that variety in Asia. Scientists believe the soil-borne fungus will make it to Latin America, home to four of the world's top five banana exporters, according to the United Nations Food and Agriculture Organization. Should the fungus devastate Latin America, the world would see a repeat of the devastation that befell the Gros Michel banana, the most shipped variety of the first half of the twentieth century. A pathogen that destroyed that

variety in Latin America pushed profits at United Fruit Co., now called
Chiquita Brands International, down 97 percent during the 1950s and
allowed rival Standard Fruit Co., now called Dole Food Company Inc., to
become the leading fruit seller, a position it holds to this day.[15]

Kenya's year-round growing season, and relatively stable economy by
African standards, holds great potential for bananas, first for local markets
and potentially for exports (see Figure 9.2), according to Henry Kinyua, a
manager for East African fruits at TechnoServe, a nonprofit with the tag-
line "Business Solutions to Poverty" that has worked with Nestlé, Google,
Lenovo Group, Procter & Gamble, and Cargill. It has been ranked as one
of the world's top five nongovernmental organizations by the *Financial
Times*.[16] Tissue-culture bananas give Kenya a chance to boost production just when the world may need new sources, Gerald Muthomi said.
While one-third of the planet's bananas are grown in Africa, only about
4 percent of all exports originate there.[17] The disparity is an opportunity for
poor farmers, he said.

The Muthomis speak excitedly about their work. Gerald, wiry and
expressive, does most of the talking. Rosemary, dignified in a light-blue business suit of jacket and knee-length skirt, interjects to keep him on-topic. We
are sitting in a bright white room with windows open while an employee
brings tropical fruit on a tray. On a separate plate is a single, fiber-rich banana
that's large and hearty, but not as curved as a typical American grocery-store
plant—and, like most every Kenyan banana, more black-bruised on its skin.
Tasting the fruit, it's sweeter and grainier, yet softer than any store-bought
Latin American variety flown from Ecuador to Minneapolis.

"That's a Gros Michel," Gerald Muthomi says, the legendary lost fruit
that still thrives in Kenya. What shippers used to affectionately call "Big
Mike" before it disappeared from northern store shelves a half-century ago.

Biodiversity may be one of the biggest selling points of African bananas,
where the lack of any need to transport over long distances gives consumers
fruit choices unimaginable to Western consumers. As many as 84 distinct
types of East African highland bananas exist, though Kenya's export potential
will come from growing the main global varieties, Rosemary Muthomi said.
In Kenya, imported types such as the Cavendish, which is growing more
prominent as Kenyan tissue-buyers demand the world-preferred variety, are
sold side-by-side with the Kampala and other bananas in different shapes,
sizes, and tastes.

Gerald and Rosemary Muthomi met in school at Jomo Kenyatta
University. They married after both became government agricultural extension agents in rural Kenya in the 1980s, advising farmers on how to grow

FIGURE 9.2 Top 20 Banana Exporters in 2008

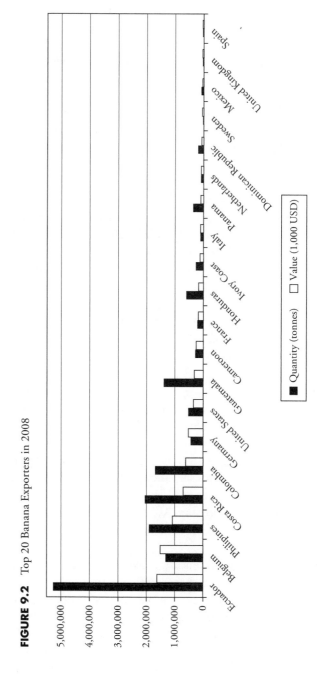

Source: UN Food and Agriculture Organization.

better crops. They were both from the same tribe, and they shared a passion for helping the poorest farmers, with whom they shared a background. Gerald said that when he was a child growing coffee in Kenya, all the children wore long shirts because pants were too expensive. The one pair of shorts available to his brother and him was available to whoever woke up first in the morning.

On the coffee farm, Muthomi's father would require him to pick 50 pounds of coffee beans before leaving for school each day. A village elder gave him some of his own coffee plants to introduce him to caring for his own crops. His real initiation into farming was the first French beans he grew, and what it represented to him:

Pants.

"When I sold them, I went to town and bought my own trousers. I would walk around with my hands in my pockets. This was quite an achievement!"

Fifteen years ago, when the Muthomis left the Kenyan government to start their business, local farmers had no sense of growing for nearby or regional markets or what practices could improve their incomes, Gerald Muthomi said. Farmers living along the equator never considered that the tropical fruits they could grow so easily would be desired by others.

"Everybody grew coffee or beans for the white man. Nobody would touch bananas or passion fruit," Gerald Muthomi said. Avocados were considered unworthy for adult consumption and were either thrown away or fed to small children and dogs, he said. "We called them 'the dog fatteners' because only dogs would eat them."

The couple started Mt. Kenya Gardens by reselling the products farmers grew, thinking food crops shipped to Nairobi might be a promising alternative to coffee exports. They first took beans to the capital by buying bus tickets to the city, placing a 100-kilogram bag of beans in their seat and standing for the four-hour drive. Once they proved that French beans weren't only for white people, they began selling fruit—papayas, then bananas. They spent no money on advertising. As Meru bananas—and their banana-sellers—became known in the Nairobi market, the Muthomis became known for their produce.

Throughout their time as business owners they've been advised by TechnoServe, which helped them master agricultural supply chains as well as suggest ideas not common to Kenya but basic to marketing elsewhere: Sales jumped, for example, when the company started putting stickers on their supermarket bananas to distinguish their brand from others. Sales at Mt. Kenya Gardens rose from more than $500,000 in 2008 to almost $700,000 in 2009 as they supplied Kenyan grocery chains with fresh produce. The couple would like to begin exporting in the next few years, first to nearby African and Middle Eastern countries where it may be easier to meet foreign food-safety standards, then to Europe, a potentially lucrative market for Kenyan bananas. Proper financing and enough farmers growing high-quality bananas could make the sky the limit for their business, they believe.

They may be right. Or, the limit may be what comes from the sky.

■ ■ ■

Navigating the paths of his 10 acres, minutes from the Sabasaba center, Samuel Ngugi Gichung'ua, a 70-year-old grower of mango, papaya, passion fruit, and avocado, says his increasing profits have prompted him to increase his biotech banana planting. Six of his 10 acres are now in banana trees, some for his own consumption, some for the market.

Lush leaves shade him from the 100-degree equatorial heat beating down from above. He points at a tree that grows Kampala bananas, a Ugandan variety, and says that while it's what he prefers to eat, it isn't a big money-maker.

Then, he stops. And admires.

"This one, here, is a Cavendish," he says, pointing at a tree that's seemingly overburdened with ripening fruit. "I sell those bananas. Some of the money I spend, and some pays the workers that are here. Cavendish pays more.

"All of the farmers who have really planted bananas, they are changing their ways of life. To live life, you need money, and we are being encouraged to plant more bananas to get money," he said. "This country is changing so much, it is changing for me and for all the other farmers."

He moves past ripening mangoes, bright bulbs of passion fruit, and bananas, and bananas, and bananas. A river runs through his property, with a single wooden plank laid across the stream serving as the only crossing to the other side of these 27 acres of fruit trees. A quiet chugging sound grows louder as he nears the river. The only piece of machinery operating on the farm—a water pump—is drawing river water to the fields to irrigate the banana trees. The pump is working hard today. The weather is dry, the stream is a trickle, and with no rain forecast, the water that's left is essential for the crop. Drought is arriving in Kenya.

We walk the plank, which bows with each step, over the gurgling flow to the other side of his land, which is hillier and more difficult to navigate. Bananas aren't only among the world's most profitable fruits, with Americans eating as many fresh bananas as fresh apples and oranges combined.[18] They're also one of the thirstiest—and Kenya is having problems with water.

Part of why famine is so endemic to parts of East Africa is that its water-distribution systems remain undeveloped. Poor resource management and a lack of technical skill have slowed irrigation in the countryside, which is subject to severe drought every three to four years. A 2009 drought put 10 million Kenyans at risk of starvation and malnutrition.[19] In mid-2011, 3.5 million were endangered because of drought as withered crops prompted the World Bank to cut the country's growth estimate.[20] Sparse irrigation makes agriculture even more dependent on weather patterns, and poor soil quality limits banana crops.[21]

Climate issues in Kenya, as in the rest of Africa, are expected to worsen, possibly costing as much as 2.6 percent of Gross Domestic Product each year by 2030, according to a 2010 study. Overall rainfall is expected to increase, the rains may become more erratic, and higher temperatures will speed evaporation, decreasing available moisture.[22] Worldwide, climate change will raise wheat prices 59 percent, paddy rice 56 percent, and livestock 39 percent higher than they otherwise would have been by 2030, a separate study said.[23] (See Figure 9.3.)

Bananas are among the thirstiest fruit. The more frequent floods and droughts predicted by climate change models increase the chance that bananas

FIGURE 9.3 Real Food Price Changes Predicted over the Next 20 Years

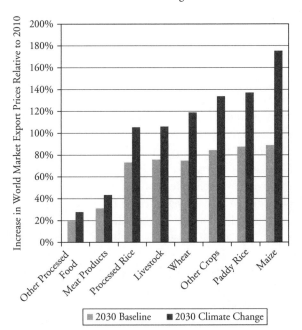

Source: Oxfam.

may be inundated with too much rainfall one season and left parched in another. Schickler of DuPont said boosting banana crops will depend on the ability of Kenyan farmers and officials to create water-management systems that keep the trees alive. The tissue-culture trees owned by Elisha Makaho are already dead. He said he's shifted focus to local varieties, which over centuries have adapted to Kenya's climate.

The ordained Anglican minister has farmed for nearly 50 years near Sabasaba. Hung on a wall in the home he shares with his wife and 48-year-old daughter is a prayer that says: "Lord, don't let me become rich and forsake you; never let me become poor and shame you, but give me my needs."

Makaho, who receives his news and weather forecasts from a solar-powered radio, decided he didn't need nonlocal varieties when they all died in a drought in 2008. His traditionally grown trees survived, as did his coffee and his maize, leading him to focus on selling those at nearby markets.

Crops aren't profitable when they don't exist, he said.

"The rains are becoming more unpredictable, and the bananas become stagnant when there is not enough rain," said Makaho.

Drought, continued with lack of adequate financing and the inability to meet international food-safety standards, are the main threats to Kenya's tropical promise, Kenyua said. "Tissue culture holds a lot of promise in Kenya, but if you have no water, forget it. Just do something else," he said. For the crop to become a serious supplier of world markets, Kenya will need to use its water more effectively and improve the quality of its soils, he said.

It will also need a better financial structure, so that erratic rain is less likely to discourage the Makahos—and the Muthomis.

■ ■ ■

The Muthomis experienced the ills of poor rainfall—and poor finance—in 2010, when a lack of rain devastated production near Meru. The farmers, to whom the Muthomis extend credit in the form of fertilizers and other crop inputs, were unable to grow food to sell to the market, making them unable to pay the Muthomis, who, as wealthier businessowners, have been supporting their production with loans that ordinary farmers can't get.

The couple reject the idea that bananas in Kenya, if successful, would become a large-scale, hired-hand business, as it is in Latin America or in the West African countries where sizable banana exports are found. "We are loyal to the smallholder," Gerald Muthomi said. "We were smallholders, and smallholders take better care of the land. This is who we serve."

Loyalty had a price when loans came due and the farmers were unable to cover their debts with production. "Last year we lost all our profits, because the drought was enormous and we couldn't deliver. And what should we do? A young boy who is finishing school and farming a 10-by-10 plot of land can't give me beans. Do you bring him to the police?

"So me and Rosemary sat down and absorbed the loss. We've been living from hand-to-mouth. Our biggest problem is finances. The droughts are unpredictable." By mid-2011, with TechnoServe assistance, they received a new round of financing, as well as access to technical training for their farmers in improving yields and fighting diseases and droughts.[24]

■ ■ ■

DuPont, and its rival, Monsanto, which have been working to increase their Kenya presence, have an answer to unpredictable weather.

The companies are both researching drought-resistant varieties of crops better able to withstand climate change. Ultimately, the battle against drought will require greater acceptance of genetically modified (GM) organisms, they maintain. Because of that, the effort to build a better banana in Kenya is in part about . . . corn.

As part of a three-year, DuPont-funded project undertaken by Africa Harvest to bring tissue-culture bananas to rural Kenya, the company also distributed free hybrid corn seeds to area farmers, with the idea that they would now buy those seeds for their own crops. By building Kenya's banana capacity, Schickler said, DuPont learns more about how to do business in Africa and also builds trust in local communities, which give them a more favorable hearing when they want to introduce new seeds to the countryside, be they hybrid seeds created through conventional plant breeding or, eventually, ones created by genetic modification.

Biotech and genetically modified crops topped a cumulative 1 billion hectares (2.47 billion acres) of plantings in 2010, according to the International Service for the Acquisition of Agri-Biotech Applications, a trade group based in Nairobi. Plantings for the year amounted to 10 percent of all crop acreage worldwide. Countries in North and South America were four of the top five planters that year, according to the group, with only one African country, South Africa, in the top 10 (see Table 9.1). Of the 29 countries that did any GM planting, only South Africa, Burkina Faso, which grows biotech cotton, and Egypt, which grew less than 50,000 hectares of corn, represented the continent.[25]

Biotechnology is viewed with deep suspicion in many African countries that rely on trade with Europe, where GM acceptance has been slow. Yet new

TABLE 9.1 Global Area of Biotech Crops in 2010: By Country (Million Hectares)

Rank	Country	Area	Biotech Crops
1	USA	66.8	Corn, soybeans, cotton, canola, sugarbeet, alfalfa, papaya, squash
2	Brazil	25.4	Soybeans, corn, cotton
3	Argentina	22.9	Soybeans, corn, cotton
4	India	9.4	Cotton
5	Canada	8.8	Canola, corn, soybeans, sugarbeet
6	China	3.5	Cotton, papaya, poplar, tomato, sweet pepper
7	Paraguay	2.6	Soybeans
8	Pakistan	2.4	Cotton
9	South Africa	2.2	Corn, soybeans, cotton
10	Uruguay	1.1	Soybeans, corn
11	Bolivia	0.9	Soybeans
12	Australia	0.7	Cotton, canola
13	Philippines	0.5	Corn
14	Myanmar	0.3	Cotton
15	Burkina Faso	0.3	Cotton
16	Spain	0.1	Corn
17	Mexico	0.1	Cotton, soybeans
18	Colombia	<0.1	Cotton
19	Chile	<0.1	Corn, soybeans, canola
20	Honduras	<0.1	Corn
21	Portugal	<0.1	Corn
22	Czech Republic	<0.1	Corn, potatoes
23	Poland	<0.1	Corn
24	Egypt	<0.1	Corn
25	Slovakia	<0.1	Corn
26	Costa Rica	<0.1	Cotton, soybeans
27	Romania	<0.1	Corn
28	Sweden	<0.1	Potato
29	Germany	<0.1	Potato
	Total	**148**	

Data Source: International Service for the Acquisition of Agri-Biotech Applications seed varieties, whether they are GM or not, are being pointed to as a way to lessen the effects of climate change and allow farming to be done on smaller areas of land as population increases. Genetic modifications have been touted as especially pertinent for bananas, given their susceptibility to disease.[26]

"Given that the annals of history of the first half of the 21st century are likely to record that climate change was the defining scientific challenge of the time, it is imperative that the role of biotech crops be fully realized as a contributor to the formidable challenges associated with climate change," the International Service for the Acquisition of Agri-Biotech Applications (ISAAA) wrote in its 2011 report on acceptance of GM crops.

Kenyan farmers were allowed to plant GM seeds sold by Monsanto, DuPont, and other companies in 2011. DuPont is developing a genetically modified type of sorghum, once again with assistance from Africa Harvest, fortified with extra vitamins and minerals that it hopes can be grown commercially in Kenya under the new law.

Francis Mwenda Kanya, who grows pineapples, sweet potatoes, and coffee, says tissue-culture bananas play a limited role on his farm, providing some cash sales without it becoming so important to his mix of crops that his family becomes dependent upon it.

Kanya, in his mid-forties, is active in the Kenya Organic Agriculture Network, which shuns fertilizers and pesticides. He sells his produce to three natural-foods supermarkets in Nairobi. Today, a daughter and granddaughter who live there are visiting his farm, which is difficult to get to not because the roads are bad, but because area teenagers are so absorbed in their cell-phone conversations they don't move quickly from the narrow pathway that leads to it. In his living room, Kanya hoists his granddaughter onto his lap and offers me pineapple juice. Pages of newsprint are plastered to his living-room wall as wallpaper.

Kanya's pineapples, avocados, and passion fruit are terraced down a steep hill that runs to a stream fed by a 50-foot waterfall. Across the stream, two men are cutting trees, presumably for lumber or firewood. Pausing near the waterfall, he says he's skeptical of large foreign businesses seeking favor in Africa. Because Kenya's politics are so unstable, foreign companies can exercise outsize influence in proportion to the public interest, he said.

"Farmers here share indigenous seeds. It is a part of our culture," he said. Poorly regulated genetically modified crops could quickly contaminate his supplies, he said.

Sylvester Oikeh manages the Water-Efficient Maize for Africa (WEMA) project, a Monsanto-funded effort to bring drought-resistant corn to the continent through conventional and genetically modified plant breeding.

WEMA falls under the auspices of the Nairobi-based African Agricultural Technology Foundation (AATF), which is also researching modified cowpeas and bananas.

The AATF for years has pushed Kenya's government toward accepting GM crops to improve its agriculture, and Oikeh said he's hoping its acceptance will be a model for Mozambique, Tanzania, and Uganda, the other countries in the corn project.

Monsanto referred questions about its corn projects in Africa to the AATF. "WEMA would not be WEMA without the partnership of Monsanto," Oikeh said. "Let Africa be open to embrace the technology. Embrace the best of it, and let us catch up to the rest of the world."[27]

The company hasn't won everyone's hearts and minds. Four firms— DuPont, Monsanto, Syngenta, and Limagrain—are responsible for more than half the world's seed sales.[28] About 300–500 companies provide around 70 percent of the food choices available to the world.[29] Large foreign companies, while a major source of investment capital, have the potential to disrupt development of local food systems that can help poorer regions develop themselves, said Olivier de Schutter of the UN.

"Different food systems serve different functions, they serve different markets, are good at doing different things, and we should recognize their specificity," he said. "If we leave it to business as usual, to the laws of the market, there is a big risk that the local food systems will be increasingly marginalized and the concentration in the hands of a small number of companies will increase, and that will be very problematic."[30]

Mistrust, or at the very least lack of familiarity, with outside businesses continues in Kenya's transmara region, where farmers still prefer to buy from local seed companies rather than from foreign giants.

"We take farmers on field days to see all these companies," said Daniel Osebe, a field officer for the Cereal Growers Association, a Kenyan grain-farmers group that works with the U.S. Agency for International Development, the World Food Programme and AGRA. "They see Monsanto, they see DuPont, but they buy Kenya Seed," he says, referring to the government-subsidized national provider. Kenya Seed is less expensive and more trusted, though some farmers are buying the more-expensive foreign varieties from multinationals as soil plots featuring their products show higher yields, he said.

In December 2010, South Africa's Competition Commission blocked a merger bid between Pioneer Hi-Bred and local company Pannar Seed Ltd.[31]

Merger opponents, led by Mariam Mayat, founder of the African Center for Biosafety, have argued that the combination, which would follow Monsanto acquisitions of South African seed companies, would allow foreign control of South Africa's seed supply, decreasing availability of conventional seed varieties, hurting export business with countries that don't accept genetically modified crops and forcing farmers to buy expensive seeds patented by U.S. corporations.

Foreign companies fundamentally misunderstand Africa, Mayat said. "They really do believe that Africa is backward. They really do think they can bring a new system. But they are not interested in social justice, they are not interested in sustaining the land. They are interested in profits only."[32]

Pioneer Hi-Bred and Pannar Seed spent much of the next year planning to log an appeal with South Africa's Competition Tribunal, which the company said it was confident it would win.

Emerging food suppliers will need to meet the rest of the world's regulations as the world seeks out new food sources and new markets to sell them, Schickler said. Building trust can take years of time—and billions of bananas. But in the end, the result is a better market for Kenya and more business for the companies, both the multinationals and the Muthomis, he said. Everyone eats, and everyone wins, as production increases, pest threats decline, and soil and water are used more efficiently, he said. Africa's agricultural development is becoming more and more about sustainability—not just environmental sustainability, but market sustainability as well, he said.

"You need to look at the big picture," he said.

In 2011, DuPont had more than 400 full-time employees in Africa, most of them in countries along the Indian Ocean, and more than 560,000 customers. In 2010 it launched an Africa Immersion Project, focusing on South Africa, Nigeria and Kenya as targets for future DuPont growth on the continent, which it expects to pick up.[33] Building customers, and bridging them, from better bananas to biotech corn, will help Africa feed itself and the world while improving the company's bottom line, he said.

"Our history, our reputation, is something we've been building for years," he said. "This is the next frontier."

CHAPTER 10

Thai Quality

In the rice paddies near Ayutthaya, a former Siamese capital that seventeenth-century emissaries of Louis XIV compared with Paris for its wealth and importance, Payao Ruangpueng is worried about insects.

Specifically, she's worried about an infestation of rice plant hoppers, slow-walking herbivores that munch their way through fields and devastate production. The hopper burn enveloping Payao's land may cut the 40-year-old farmer's crop yields by more than half.

Holding hopper-heavy grasses in her hands, she laments the brown bugs that become dozens of bumps on her rice grasses, ignore her pesticides, and stymie her best efforts at eradication. They might ruin the second of her three harvests this year.

"We can't grow other crops in this plain," said Payao, who has farmed in the region her entire life. She wears loose-fitting clothing on her five-foot frame and a mesh straw hat to shield against the March sun, which will only grow hotter as spring continues. Her 20-acre farm would be large by African smallholder standards, but isn't unusual in this part of Thailand.[1] The hopper isn't the only threat to her income. While high prices created unrest elsewhere, in Thailand's rice bowl where Payao farms, the problem in early 2011 was lower prices that combined with the hopper to eat away income—a double scourge for farmers in the country that's responsible for almost one-third of the world's shipments of the grain.

"We're suffering from a rice price slump, crop damages, and lower-than-expected production," Payao says, standing on the outside edge of a rain-soaked, green-and-gold paddy field where green means a healthy crop and gold means a matted clump of dead stalks is developing, the hopper calling card. "Production costs are higher than income," from rising fertilizer and pesticide costs. "We can't afford to continue planting."

The rich and developed nations of the Pacific Rim, the poorer nations of Asia, the burgeoning global economies of India and China, and increasingly, Africa, all have come to rely on Thai farmers like Payao for their rice, and their appetites will only increase further. Yet, prosperity is elusive for her, a problem Thailand is trying to solve as it faces lower-cost competition from rivals. The struggles of Thai farmers, two-fifths of the nation's workforce, were pivotal to the country's elections in July 2011, when both of the leading political parties promised more money for rice farmers. A farmer needs a market, but the desire to rely on markets declines when prices fall.

Food security isn't only about poorer nations growing and selling more food. It's also about the role more developed farm economies play as consumers want more variety, better nutrition, and higher food quality along with the calories needed to live. For smallholders in Africa, it can mean growing coffee or cocoa for premium certified markets such as fair trade, shade-grown, rainforest, or other categories. In the United States, the farmer's market may be . . . the farmers' market, which provides growers near urban areas with extra income and consumers with greater choice. In Thailand, it may mean greater focus on higher-quality rice as export rivals emerge—with outcomes that reverberate through world supplies and prices.

■ ■ ■

Payao may not be able to afford continued planting. The planet may not want her to stop.

The world's most acute hunger problems are in sub-Saharan Africa. In sheer numbers, Asia has more than twice as many people suffering from malnutrition. In some ways, its hunger problem is more vexing because, if growth alone were the answer, the problem should be gone.

Asia has already had a Green Revolution, with higher production to prove it. Many of its economies are well-developed. The continent's growing prosperity touches every aspect of life in the rest of the world. China and India have driven growth for two decades. The industrial success of Japan, Taiwan, South Korea, Singapore, and Hong Kong served as a model for Indonesia, Malaysia, the Philippines, and Thailand, the Tiger Cubs that diversified their economies over the past 30 years. Thailand's national income rose 72 percent during this century's first decade. Even a currency crisis that hit the country first and worst in the late 1990s proved a temporary setback, as Southeast Asia continued to benefit from greater exports and trade with its dynamic, ever-expanding neighbors. Better technology, seeds, and fertilizers that help grow more food, combined with rising affluence, would seem an effective recipe for fighting hunger.

It hasn't worked out that way.

The proportion of Asia's population that experiences undernourishment dropped from 20 percent in the early 1990s to 16 percent 15 years later, but hunger persists both in areas that have completely missed out on growth—in famine-struck North Korea malnourishment has risen from one-fifth to one-third of the population—and in places where growth is unequal. In the early 1990s, near the end of decades of slow income growth, India's percentage of undernourished was 20 percent. In the mid-2000s, the percentage of undernourished people in India, after the economy had grown 400 percent, was . . . 21 percent (see Table 10.1). By that measure, the Green Revolution contains shades of gray.[2]

Population is part of the problem. More food plus more mouths creates a treadmill where plants and livestock keep up with people, but nothing more. Policy provides another puzzle piece. Trade barriers that keep food prices low for one country raise them elsewhere, even as domestic farmers lose their incentive to grow. Poorly constructed subsidies encourage farmers to reduce

TABLE 10.1   Prevalence of Undernourishment in Developing Countries

Year	Total Population 2005–07 (millions)	Number of People Undernourished				Proportion of Undernourished in Total Population			
		1990–1992	1995–1997	2000–2002	2005–2007	1990–1992	1995–1997	2000–2002	2005–2007
Asia and the Pacific	3558.7	587.9	498.1	531.8	554.5	20	17	17	16
Latin America and the Caribbean	556.1	54.3	53.3	50.7	47.1	12	11	10	8
Near East and North Africa	439.3	19.6	29.5	31.8	32.4	6	8	8	7
Sub-Saharan Africa	729.6	164.9	187.2	201.7	201.2	34	33	31	28

Source: UN Food and Agriculture Organization.

planting in some cases and make bad crop decisions in others when government policies distort price signals. A well-functioning market helps them decide what and how much they should plant. It also increases risk—but without it, world prices stay volatile, production doesn't match needs, and hunger persists. Farmers lose opportunity, and consumers don't benefit from what farmers could grow.

The rice bowl has already had its production revolution. The market evolution is happening now, in sometimes violent fits and starts.

■ ■ ■

Millennia of cultivation have deeply engrained rice in the culture of rural Thailand, where the legend of Me Posop, the rice goddess who rewards those who are good stewards of her grain, remains part of folklore. Young children, sometimes even in Thailand's cosmopolitan capital, will salute the rice mother after a meal. Farmers give ceremonial offerings at the beginning of planting as well as during the crop's growth to ensure productivity, and colloquial exhortations for the goddess to bless the land with fertility are still part of the culture.

In art, she is shown as a young, traditionally dressed woman holding rice and placed near representations of fish, the other staple food of Thailand's rice-growing regions. The goddess and the sea are the foundations of famous Thai dishes—*khao phat kung, phat thai, khanom chin*. Allowing rice to fall to the floor is considered both impolite and an affront to Me Posop, who remains respected even as tractors and fertilizers join prayers and offerings as yield-boosting techniques in Thailand.[3]

Me Posop hasn't seemed terribly offended, given Thailand's exploding rice production of the past half-century. The Rice Mother has been kind, as have regional politics. Neighbors lived through war and communism, while Thailand became Southeast Asia's second-biggest economy after Indonesia, which has nearly four times as many people. Farm production accelerated even as it became a smaller share of the Thai economy, the normal trend of developing nations. The country's top five exports include manufactured goods and jewelry; among commodities, it's a major shipper of rubber and tapioca to China, processed chicken to Japan and shrimp to the United States. It has even been a major source of corn, and it's a top-five sugar exporter. The country surpassed Myanmar as the world's top rice shipper in the 1960s and has stayed there ever since.

Thailand has had its share of political turbulence. Ethnic and social differences between northern farmers—descendants of the nineteenth-century

Lanna kingdom annexed by what was then called Siam—and urban, Bangkok-based elites have fueled nine military coups since the current king took the throne as an 18-year-old in 1946. The north and northeast, where average incomes are one-third those of Bangkok's, was the base of a communist insurgency active into the 1980s. It's now the base of support for Thaksin Shinawatra, the country's populist leader from 2001 to 2006, when he was deposed by the military. His influence from exile in Dubai remains strong. In 2010, about 90 people died in clashes between "red shirt" demonstrators loyal to Thaksin and armed troops in Bangkok, and the specter of violence loomed over the next year's elections. All the while, Thailand's farmers have kept the rice bowl overflowing, with annual exports nearly equal to domestic consumption.

Wichian Phuanglamchiak, an admirer of Thaksin, grows rice near Ayutthaya. The frenetic farm activist began working in his parents' field when he was six years old. Now in his seventies, he remembers the shift that made Thailand's farmers suppliers to the world.

"Every morning before school, I hooked up the plow with [water] buffaloes. After school, I came back to help them, pounding paddy rice to separate rice shells, so we had unpolished rice."[4]

The next day, after school, he pounded the rice again, polishing it to make it whiter and rid it of the bran dust to give it a glossier appearance that was more pleasing to consumers. After that, the rice was stored in a barn.

His routine changed in the 1960s, when his family began to use fertilizer and chemicals. Production increased more than sixfold. By 1964 the family had ditched the water buffaloes for a tractor. Today he has nine sons and daughters, two of whom have their own rice farms. With the tractor, the productivity and the income came debt, the first his family had ever had. That cycle troubles Thai farmers today, he said, as costs and competitors catch up with them.

It also troubled Thailand's government, which in the spring of 2011 was engaged with Thaksin's supporters in what was expected to be a close, tense election. Rice subsidies were crucial to rural voters. Abhisit Vejjajiva, the country's Oxford-educated prime minister, scrapped the Thaksin-era system of paying farmers above-market prices to turn over their crops to government warehouses and replaced it with one that paid farmers varying subsidies based on market prices. Thaksin's "pledging" system gave the government huge stockpiles to control prices but was prone to corruption among traders, millers, and authorities. The new system of guaranteed incomes distorted markets less, but became confusing and tough to administer as prices moved up and down. Total rice supplies didn't change, and lower subsidies made it more difficult for farmers to deal with rising oil and fertilizer costs, making it unpopular.

Abhisit's opposition coalesced under the Pheu Thai (For Thais) party, an iteration of Thaksin's earlier following that made his youngest sister, Yingluck Shinawatra, its leader. Both Pheu Thai and the incumbent Democrats promised generous farm subsidies, and Pheu Thai promised to revive pledging.[5] As the election progressed, the army, in recent years the true power broker and a backer of Abhisit, was warning voters to pick "good people" in the election and reminded them that criticism of the monarchy—an offense punishable by up to 15 years in prison and a limit to freedom of expression in Thailand—would not be tolerated.[6]

Thai farmers, like farmers around the world, are on the whole less prosperous than city-dwellers. Also like farmers in many countries, they are a media-savvy, well-organized, and politically powerful force. Farmer strikes and protests in recent years have crippled exports in Argentina, stopped land development in India, and supported subsidies in the European Union. Wichian is speaking rapid-fire on his cell phone and coordinating his fellow activists in what has become Media Day for the struggling Thai farmers as a Bloomberg colleague and I travel with him to the rice paddies of the Pak Hai district, about 50 miles north of Bangkok. We arrive at roughly the same time as a Bangkok television crew of two cameramen and a female newscaster who is also interviewing the farmers as they explain the hopper plague and why they need more government assistance.

My colleague is talking to farmers, working on her own stories and helping with my interviews while I formulate questions and take photos. In the distance a grower is working his land wearing long, gray pajamas, heavy gloves, and a paddy hat. I zoom my lens to photograph the lone, silent man. My view is obstructed by a motorcycle vendor, who is selling sandwiches and juices to farmers along the road. The motorcycle buzzes away. I raise my camera, and a pickup enters the frame. The pickup passes. It's followed by a slow, lumbering tractor pulling a cart of pesticides. I could switch to video, but the sound wouldn't pick up well. Someone's playing a boom box. And so on. This is a busy place, and people have work to do.

The ease with which Thailand achieves rice surpluses was crucial to keeping the world fed in 2008. When other exporters, including Vietnam, were shuttering their borders, Thailand stayed open, keeping markets from seizing up completely. The country today is not only a major supplier to large Asian markets such as Malaysia and Indonesia. Its biggest shipping destination in 2010 was Nigeria, followed by Ivory Coast and South Africa. China, Iran and the United States have also been recent top-10 export sites.[7]

But dramatic increases to the quantity of Thai rice and exports may not be the country's future, regardless of who holds power. The Thai rice bowl is becoming less central to Southeast Asia production as regional rivals emerge for the first time since Myanmar, then named Burma, fell under military rule. Thai exports are still rising—shipments have increased 33 percent to 10 million tons in the past decade, according to the U.S. Department of Agriculture (USDA). Vietnamese exports are up 70 percent to 6 million tons in the same period (see Figure 10.1). Vietnamese wholesale rice prices can be two-fifths of their Thai rivals, and their farms carry lower expense: Thailand as a whole has 35 percent more tractors than its eastern neighbor, and Vietnam has 65 percent more draft animals.[8] Vietnam's effectiveness in rice-growing allowed it to halve its national hunger five years sooner than the date spelled out in the Millennium Development Goals. The country, said Nguyen Van Bo, the president of the Vietnamese Academy of Agricultural Science, is playing an increasingly important role in food security because many of its customers are nations with high poverty rates. Vietnam also offers technical assistance to African and Latin American countries developing their own rice industries, he said.

"As a developing country, our technology is not too modern and costs less," making it more suitable for poorer nations, he said. "For Vietnam, exporting lower-quality rice is still more economical."[9]

Cambodia, which has stabilized after a generation of violent political turmoil but still has deadly border clashes with Thailand; Laos; and eventually even Myanmar will emerge and reemerge as global rice powers, said

FIGURE 10.1 Rice Exports from Southeast Asia

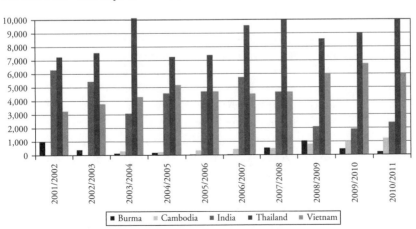

Source: United Nations Food and Agriculture Organization.

Pramote Vanichanont, honorary president of the Thai Rice Mills Association. Thailand has priced itself out of much of its own market because its prosperity increases production costs as land, equipment, and living expenses rise, he said.

Vietnamese competition affects Thai prices. The country's harvests flood the market with inexpensive rice, driving sales prices below Thailand's cost of production. Meanwhile, Thailand's high-priced, high-quality Hom Mali or jasmine rice crop is supposed to increase production 20 percent by 2015, he added. The future, Pramote said, is in taking Thailand's head start on rice and using its better roads, warehouses, and millers to become the hub of Southeast Asia's rice marketing, processing, and trading. "We don't aim to be the world's largest exporter," said Pramote, a member of his country's National Rice Policy Committee that advises the government on the future of Thai rice. "We've learned from past experiences of being a key player in the market that farmers have been suffering losses because we can't set appropriate prices by ourselves."

And to get the most advantageous price for the most profitable product, a farmer needs to be producing for the right market.

■ ■ ■

Just as quality and quantity aren't conflicting terms, which path gets emphasized isn't a simple question of economic development. Vastly different markets exist side by side, and the hunger for variety will only continue as the world grows wealthier.

I had spent the day in Ayutthaya immediately after leaving the Bangkok airport, a 24-hour trek with a layover in Doha and no break for jet lag. By 5 P.M. I was struggling to keep my eyes open in the car, and we checked into a hotel in Nakhon Sawan, near the next day's interviews. I fell asleep at 5:30. And was wide-awake at 3 A.M. I transcribed notes for a couple of hours. I was getting hungry, and I needed toothpaste, so I decided to see what might be available as dawn quietly urged the city from its slumber. Across the street from the hotel was a shining orange-and-green universal beacon of 24-hour caloric availability: a 7-Eleven store. I walked into the 7-Eleven, found some toothpaste and some packaged sweet buns for 50 baht (a little under $2), plunked my money on the counter, took my nutrition in a white plastic bag, and stepped outside.

Clouds had burst during the night, leaving a heaviness in the air that smoothly pressed upon my face and left a touch of texture. The predawn suggestion of sunlight, disturbed only by the fluorescence of the 7-Eleven, seemed to become more insistent with each solitary car and motorcycle that passed through the streets of Nakhon Sawan, whose name translates as "Heavenly City," splashing water that was already rising into steam. I decided it was time to see the sunrise, take a walk and enjoy my prepackaged, convenience-store breakfast bun. I struggled with the wrapping as I crossed the street and turned the corner.

A block away from the 7-Eleven, on a side alley, a local market was setting up shop for the day: Nam Wah bananas, plum mango just getting into season, guava, papaya, and rose apple, brought in by scooter from nearby farms; fresh meat, fresh breads, and, of course, rice, its steam fading into the humidity that hugged the morning. Conquering the crinkly plastic, I bit into the bun. The super-processed, tightly packaged bread-based substance wasn't bad, not for 50 baht, including toothpaste, I thought. But not as good as what I had seen around the corner.

A globalized food world is a diverse food world. McDonald's restaurants open across Asia; Europeans prize African fruits; and in the United States, more than one-third of its goats are slaughtered in New Jersey, the center of halal meat-packing to serve Islamic dietary needs. The United States, the world's richest nation, is also the biggest exporter of low-cost, bulk staple crops, even as its organic foods consumption rises from a miniscule fragment of grocery sales in the mid-1990s to about 4 percent today. U.S. imports rise in tandem with exports because consumers demand bananas in New York in November—but that doesn't affect needs elsewhere for corn, which can be grown at large scale and competitive prices by U.S farmers. The world's most expensive coffees are grown by smallholders in Africa and Latin America who benefit from favorable climate conditions that give them their best chance at income even as they sometimes starve for grain. In India, the heart of the Green Revolution, small organic farms are beginning to supply prospering cities even as bulk rice and wheat remain staples.[10] Rich countries develop local foods movements that prize outdoor markets, where you can meet the farmer who grew your food; poorer countries build supermarkets that wouldn't look out of place in suburban Paris. It's a mixed-up world, and only getting more so.

In Nicaragua, Wilfredo Meneses has added three acres of organic cabbage to the 34 acres of potatoes he grows for supermarkets across the country. He is an insistent and powerfully built man who plans to expand his farm and invest in more modern equipment as his income rises. He insists I stay for dinner, offering tortillas made from nearby corn that are wrapped around cheese his wife had made from their dairy cow's milk. Coffee from freshly harvested beans accompanies the meal, topped with homemade breads for dessert.

For the most part I've passed up fresh foods, a potential source of stomach bugs, with great discipline. Meneses is ever-insistent. If my American stomach can't handle his food, at least I have good hospitals to visit when I get home, he jokes. I don't have any problems, and were it not for my overriding desire to clear through customs without too many questions and a conscientious fear of introducing a previously unknown pathogen that could wipe out the U.S. potato crop, I would certainly have left Nicaragua laden with coffee and cheese.

Organic cabbage is a newer crop for him, he said. It's more expensive to produce than one using standard growing methods. An organic cabbage sold in Estili, the nearest city, may cost about 2.5 cordoba (about 12 U.S. cents) more to produce, but it will sell for 5 cordoba more than a non-organic variety. The potatoes are Meneses' main investment—with the storage facility built on his land he can protect his produce for up to three months instead of one. He's ready to expand his cabbage planting if the expected returns materialize. Meneses said his choice is somewhat motivated by his concerns about climate change and the impact of farming on the environment. Mainly, he's interested in higher profits.

"People demand it in the supermarkets," he said.[11]

Global organic production holds potential for smallholder farmers whose yields and soil quality can improve at little expense simply by improving farm management practices without reliance on more expensive crop inputs, said Gary Hirshberg, chief executive officer of Stonyfield Farm, the largest U.S. producer of organic yogurt. And as alternative-food production gains greater scale, cost differences should decline, he said.[12] Cultivating niche markets alone doesn't bring food security. Ray Offenheiser, the head of Oxfam America, which has supported organic projects worldwide, cautions that farmers first need to feed themselves and their neighbors, and simply creating markets that cater to rich-world tastes may not be the first priority.[13] It may even have unwanted consequences. When quinoa, a grain-like staple of Bolivian diets, used centuries ago to feed Inca soldiers, was anointed the latest superfood by health-conscious, affluent U.S. and European consumers, exports soared and prices skyrocketed—good news for farmers and bad news for Bolivian consumers forced to buy less-nutritious foods because they couldn't afford their traditional diet.[14]

Still, such production yields environmental improvements and creates yet another market for farmers—if "What's it worth?" is answered a little more lucratively when sustainability is an added benefit, then more is enriched than the farmer and the consumer.

Markets adapt to fill needs as worldwide tastes evolve. In Nakhon Sawan, the heart of the Thai rice bowl, the country's millers are trying to do exactly that.

■ ■ ■

The traders begin gathering in the warehouse shade around 10 A.M. Buckets of ice filled with sealed plastic cups of water are already placed near tables and chairs set up in a side room to deal with the approaching midday heat. Rice buyers and sellers are examining pink and yellow sheets, dropping their offers into orange plastic bins numbered 1 through 19—one for each variety of rice offered in the first day of trading at a new spot-price market designed to establish a private mechanism to set a benchmark global price for Thai rice.

Or, the revival of an older tradition. For decades, privately owned and managed paddy markets helped establish prices for the rice sold by Thai farmers, helping them decide what to plant, how much, and when.

Prakit Narongtanupon, a native of the region who holds a PhD from the University of Indiana, helped set up the market, even down to selecting the colors—pink for sales offers, yellow for buyers. For Thailand to make the right decision for the future of its rice, it has to know what buyers want. Figuring that out starts here, he said.

"Right now the market flies in the air and nobody has any ideas what's going on," he said. "You need to organize and make things more systematic. Then, when things are more systematic, everything works."

The varieties on sale run the rice spectrum. Jasmine. Parboiled. White rice—5 percent broken, 10 percent broken, 15 percent broken, 100 percent broken. Most of these varieties would never have the volume to be traded on a Chicago-style exchange, but prices for goods bought on the spot will still help farmers know what they should plant and what they should charge, as well as give information to help Thailand's own rice futures exchange, the Bangkok-based Agricultural Futures Exchange of Thailand (AFET), develop, he said.

In 2011 AFET, the nation's government-backed rice and rubber futures market, rolled out a new contract intended to be a regional benchmark for standard-quality rice that could be traded worldwide. The exchange and the spot market interact, said AFET senior officer Archvis Vorapanya, by giving big buyers who want to hedge their risks on the Bangkok exchange an idea of sales trends closer to the farmers. The spot market also indicates supply and demand for a wide array of rice—the many varieties that, even if not directly traded on AFET, give traders an idea of Thai production trends, which then reverberate through world markets via Thailand's export power, Prakit said.

These mechanisms can keep Thailand at the center of rice trading at the same time it focuses on producing higher-grade varieties popular in Singapore, Hong Kong, Japan, and the West, Pramote said. That would allow Thai farmers to cover their expenses and let other, emerging countries provide basic food security.

Thailand's future revenue growth will be in rice quality, while for Cambodia and Vietnam it will be quantity, he said. Even so, Thailand and the world will need to continue doing both. Some world appetites will need more food; others will want more varied diets. That distinction's already found throughout Asia, notably in China, where rich and poor consumers together shape the biggest food market of all.

Feeding China, India, and the rest of Asia looms as one of the future's biggest food-security challenges. Food demand in the world's most populous nation, where the percentage of malnourished people has stabilized at about 10 percent, down from 18 percent 20 years ago, will rise further as both population and living standards rise.

■ ■ ■

Higher incomes change what people eat. Consumers first step up food purchases as they become wealthier, eating more food and diversifying their diets (see Figure 10.2). At some point, additional food spending shifts toward quality, variety, and convenience. Balanced diets and obesity become greater concerns. China's a massive example of all three dynamics—the poor and food-insecure calorie-seekers, the rising diet-diversifiers, and the wealthy quality-buyers— happening at once. Different markets have different needs. A big challenge of the global food marketplace is figuring out how to best serve each.

China's growth has dramatically increased its food security as it has become richer and more urban, in part because of social-welfare programs that aid its poorest. From 1981 to 2004, its impoverished population fell from 652 million to 135 million, according to the UN. China has gone from being the world's largest food aid recipient to becoming largely self-sufficient. Its highly regulated grain exchanges and its ample reserves help smooth out price spikes. All this, created by 200 million smallholder farmers whose farms average less than two acres in a country that has less than 7 percent of the world's water, less than 9 percent of its available cropland and more than 20 percent of its population.[15]

FIGURE 10.2 The Changing Global Diet

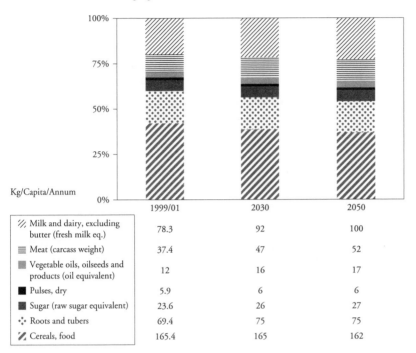

	1999/01	2030	2050
/// Milk and dairy, excluding butter (fresh milk eq.)	78.3	92	100
≡ Meat (carcass weight)	37.4	47	52
▓ Vegetable oils, oilseeds and products (oil equivalent)	12	16	17
■ Pulses, dry	5.9	6	6
■ Sugar (raw sugar equivalent)	23.6	26	27
∴ Roots and tubers	69.4	75	75
/ Cereals, food	165.4	165	162

Source: World Agriculture: Towards 2030/2050. Interim Report. Prospects for Food, Nutrition, Agriculture and Major Commodity Groups. Table 2.7 UN Food and Agriculture Organization, Rome, June 2006.

China has doubled its meat consumption in the past two decades as wealthier Chinese eat more protein. Half of the world's pigs live in China, and the average Chinese person was consuming 87 pounds of pork in 2011, compared to 43 pounds in 1990.[16] The long march to food self-sufficiency of the world's second biggest economy—a dramatic shift from Mao Zedong's Great Leap Forward of the 1950s, a man-made famine worse than Stalin's starving of Ukraine—faces obstacles that may make future self-reliance difficult. Environmental degradation, including depleted aquifers and soil erosion, is growing even faster than China's runaway GDP. Climate change may cut crop yields 5 to 10 percent. And usable cropland is also declining, lost to erosion and cities.

Cracks in China's self-sufficiency are beginning to show.[17] In 2009, in the midst of a drought, the country started buying significant amounts of overseas corn for the first time in nearly a decade while the world, unable to rely on government estimates, tried to figure out how much grain China actually had. A 2011 sale of 1.25 million tons of U.S. corn, the sixth-biggest in the history of U.S. corn sales, was believed to be from China, though the sales destination was initially listed as "unknown."[18] China bought at least another 540,000 tons during the summer, as some experts questioned how forthcoming the country was being about its own food supplies.[19] Large food reserves are a part of Chinese national policy. China holds about two-fifths of the planet's supplies of the grain, according to U.S. government statistics. The bigger question is, as urbanization continues and the environment is strained, whether that can be sustained for decades.[20]

Chinese droughts and imports weigh in the back of exporter minds, said Chookiat Ophaswongse, the head of Huay Chuan Co., a Thai shipper of rice and rubber. China seems to have enough food until it doesn't, and a China food shock would create a price spike that would reverberate throughout the region and the world.

"They could order three million, five million tons of rice, just like that," he said. Five million tons would be half of Thailand's annual exports and about one-sixth of all rice traded worldwide in a year. For China, it would represent less than 4 percent of annual consumption—not an unimaginable shortfall.

Strains on China's farms have the potential to feed civil unrest. Forced dislocation of farmers for urban development, an internal land grab with Chinese characteristics, has been a less-publicized source of social tension. "You should be talking to the farmers," Jin Qiansheng, a Chinese aviation official, told me in an interview in Xi'an in 2005. Xi'an, a central Chinese city that had been the terminus of the fabled Silk Road trade route and claims the famous terra-cotta warriors nearby, is now an aerospace town in transition to joining the world economy. In the streets just off the town square, which boasted a shopping mall complete with Western luxury goods and a fashion-store pianist playing Gershwin, lie vast neighborhoods of one-room homes and heaping piles of garbage, its smells intermingled with the spices added to dishes prepared on outdoor cooking stoves. An aerospace center the government was building outside town was a big slab of sod, with a headquarters building in the middle, a bunch of holes dug at the edges and some soon-to-disappear farmhouses ringing the perimeter.

The base, designed to house 50,000 workers in a five-kilometer square complex for manufacturing, living, and shopping, was being taken from farm-land. Jin guided me to a greeting area where, proudly placed for observation, was the model of a Chinese city built on forbidden farms. Gleaming white buildings, plants for manufacturing, clean dormitories for workers from the countryside, another sign of China's rush from earth to sky.

He looked out a window, past the construction and toward the rural homes beyond. "Some of their families have lived on their land for 500 years, and they are all being moved somewhere else," he said.[21]

Details differ, but China's story of rising demand also is being played out in India, which offers generous farm payments, protects its farmers from trade competition, and stresses food self-sufficiency, and in Indonesia, where the government heavily subsidizes fertilizer to boost production. Those three countries account for two-fifths of the world's population. Rice is in no danger of disappearing from Asian diets, and Thailand is in no danger of disappearing as an exporter. But its market is evolving. While Bangladesh buys lower-priced white and parboiled rice from Thailand, the majority of Singapore's purchases are Hom Mali rice, a source of Thai national pride for its nutty, rich aroma and subtle flavor. One type of rice offered for export becomes 19 varieties. Thai farmers have kept Thailand well fed as its cities have prospered and national wealth has grown. Higher living standards have made land, labor, and machinery more expensive, making Thai rice uncompetitive for the lower grades even as poorer consumers still need it.

And thus, the heart of the Asian rice bowl is at a crossroads—just as demand is intensifying both for more food and for better quality and greater variety.

■ ■ ■

Thailand's sellers and shippers grew nervous as spring turned to summer and Yingluck, telegenic, articulate, and relatively untainted by the turbulent past, built a lead over Abhisit in the polls. Traders and shippers worried that more heavily subsidized rice, meant to help farmers, would make the country less competitive with Vietnam, reducing Thailand's exports and raising world food costs.[22]

The farmers disagreed. Yingluck convincingly won, enough to persuade the military to stand down and Pheu Thai to gain control of nearly three-fifths of the country's parliament. Wichian said the victory gave hope for farmers who would benefit from new subsidies. "It will help farmers to have a better life," he said. "Farmers will be able to sell rice at high prices, without being pushed down by traders like before."[23]

While the new government planned its agenda, traders and exporters waited to see the impact, with the effect on efforts to expand trading and transparency unclear. Rice rose to its highest prices since 2008 by mid-July as traders worried that new payments to farmers would raise export costs. The evolution toward quality is likely to continue regardless of who is in power, said Korbsook Iamsuri, president of the Thai Rice Exporters Association, in an interview before the election.

Korbsook, a tall, impeccably dressed woman, speaks of rice with the confidence and poise one would expect from a third-generation rice shipper and the chief executive officer of Kamolkij Co. Ltd., one of the country's most important rice-trading companies. She said her country's grain growth hinges on freer markets and regional integration. The formation of the ASEAN Economic Community, a single regional trading bloc promised in 2015, may be Thailand's best bet at staying on top, making the country's more developed economy a better target for foreign investment even as Thai exporters consider investments in Cambodian rice mills and expand trade across Southeast Asia, she said.

The export market for higher-quality rice itself will expand as rising population will be accompanied by increased incomes that whet consumer appetites for more rice variety. How farmers handle the transition will play a crucial part in its success, she said. In 2011, Thai farmers wanted what they considered to be greater security.

"Farmers don't fully get compensation" for their work, Payao said. "If the government covers the difference, farmers can live happily."

Or at least some can, in some places.

CHAPTER 11

Steps Up

Suleymane Soro always grew cotton on his 17-acre farm in Ivory Coast, supporting his wife and six children in a mud home he built himself, with no running water or electricity. And in the fall of 2007, no cotton.

"We are completely discouraged," Soro said at the time, smoking a cigarette as he sat in the shadow of a tree, his three youngest children and those of a neighbor plowing a field with two oxen. The village leader—considered such as one of the few French speakers in the area—couldn't buy seeds and fertilizer after the local ginning company failed. From 2000 to 2006 his annual profit fell two-thirds, to 120,000 CFA francs, about $250. He turned to corn to feed his family, but the lack of cotton income deprived him of his best chance to improve his farm production and his family's standard of living.[1]

Cotton incomes fell by 30 percent in the early 2000s in Soro's West Africa, where about 10 million people depend on the fiber for their livelihoods. The struggle he and other farmers faced stemmed in part from rich-nation subsidies that artificially lowered prices and flooded markets with cheap cotton, prompting a labyrinthine World Trade Organization case that by 2011 had led to the bizarre situation of the U.S. government paying one of its biggest agricultural competitors, Brazil, $147 million a year to stave off greater retaliation by the World Trade Organization (WTO). The Brazil cotton saga may continue for years, part of a familiar narrative of rich countries lavishly supporting their own farm lobbies at the expense of the world's poorest. It remains relevant in determining how the world deals with situations when overproduction pushes income below the cost of growing a crop.

Times have changed. Cotton prices quadrupled from 2008 to 2011 when rich-nation farmers switched to corn and soybeans to feed hungry food markets. When cotton contracts traded in New York reached $2.197 a pound in March 2011, the price wasn't only a record—it was nearly double what futures had ever been in the history of cotton trading before 2010. West African cotton farmers certainly still face problems: In Ivory Coast, simply getting bales out of the country was a challenge during its brief civil war.[2] In Mali, farmers stopped growing the fiber because the state-owned textile company wasn't paying them quickly.[3] Still, low crop prices are no longer the central issue as a world of surplus becomes one of scarcity. How to take advantage of high prices and new market opportunities has created a new set of problems as tight supplies meet expanding demand.

We now live on a planet where a grain-seller in Ethiopia bases his prices on Chicago wheat markets; where wheat futures in Chicago are shaped by the needs of a pension fund; where a dry spell in Russia sparks riots in Mozambique and revolution in Egypt; where a cold-storage unit in Kenya may affect the future of bananas in Europe; where Walmart tomatoes depend on decaying Nicaraguan roads; where an election in Thailand may determine who sells rice to Nigeria. Where a Tunisian street vendor's death in a dispute over vegetables inflames a region and changes the order of the world.

■ ■ ■

Countries that increasingly depend on one another for food and fiber are still wrestling with global trade and local subsidies even as the vehicle for worldwide agreement, the Doha Round of world trade talks, begins a second decade with no resolution in sight. Export restrictions, not even part of the original Doha agenda, feed price shocks unforeseen a decade ago. Disputes over food safety standards, long a tricky trade barrier, are emerging as larger, and highly complicated, concerns as traditional tariffs are used less to block food flows. Subsidies still send incorrect signals of the world's wants and needs, but in a high-price world programs that raise prices may cause more immediate harm than ones that lower them. Meanwhile, smaller groupings of countries are working to make their markets function better as hope for a global agreement ebbs.

The questions posed by globalized food will never be resolved once and for all. Grappling with them is necessary to make sure all that food gets where it needs to be at a price that's affordable for everyone.[4]

■ ■ ■

A trade paradox that makes agreement difficult is that while everyone ultimately benefits from open markets, for an individual, an interest group, or a particular country, it often makes sense to keep them closed, or at least try to skew the results in one's favor. It's understandable why Russia would keep its wheat, India would keep its onions, and Nicaragua would keep its beans during a drought: In mid-2011, after it was lifted, Russia, in fact, could look back on the ban that helped destabilize North Africa and the Middle East as a domestic success, as it helped limit its own inflation.[5] Foreign buyers may be forced to scramble for supplies at even higher prices, but that's not the exporter's primary concern. It's more worried about feeding its own people, preventing internal unrest, and maintaining power. And it always will be.

Proliferating bans choke off trade, with all sorts of undesirable consequences for production and the planet. Saudi Arabia may decide it's better to grow its own wheat, depleting an aquifer by irrigating deserts when it would be cheaper and sustainable to just buy grain from the Black Sea.[6] South Korea, the world's third biggest corn buyer, may decide it should secure corn supplies by buying land in Tanzania when Tanzanians would likely ship surpluses to Korea if they could feed themselves first.[7] Indonesia may decide it needs to become self-sufficient in rice and as a result ban imports of the grain—forcing prices higher for its own consumers when Thailand and Vietnam would be more than happy to sell to what once was the world's biggest rice buyer.[8] These are not theoretical examples. These are things that have already happened, and will continue to without some sort of global response.

Trade restrictions continue to complicate global food movement. One study found that reducing trade barriers to the level of the nation most open to imports reduced global consumer food prices 57 percent. In one model, only Argentina, Brazil, and the United States saw crop prices rise when trade barriers fell, simply because their products were so attractive as exports. Farmers in most countries would experience lower crop prices while raising incomes by producing more of what would make the most sense in world markets. Falling food prices in the world's poorest countries would leave money to alleviate poverty, the main cause of hunger.[9]

The Doha round of global trade talks, which started in 2001, has focused on opening markets for imports. That's a key concern when international negotiators are worried about surpluses. Export bans become a problem when surpluses don't exist. They will need to be addressed at a global level, said Joe Glauber, chief economist at the U.S. Department of Agriculture, the country's chief negotiator on farm trade for much of the Doha Round—and, for two years in the 1970s, a Peace Corps volunteer in Mali. "It's very difficult to get an agreement within the WTO because there are a number of countries that have used these policies to insulate their own consumers from high prices," he said.[10]

Russia and Ukraine, its consumers calmed by larger crops, lifted wheat restrictions in the first half of 2011. Egypt bought its first Russian wheat of 2011 in July, wary of relying on its once-biggest supplier and planning to maintain its ties with other customers.[11] India increased rice shipments shortly afterward and contemplated lifting its ban on wheat while trying to keep consumer prices below market costs.[12] Efforts to curb export bans have stalled, even as the Group of 20 agricultural ministers moved to ease restrictions involving humanitarian food-aid shipments. Japan, the world's leading importer of corn, wheat, and pork in 2008, in 2011 tried to rally support against export bans at the WTO, asking for prohibitions to be limited to "strictly necessary" situations, taking into consideration a potential banner's "production situation, stocks, and volume of domestic consumption."

Seeking international support for its proposal, Japan was joined by . . . Switzerland. The proposal was tabled.[13]

■ ■ ■

Negotiators on the Doha Round were trying to salvage some sort of agreement as it neared its 10-year anniversary.[14] Even without an agreement, the global trend on tariffs is toward reducing them (see Figure 11.1). When direct trade barriers lessen, the desire to protect domestic farm interests remains strong. Countries find other ways to protect their markets and thwart competitors, making restrictions based on food safety a favorite barrier used to keep goods out, keep prices higher, and distort global trade. The line between legitimate food safety worries and outright protectionism is difficult to draw. Russia, which in 2011 was trying to become a member of the WTO, routinely banned pork, poultry, and other agricultural goods from outside its borders for health reasons, to the chagrin of countries trying to sell it food.[15] Worried consumers prompted the rash of bans against Japanese farm products on fears of nuclear contamination after the reactor leaks at the Fukushima Daiichi power plant. Government actions reassured voters—and also knocked a competitor off the market. The principle that food-safety bans be rooted in a scientific assessment of risk, established in a world trade agreement that predates Doha, wasn't followed at least half of the time, according to a study of measures taken before the WTO from 2006 to 2009.[16]

Food safety barriers, called Sanitary and Phytosanitary (SPS) restrictions, have existed in some form as long as trade itself: When a country says it doesn't consider a competitor's product to be safe, it's hard to force that country to let that product in without some sort of global standard that everyone is supposed to follow. SPS disputes will only rise as more countries

FIGURE 11.1   World Tariff Rate Applied to All Products (Simple Mean, %)

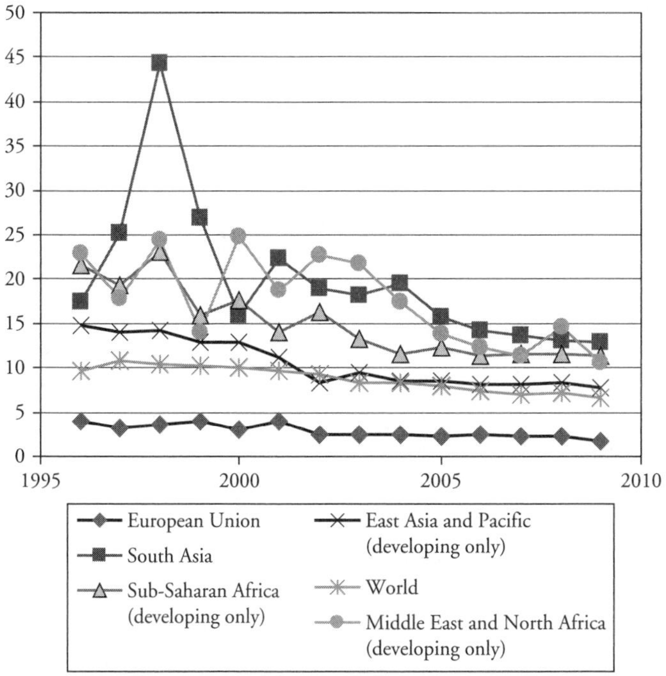

Source: World Bank.

become more dependent on one another for products, and especially as less-developed competitors with food-safety systems more vulnerable to criticism come online. Safety-related bans can cost exporters billions of dollars, fairly or unfairly: Slow resumption of trade after the first U.S. case of mad-cow disease pushed more than 30 countries to ban the nation's beef cost companies at least $11 billion, according to one study.[17]

Food-safety strictness can encourage development. It provides an incentive for countries to upgrade their processing and export capabilities to meet the requirements of promising new markets and improves the quality of food consumed domestically—the Muthomis, in Kenya, are improving their facilities with an eye toward selling bananas to the Middle East, and with further investment, they hope to sell to Europe. For poorer countries trying to enter the global marketplace to benefit their farmers and everyone else, investments in meeting rich-world food-safety standards will become crucial.[18] As Franz Fischler, a former European Union agriculture commissioner who negotiated—and disagreed with—Glauber at the WTO, said, lower tax barriers "don't help at all if you don't have a product that's tradable."[19]

■ ■ ■

Subsidies continue to limit competition even as export bans and food safety challenge markets. Nearly every nation has them, in some form or another. In 2010, total payments for agricultural producers, including subsidies, was $120.8 billion for the EU, $46.5 billion for Japan, $30.6 billion for the United States, $17.5 billion for South Korea—and $35 million for New Zealand, which largely has done away with farm supports.[20]

The United States, which tends to gain the most criticism for its payments as the world's leading food exporter, is far from the worst: Measured by dollars per acre, Japanese farmers are the most heavily subsidized, receiving $2,235 an acre, according to a 2009 analysis. European benefits are also generous: German farmers receive $1,440 an acre, French farmers $1,237, and UK producers $889 an acre, while U.S. farmers get by, in comparison, on a paltry $225. Still, richer nations give much more support to their farmers than poorer ones: Growers in Malawi, which went against international advice and steeply increased its farm subsidies in the mid-2000s, are paid $106 an acre. Kenyans get $15.[21]

Who receives subsidies, as well as the subsidies themselves, can be poorly targeted. Subsidy recipients worldwide have included noted farmers such as basketball Hall of Famer Scottie Pippen and at least a half-dozen billionaires, according to U.S. records.[22] Queen Elizabeth and Prince Charles have also received public farm funds, although the Prince of Wales, a champion of organic farming, criticizes subsidies for large-scale agriculture.[23]

The Brazil cotton case, also called the "Step 2" case because of the name of a U.S. cotton payment program, was an attempt to take action against a subsidy that benefited rich farmers over poor ones. Step 2 pitted the developed world against the developing world, with the prosperity of some of the world's poorest farmers at stake. The United States is by far the world's biggest cotton exporter, making U.S. cotton farmers on overseas shipments. Brazil is the number-four shipper; the main African cotton-growing nations combined ship about as much cotton as it does. Brazil, joined by African countries, argued they would sell even more fiber if the United States didn't support its farmers so heavily, particularly in programs they said subsidized exports, a practice frowned upon by the WTO.

In years of rulings, appeals, arguments, and counterarguments dating to 2002, Brazil consistently won, eventually gaining the right to impose up to

$830 million in trade sanctions on products ranging from ketchup to cars. The United States warded that off by agreeing to aid Brazil's cotton producers. That fix is only intended to last until 2012, when the United States is scheduled to rewrite its subsidies.[24]

U.S. farm payments made to a rival to stave off retaliation are "pure lunacy," according to Representative Barney Frank, a Massachusetts Democrat who in 2011 introduced legislation to stop payments to Brazil.[25] Congressional committees and the House of Representatives had passed measures by mid-2011 rolling back the payments—none were binding—yet the signal was clear the makeshift measure would be attacked until it went away.[26] Countries subsidize their farmers and restrict trade for reasons of varying validity—because well-organized farmer groups can swing elections, because subsidies may be a means of fighting poverty, because food security is considered national security—whatever reason is deemed the crucial self-interest. And not every payment encourages oversupply. Some subsidies, notably incentives to produce biofuels, may actually drive prices up, making them more of a concern when food costs are high.[27]

Subsidies are unlikely to go away—and in some cases, experience has shown, they shouldn't. Subsidies for consumer nutrition purchases ranging from the Supplemental Nutrition Assistance Program, more commonly called food stamps, in the United States, to Brazil's "Fome Zero" (Zero Hunger) initiative and school feeding in Ghana, for which former presidents Luiz Inacio Lula da Silva of Brazil and John Agyekum Kufuor won the World Food Prize in 2011, can keep costs under control for poorer citizens. Farm payments can give farmers a safety net to fall back on when weather and low prices threaten to knock them out of business. While African nations develop, government policies must "include comprehensive support for African farmers to access agricultural technologies, to be able to have access to finance, to be able to have access to markets, both local regional and international markets," said Akinwumi Adesina, policy vice president for the Alliance for a Green Revolution in Africa. "If you don't have that sort of system they can't even produce anyway to compete," he said.[28]

What isn't desired, Adesina said, is a return to the so-called structural adjustment programs of the International Monetary Fund and World Bank in the 1980s and 1990s—when governments, on the advice of Western economists, privatized state-owned agribusinesses and slashed subsidies—which were meant to unleash market forces in agriculture. In many places, linked-up, finance-ready markets didn't exist. When the payments went away, farmers freed to fly from their subsidized nests fell with a thud, actually increasing poverty in some instances. "Structural adjustment in the 1980s dismantled the elaborate system of public agencies that provided farmers with access to land, credit, insurance, inputs, and cooperative organizations," the World Bank wrote in 2008. Incomplete markets, it said, threatened "their competitiveness and, in many cases, their survival."[29] A farmer needs a market, but a market alone doesn't guarantee prosperity.

Higher prices are reducing farm subsidies worldwide. U.S. payments fell by more than half from 2005 to 2007 and have stayed at lower levels. Nations from Indonesia to Turkey to Peru have lowered taxes on imports to make food less expensive for their citizens. Still, trade and farm payments tie up policymakers. The WTO has a role to play as a forum for grievances, for proposed solutions, and for peer pressure to correct the world's worst trade and subsidy offenders. Without an agreement, actions are being taken by individual nations themselves, or small groups of nations acting together, or by a global consensus outside the WTO against activities that have negative effects on consumers and producers.

In Malawi, the solution has been to subsidize corn like crazy.

■ ■ ■

Malawi, a landlocked, Pennsylvania-sized country in southern Africa, is among the world's poorest and least developed, with half of its population living in poverty, about 80 percent residing in rural areas. Agriculture accounts for 90 percent of its exports, with tobacco the biggest cash crop. In 2005 it was struggling with a poor corn harvest that put 5 million of the country's 13 million people on food aid. That prompted its newly elected president, Bingu wa Mutharika, to put his country, where four-fifths of the population farms and two-fifths of the national GDP comes from agriculture, on a crashcourse in production. The country dramatically stepped up its subsidies for crop inputs, offering coupons to buy seeds and fertilizer at well below market prices. The decision trashed structural-adjustment thinking and focused on food production first.[30]

The policy shift was immediately followed by record Malawi harvests in 2006 and 2007, aided by good rains, more fertilizers and better seeds. At first, some analysts thought Malawi just got lucky with rain. But the trend has continued. Crops in 2010–2011 were estimated to be nearly three times what they were five years ago. The worst year of the half-decade leading up to those crops was still better than the best of the five years before (see Figure 11.2).

Malawi's example has spurred new payment programs for farmers in Ghana, Zambia, Nigeria, Rwanda, and Tanzania. Higher subsidies helped

FIGURE 11.2 Malawi Corn Production (1,000 Metric Tons)

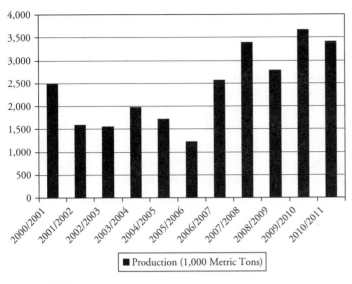

Source: USDA.

Senegal, a West African country that was once the continent's second-biggest rice importer, to become self-sufficient in 2011, according to its government, part of a wider trend in which boosts in farm spending in all areas have increased productivity.[31] The perception that Malawi improved itself by ignoring the advice of global financial institutions and richer nations to cut back on subsidies has prompted those advisers to clarify just what is a good subsidy and what's bad. The World Bank, in a statement on Malawi, says it supports "smart subsidies" that are targeted to poor farmers and help transition them to private markets.[32] It also urges exit strategies to phase out payments and ensure that the subsidy doesn't become an excessive burden on national governments. Malawi's subsidies took up 6 percent of its national budget in 2005. By 2009, it was 14 percent.[33]

The WTO has mixed feelings about subsidies for seeds and fertilizers, seeing them as trade-distorting while acknowledging they can be useful to boost production. And Malawi's policies aren't without side effects. A ban on raw cotton exports in 2009, combined with a government-set minimum purchase price, was meant to ensure good prices for farmers and nurture Malawi's cotton-processing industry. Instead, it caused some companies to stop buying Malawi cotton at all, forcing prices even lower.[34] Poor and rich nations alike risk unintended consequences when meddling in markets. The question becomes what mix works best for each country or region, and how that balances with the world's needs as a whole.

One way to work out solutions locally is to leave it to the farmers to figure it out themselves. Farmer cooperatives, a fixture in the United States for more than a century, give small farmers access to economies of scale and help link farmers to markets, said Kanayo Nwanze, the head of IFAD.[35] They've found success in South Asia; in India, dairy cooperatives alone are 100,000 in number and have 12 million members. Sub-Saharan Africa's success, as in many areas, is spottier, in large part due to finances. Land O'Lakes Inc., a St. Paul, Minnesota–based co-op that's the second-biggest in the United States, is advising African dairy businesses on improving their technologies. It's also worked with the U.S. Agency for International Development in bolstering the capacity of Africa's farmer cooperatives, which can play a similar role in that continent's development that U.S. farmer co-ops played in American farm growth if they're truly set up to serve their members, said Chris Policinski, CEO of Land O'Lakes.

"For cooperatives to flourish, they must truly serve the needs of their owner-members," rather than serve state, he said. "Small-scale farmers working independently typically lack the purchasing power to pay for these inputs themselves. But by marketing their goods and services to cooperatives, multinationals can grow their businesses."[36]

Cooperatives can also help develop insurance against bad weather, traditionally unavailable because small farmers aren't worth the transaction costs—a $10 policy takes as much time for a claims adjuster as a $10,000 policy. Crop insurance is being helped along by cell phones, which enable easier cash transactions, and solar-powered weather stations, which make forecasting and data across the region more complete than would have been possible a decade ago. In Kenya, where 40 percent of the country's savings are in M-PESA ("mobile money" in Swahili) accounts, mobile technology is bringing risk management and market information to areas that didn't have access.[37] Syngenta, the global chemical and seed company, has tapped into telecom by offering a pay-as-you-plant program to protect Kenyan farmers against increasingly erratic weather and make it easier for them to plant without fear of failure. Services that are local help make the system global.

It also helps to have friends in your neighborhood. The planned ASEAN Economic Community Trading Bloc in 2015 is already reordering rice in Southeast Asia, pressuring countries to be better neighbors to one another to increase the region's potential. African partnerships such as the Economic Community of West African States (ECOWAS), the Common Market for Eastern and Southern Africa (COMESA), a 19-member free-trade area launched in 2000 that's the continent's largest, and the East African Community (EAC), which includes Kenya, Uganda, Tanzania, Rwanda, and Burundi, are lowering trade barriers and increasing farm investment.[38] Sometimes the benefit is even more basic: Simply cutting down the amount of time it takes for goods to clear customs and setting common transportation standards can create new markets and boost income.[39] High trade barriers against neighbors and colonial-legacy infrastructure that makes it easier for some nations to ship goods to Europe than to one another both have hampered opportunities for countries to profit from markets nearby. That's changing, fitfully.

Trade and subsidies on a competitive planet will always be imperfect, shaped by self-interest, and inevitably unfair. Yet policies show signs of catching up to the problems. Beyond byzantine trade cases and farmer and consumer anguish, there is reason to believe that global food markets can be made fairer and better for everyone.

But it also requires everyone.

CHAPTER 12

Harvest of Hope

Bill Gates rocks forward and back in his chair and taps his foot against the floor, trying to address a challenging question. He's talking to a small group of journalists about how to keep people focused on the long-term growth of farming in Africa, a topic that usually hasn't been high on many people's minds elsewhere in the world.

"Agriculture, it's about the long term," he says.[1] Rock, *tap*. "Many of these new seed varieties we work on, it's a decade before you're out to hundreds of thousands or millions of farmers." The efforts of Gates and governments have an advantage they didn't have in 2006, when the Bill and Melinda Gates Foundation started investing in agricultural development. The commodities casino that jolted short attention spans back to the slow, but rewarding, process of feeding the poorest, lifting them from poverty, and connecting them to world markets has brought politicians, nonprofits, banks, businesses, and traders together in ways not seen before.

"Agriculture got off the priority list," said the Microsoft co-founder. "Now, looking at the food prices we've got, the food insecurity, and the fact that three-quarters of the poorest people in the world are on these small farms . . . there are some amazing things on the positive side." Nonprofit foundations working with banks, governments working with corporations, investors taking an interest in places previously passed over, all are ways to calm the casino and reduce suffering and unrest. The result, he said, will be "more nutrition for the poorest, somewhat lower prices off of these highs that we have now—which is huge for the urban poor," and greater food security worldwide. "We think it's very achievable."

Gates is in growing company in his push to eliminate hunger and build better markets. For reasons ranging from the end of Cold War rivalries to the challenge of climate change to the attention that food riots force, sometime-rivals are increasingly working together, bringing results from the bottom-up and the top-down. That bodes well for food security, as long as the spotlight doesn't fade. The global food market, with bigger crops coming from more farmers and better ways to distribute them, can and will show that hunger is fixable. The response to short-term pain, if sustained, can meet its twin goals: cutting poverty while meeting the endless appetites.

■ ■ ■

The Gates Foundation established its track record with health initiatives against HIV/AIDS, malaria, and other scourges of poorer countries. It turned its attention to farming after deciding that better health is a tough goal to achieve if people aren't fed first. Its early focus was on improving seeds. That's still its signature, but it has expanded its reach to include market access, technology, and policy. It's also becoming a bridge between small-holder farmers and banks, traditionally one of the toughest relationships to build. As of mid-2011, the foundation had committed $1.7 billion in African farming, with the expectation it would take 20 years to see the results of the work.[2]

The Gates program is driven by a belief that the right approaches to development can greatly reduce poverty and increase wealth, creating a more livable planet. He did not become someone who's held the title of World's Richest Person by being starry-eyed. "In Africa, you pretty much name the barrier—whether it's roads, cost of fertilizer . . . even the basic science" presents a challenge, he said. To meet that, it will take more than Bill and Melinda Gates—but foundation funds can leverage more support from other sources. In 2009, South Africa–based Standard Bank Group Ltd., the continent's larg-est lender, agreed to provide $100 in loans over three years to small-scale farmers under the Alliance for a Green Revolution in Africa (AGRA), a pledge followed by a $50 million commitment from Equity Bank Ltd., Kenya's big-gest bank, and $10 million from the National Microfinance Bank of Tanzania Ltd.[3] AGRA provides the confidence that an investment can work with their development know-how.

Higher food demand and expertise from foundations and nonprofits helps banks expand their portfolios beyond traditional minerals investments, said Clive Tasker, the CEO of Standard Bank's Africa division. The projects show how profit-making enterprises and nonprofit development programs, previously worlds that reacted to one another with indifference or distrust, can build a continent. A similar deal with the Central Bank of Nigeria will leverage $3 billion in loans from Nigerian banks, making finance available for 3.8 million farmers.[4]

"There's a convergence" among groups that all have an interest in boosting production, be it to reduce poverty or expand profits, he said.[5] Unlike previous initiatives that may have been done more to check off the "social responsibility" box for an annual corporate report than to actually create long-term suppliers and markets, the food crisis has made African agriculture a genuine business opportunity.

"One hundred million dollars is not a small amount of money. It's mainstream business, it's business we believe we should be involved in," he said. It also illustrates the connections he's seeing between the government, private, and nonprofit sectors, he said. "Each has different qualifications, competencies, and capacities. It's a very healthy thing, and it is going to do a lot for the projects that are required.

"It's an interesting challenge to talk about Africa," he continued. "What is Africa? There are so many different component parts, there are so many different countries that make up what we put together as Africa. We certainly try not to take a big paintbrush to it. . . . Projects in Africa should be considered because they can render returns and perform on a global basis. I would not have said that 10 years ago."

And 10 years from now, the differences between investment challenges in Africa and elsewhere will be even less, he said. Meanwhile, as developing regions build themselves—with literal and figurative seed money—the rest of the planet is shifting its own priorities.

■ ■ ■

Bill Clinton, who said in 2008 that he and world institutions "blew it" on food, wasn't going to do it again in 2011. The William J. Clinton Foundation includes food security in its portfolio, so it wasn't odd to see him speaking at the U.S. Department of Agriculture's annual outlook conference, where the usual highlight is the agency's first U.S. crop estimate for the upcoming year, not an address by a former U.S. president talking about hunger, poverty, and the new food crisis that had helped topple two governments and spark a civil war in the previous six weeks.

The USDA conference, held every year at a Marriott in Crystal City, Virginia, just outside the capital, typically draws about 1,500 attendees. The 2011 edition topped 2,000 for the first time, running the gamut of agribusiness, farmer groups, academics, lobbyists and crop traders, everyone in some way connected to the global food market. A decade out of office, Clinton combines global celebrity with a greater candor than he could afford in the White House. On this day, he was being candid about corn.

"If you produce more biofuels, you produce less food. Well, that means food prices will be even higher, and you will have more food riots," he said. "Everyone should be talking about and not pretending that there's not inherent contradictions and dilemmas here" between energy and nutrition needs. "We have to become energy independent, but we don't want to do it at the cost of food riots."[6]

The remarks drew responses appropriate for the topsy-turvy world of volatile food prices. Longtime Clinton supporters in the biofuels industry criticized his link between ethanol and riots.[7] The editorial page of the *Wall Street Journal*, which had called for his resignation when he was president, applauded his stance.[8] After decades of steady support for programs that put cropland in the service of energy, better balance seemed certain as 2011 crops were planted in the United States.

Biofuels still commanded wide support in Congress—and always will, as long as South Dakota has as many senators as New York. Food and fuel balance became more likely as the period of the industry's dramatic ramp-up, spurred by federal support, was set to plateau under the same rules, relieving supply pressures as corn yields increase. Ethanol supporters as well as opponents acknowledged the industry was outgrowing its government supports in the first half of 2011.[9] When Republican Senator Tom Coburn of Oklahoma and Democratic Senator Dianne Feinstein of California proposed to immediately end the credits, ethanol stalwarts replied with legislation that would extend it—lower levels.[10]

A group of 23 countries led by the United States and China created a potential model for biofuels agreement with guidelines on producing diesel fuel from palm oil, linked to rainforest destruction. Fuel demand had helped push prices for the popular cooking-oil ingredient back to near its 2008 peaks early in 2011. A report the group released said that bioenergy held potential for poor countries if well managed, but also have "been a cause for deep concern regarding their economic, social, and environmental viability."[11] Biofuels backers in the United States, meanwhile, proposed to link subsidies to the price of oil, the ultimate driver of ethanol demand. Nothing focuses attention on high energy costs like expensive gasoline, complete with presidential speeches and congressional hearings. Investments in cleaner, sustainable energy seemed most likely to have the greatest pay off in the long term—in 2008, global investment in renewable energy outpaced funding for fossil-fuel technologies for the first time, and in 2011, green-fuel investments were greater in developing countries than in developed ones.[12] Solutions that would create a greener, less oil-thirsty planet would be food solutions as well.

■ ■ ■

Food-and-fuel adjustments addressed one set of concerns. Changes in financial rules engaged another.

Progress in implementing financial reform legislation Congress passed in 2010, mainly in response to the banking meltdown but also influenced by commodity prices, slowed to a crawl the next year. Financial, business, and banking groups, along with congressional allies whose numbers had been boosted by the previous fall's elections, fought to delay regulations. The Commodity Futures Trading Commission (CFTC) pushed back timelines for changes, and some lawmakers wanted them to push them back further. The delays were piling up by July 16, 2011, with dozens of rules yet to take effect on the one-year anniversary of the law,

The idea that speculation in food may drive up prices, increasing volatility and aggravating global hunger, remains highly controversial, and not only to the traders and banks who profit from volatility: Many of the dozens of academic studies completed since the food crisis question the connection. Speculators don't drive crop markets because futures contracts, which can be bought, sold, and rolled over into infinity, are separate from physical markets, argues one school of thought. Those studies attempt to debunk what the authors consider fallacies and misinterpretations of how speculation affects commodities markets.[13] In these studies, the jump in commodity prices that rose with new money is dismissed as coincidence—they maintain that commodities exchanges would have seen the same sharp price gains whether index funds had been there or not. Other research doesn't let speculators off the hook, finding that prices of publicly traded commodities linked to index funds are moving increasingly in lockstep, indicating that commodities have become financialized as an asset class. Still more papers argue that the introduction of multibillion-dollar index funds that hold onto futures for decades regardless of immediate circumstances—the elephants in the kiddie pool—makes futures prices less likely to fall and more likely to rise, since the funds will buy a futures contract expecting it to increase over the longer term, even when shorter-term prospects aren't clear.

The research debate is of intense interest to CFTC Commissioner Bart Chilton, who emerged during the 2008 food crisis as the panel's top critic of the role investors may play in driving up food costs. Early in 2011, he was staying more quiet on regulation—"I'm keeping my powder dry," he joked—because the price and political situation was different in 2011 than in 2008.[14] The second food shock saw stock markets rising with commodities prices as the global economy grew, a classic story of supply and demand. Real-world explanations for price gains—China, oil, weather—were more up-front the second time around.

The CFTC, led by Gary Gensler, an Obama appointee and 18-year Goldman Sachs veteran, was at its most willing to limit big-bank trading since the Clinton administration. The Dodd-Frank bill, named for its Senate and House sponsors, tightened limits on how many crop futures a speculator could hold even as it continued to exempt buyers of actual physical commodities, called end-users, from limits. It also brought under regulation many trades done outside exchanges, and it expanded the agency's ability to collect information on exactly who was doing what in which commodities markets.

The legislation inevitably attracted a swarm of lobbyists to the once-quiet CFTC building on M Street. In 2010 the commission met with 199 different lobbying clients, according to records examined by the Washington-based Center for Responsive Politics—the most since the center began tracking the records in 1998, 90 percent more than in 2009 and 165 percent more than in 2008. (See Table 12.1.) Chilton said he met with the same lobbyist, representing three different companies, in the space of two weeks. Each time, the attorney argued that his client was exempt from the law, or that implementation ought to be put off.[15] Financial interests called for caution and gained new allies in Congress, as Republicans skeptical of government regulation took control of the House of Representatives and eroded the Democratic majority in the Senate. The voices urged restraint, for fear that wrong moves could actually drive trading from U.S. markets, sending them to less-regulated areas overseas.

"It is critically important that the implementation of these complicated reforms be done in a manner that avoids disruption and allows continuing access to derivative instruments," said Steve Bunkin, a managing director at Goldman Sachs, before the committee.[16]

The rest of the world watched the United States and worked on its own rules. European markets—the ones to which U.S. capital would allegedly flee should speculators be reined in too tightly—would put their own limits in place to ensure that flights of capital across the ocean wouldn't occur, said the European Union's financial services commissioner, Michel Barnier.[17] The rising economies of Brazil, Russia, India, China, and South Africa called volatile prices a threat to their growth and asked for greater global regulation of derivatives markets.[18] The academic speculation debate remained unresolved. By the middle of 2011 the CFTC was delaying new regulations, needing

TABLE 12.1 Annual Number of Clients Lobbying the Commodity Futures Trading Commission

Year	Number Lobbying
1998	28
1999	33
2000	54
2001	17
2002	39
2003	19
2004	21
2005	34
2006	39
2007	37
2008	75
2009	105
2010	199

Source: The Center for Responsive Politics.

more time to complete them.[19] Chilton predicted that in the end new rules would make markets less vulnerable to wild swings than before.

"The limits will decrease volatility both up and down, and keep swings from being wider," he said. "I think we're going to get to the right point, ultimately."[20]

■ ■ ■

International cooperation on food security entails everything from new trade agreements to a reexamination of grain reserves as a potential buffer against price shocks. World Bank President Robert Zoellick suggested that a system of emergency food-aid warehouses be created near potential famine trouble spots, possibly managed by the World Food Programme (WFP), an idea endorsed by G-20 agriculture ministers; the WFP, United States, and EU, meanwhile, already have some storage in place, and are planning expansion.[21] Supplies earmarked for emergencies would not have a significant impact on smoothing prices, but would make immediate responses to price shocks more effective.

Climate change, export ban, trade and land-grab agreements remain elusive. A gathering of officials from 21 Pacific nations in Montana in May 2011 generated a statement recognizing "the important role that open and transparent markets for food trade play in ensuring global food security by increasing reliability of supply, mitigating price volatility, and providing farmers with accurate price signals." A 20-nation group of agriculture ministers in France the next month reiterated that position and called for more public disclosure of national crop inventories. It stopped short of eliminating export bans, an idea eyed warily by China and other nations.[22] And the world's food needs kept rising with population set to surpass 7 billion.

Cooperation to prevent future food-price spikes is rising as well. Long-standing battle lines drawn between what's called production agriculture—industrial-scale farming relying heavily on the latest technology—and sustainable agriculture of often-smaller farms where environmental stewardship becomes an organizing theme, started to blur. As traditional production agriculture grows more sustainable, with more attention to soil and water improvement, sustainable agriculture is becoming more productive, with moves toward international organic foods standards that could create new markets for smaller farmers worldwide. Other approaches to food production, such as aquaculture and water desalination, also hold potential to relieve land and environmental strain.[23]

Business projects and development initiatives involving everything from trade rules and bank loans to water use and seeds are becoming less distinguishable as food needs grow more complex, said Paul Bulcke, the chief executive officer of Nestlé SA, the world's biggest food company. If the convergence is "done coherently, it is something that creates value for society."[24] Nestlé, which has been in Africa for more than 100 years, is focusing on improving water availability and efficiency—which will help consumers as well as shareholders, he said. "We as a company have to be part of the discussion," he said. "That's part of our responsibility."

"Business, in my eyes, is development."

■ ■ ■

Mohamad Bouazizi's mother, clad in black hijab, had finished a 10-minute meeting with the secretary-general of the United Nations when she told reporters in Tunis that she is sure her son, whose self-inflicted burns took his life and started a revolution, is happy.[25]

"I am proud of my son, my son who contributed to the liberation of Tunisia," she said.

Tunisia's liberation was a starting point, not an end, for unrest and opportunity. A chance at a better life is exactly that—a chance. A revolution is meant to create a world anew, but problems that plagued one era don't simply go away because a new dawn is proclaimed in a capital city or at an international conference.

The world isn't static either, and it is far, far from hopeless. For all its problems, in many ways and for several billion people, the world is a more just, more humane, more comfortable place than it was 50, 30, or even 10 years ago. That progress can continue. Hunger was on the decline for a generation, and it has risen in the past half-decade because of turbulence in the global food system that, sorted out, can feed everyone now and in the future. Unlike some global problems, ending hunger is a universal value only violated by monsters—the Stalins, Maos, and Mengistus who are recognized as such and are, in time, overcome. That creates hope that this problem can be solved. Every child fed, every woman who gains power over her livelihood, every family that prospers past the previous generation, every life saved is another success. Millions upon millions of successes are possible.

To have more food you have to grow more food. The concept is simple, the best way to do it isn't. Those questions will be answered differently in different places with different needs. One factor that will make them easier to answer—and without which even asking these questions becomes irrelevant—is by creating markets where farmers have access, knowledge, means, and ability to fairly compete with one another and earn a meaningful living from their work. This includes everything from research, roads, and radios to trade and training. A farmer needs a market, from the United States, Russia, and Brazil to the farms of Haylar Ayako, Hugo Alejandro, Christina Chebi Ngogi, and Wichian Phuanglamchiak.

The risks markets present are manageable, even as they provide greater opportunities to serve more people, meet global needs, and help banish one of humanity's most debilitating forces—hunger—to history. The key is to take advantage. Hunger and the importance of food security have returned to global attention. High prices—and violence—underscore that the problem will not take care of itself. Meanwhile, hundreds of millions of farmers, many of them the same people at the greatest risk of famine, can work to solve these problems—if only there were a market. A globalized world can make those connections.

■ ■ ■

The East African rains had fallen more steadily than in recent years, leaving a bountiful crop in the year's early months. The grain bins are emptying, but they'll last until the next rains, and assuming those rains occur, food will remain plentiful. On the road from Sodo in southern Ethiopia, the farm houses are close enough for one neighbor to shout from his door to another, which some did as I walked to the end of a ruddy dirt road.

The sun was retreating behind the highlands. A steady traffic ambled along the road, from the farmhouses to a local market where corn was sold by the cup and families were returning with food to prepare for dinner, including vegetables brought by the wife of Kosa Koyo, who is setting up his family's outdoor kitchen outside his 10-foot by 10-foot mud hut. Inside, his 80-year-old mother watched the youngest of his eight children. Nearby were his cattle and goats, resting in a shed connected to his home. On his five acres he plants teff, cassava, coffee, and *ensete*. In the middle of his land is what looks to be an oddly placed, above-ground shed.

"That is the grave," he said.

Two of his children died from fevers in 2008, when illnesses swept his community. Today the local cooperative has fertilizers and seeds that are affordable to buy, which Kosa Koyo is using to boost his yields. Not only is he more productive, he is also more efficient. He is adding less fertilizer to his soil, he says, because his training has given him a better sense of how and when to use it. The rain is always a struggle, but with water there is life, and with the market there is opportunity.

On his wall he has a sign, in English, that says "I am the Way, the Truth and the Life." On his door he has written "God" in his local language. Koyo prays for the health of his family, and he prays for better days, and he prays for rain—but is that really enough? Couldn't he use roads, and irrigation, and information, and insurance? Couldn't he use better policies, and better governments, and help from others that would cost us each less than the price of a cup of coffee?

Couldn't his two children be alive?

He continues. "Things are better now," he says. "I am hopeful. I thank God."

Silence.

The driver is motioning back toward the vehicle. The sky is darkening, and it is time to leave. Tonight, when his wife returns from the market, Kosa Koyo's family will share a simple dinner together. For that he is thankful, as he tends to his children, and his fields, and his grave.

He hopes for a better harvest ahead.

Notes

Chapter 1: Floors, Fields, and Famines

1. Whitney McFerron, "Wheat Futures Increase as Egypt, Jordan Buy Supplies from U.S.," Bloomberg News, December 15, 2010.
2. Yi Tian, "Commodity Assets under Management Rise to Record, Barclays Says," Bloomberg News, December 15, 2010.
3. Interview, Chicago, December 15, 2010.
4. Kareen Fahim, "Slap to a Man's Pride Set Off Tumult in Tunisia," *New York Times*, January 22, 2011.
5. Bouazza Ben Bouazza, "Youth at Heart of Tunisia Unrest Dies," Associated Press, January 5, 2011.
6. Lester R. Brown, "The New Geopolitics of Food," *Foreign Policy* (May–June 2011).
7. Anna Badkhen, "The Baguettes of War: Inside the Middle East's defiant kitchens," *Foreign Policy* (May–June 2011).
8. Interview, Nicaragua, April 30, 2011.
9. Interview, Ethiopia, January 31, 2011.
10. Alan Bjerga, "Biotechnology Is Key to Fighting Hunger, Clinton Says (Update 1)," Bloomberg News, October 16, 2009.
11. Rabah Arezki and Markus Bruckner, "Food Prices and Political Instability," International Monetary Fund Working Paper, N. 11/62, March 2011.
12. Tony C. Dreibus, "Food Costs May Top Record as Global Inflation Accelerates," Bloomberg News, April 26, 2011.
13. Telephone interview, February 24, 2011.
14. The UN Food and Agriculture Organization, the International Fund for Agricultural Development, and the UN World Food Programme, "Reducing Poverty and Hunger: The Critical Role of Financing for Food, Agriculture and Rural Development" (2002). Prepared for the International Conference on Financing for Development, Monterrey, Mexico, March 18–22, 2002.
15. Michael A. Trueblood, Shalah Shapouri, and Shida Henneberry, "Policy Options to Stabilize Food Supplies: A Case Study of Southern Africa," U.S. Department of Agriculture, 2001.
16. The distinction between the existence of food and access to it as a cause of hunger is crucial to understanding the dynamics of why people starve when adequate

food exists. See Amartya Sen, *Poverty and Famines: An Essay on Entitlement and Deprivation* (New York: Oxford University Press, 1981).

17. Alan Bjerga, "Record Number of People Faced Hunger Last Year in U.S. (Update 1)," Bloomberg News, November 15, 2010.

18. Based on OECD data for entire adult populations, 2007–2008, from "OECD Health Data 2010," www.oecd.org/document/16/0,3746en_2649_37407_2085200_1_1_1_37407,00.html (accessed May 29, 2011).

19. Jenny Gustavsson, et al., "Global Losses and Food Waste: Extent, Causes and Production," UN Food and Agriculture Organization, 2011. In the developed world consumer waste is a larger problem: Waste in industrialized countries is roughly equal to the farm production of sub-Saharan Africa, according to the study.

20. World Bank, "Missing Food: The Case of Postharvest Grain Losses in Sub-Saharan Africa," April 2011.

21. UN News Centre, "Global Population to Pass 10 Billion by 2100, UN Projections Indicate," May 3, 2011.

22. UN Food and Agriculture Organization Media Centre, "2050: A Third More Mouths to Feed," September 23, 2009.

23. Ronald Trostle, "Global Agricultural Supply and Demand: Factors Contributing to the Recent Increase in Food Commodity Prices," U.S. Department of Agriculture, July 2008.

24. UN, "A Third More Mouths to Feed."

25. Rudy Ruitenberg and Tony C. Dreibus, "Farming Needs 'Major Shift' as Food System Fails, FAO Says (1)," Bloomberg News, June 13, 2011.

26. Whitney McFerron and Alan Bjerga, "U.S. Farm Income May Rise 20% to Record, USDA Says (Update 2)," Bloomberg News, February 14, 2011; Alan Bjerga, "U.S. Farm Exports May Increase to Record $137 Billion (2)," May 26, 2011.

27. Alan Bjerga, "Food Prices Changing Diets, Oxfam-Backed Survey Says (1)," Bloomberg News, June 15, 2011.

28. Rudy Ruitenberg and Lorenzo Totaro, "Food to Stay Costly on Finance Contamination, New FAO Head Says," Bloomberg News, June 27, 2011.

29. Claudia Carpenter, "Food Prices to Double in 20 Years without Action, Oxfam Says (1)," Bloomberg News, May 31, 2011.

30. Hugh Turral, Jacob Burke, and Jean-Marc Faures, "Climate Change, Water and Food Security," UN Food and Agriculture Organization, 2011.

31. Oxfam International, "Growing a Better Future," June 2011.

32. Interview, Kenya, February 10, 2011.

33. Interview, Thailand, March 21, 2011.

Chapter 2: Chicago Makes a Market

1. Interviews conducted in Chicago, December 15-16, 2010.

2. For the story of the birth and rise of the Chicago Board of Trade, I am heavily indebted to William D. Falloon's *Market Maker: A Sesquicentennial Look at the*

Chicago Board of Trade (Board of Trade of the City of Chicago, 1998); Erika S. Olson, *Zero-Sum Game: The Rise of the World's Largest Derivatives Exchange* (Hoboken, NJ: John Wiley & Sons, 2011); and telephone interviews with Dan Lehman and Charles Carey conducted in December 2010.

3. Ulrike Schaede, "Forwards and Futures in Tokugawa-Period Japan: A New Perspective on the Dojima Rice Market, *Journal of Banking and Finance* 13, nos. 4–5 (1989).

4. Commodity Futures Trading Commission, "Establishment of Speculative Position Limits," 46 Federal Register 50938, October 16, 1981.

5. For more detail on the promise of commodity investments, see R. Greer, "The Nature of Commodity Index Returns," *Journal of Alternative Investments* (Summer 2000): 45–52. Greer in 2002 helped Pimco launch the largest commodity mutual fund, with $25 billion under management. The fund as of 2011 uses over-the-counter swaps and structured notes in its trading, not futures. See also Gary B. Gorton and K. Geert Rouwenhorst, "Facts and Fantasies about Commodity Futures," Yale ICF Working Paper No. 04-20, New Haven, Connecticut (2005).

Chapter 3: Elephants in the Kiddie Pool

1. Silla Brush, "Dodd-Frank Rules Will Help Derivatives End-Users, Gensler Says," Bloomberg News, June 2, 2011.

2. Sections of the history of the regulatory tug-of-war arising from the rise of swaps taken from an unpublished memo by Asjylyn Loder of Bloomberg News.

3. Interview, Chicago, December 16, 2011.

4. Discussion of commodity-fund marketing and physical assets owned by banks taken from Peter Robison, Asjylyn Loder, and Alan Bjerga, "Amber Waves of Pain," *Bloomberg Businessweek*, July 22, 2010.

5. All statistics taken from World Bank and OECD data.

6. Philip C. Abbott, Christopher Hurt, and Wallace E. Tyner, "What's Driving Food Prices in 2011?" Issue Report, Farm Foundation, July 2011.

7. Data from USDA Food Dollar Series, www.ers.usda.gov/Data/FoodDollar/app/ (accessed June 11, 2011).

8. Broin statement taken from testimony before Senate Agriculture Committee, March 30, 2011.

9. Bruce A. Babcock, "The Impact of U.S. Biofuel Policies on Agricultural Price Levels and Volatility," International Centre for Trade and Sustainable Development, June 2011.

10. Tim Josling, David Blandford, and Jane Earley, "Biofuel and Biomass Subsidies in the U.S., EU and Brazil: Towards a Transparent System of Notification," International Food & Agricultural Trade Policy Council, September 2010.

11. Joe Leahy, "Brazil Seeks to Curb Volatile Ethanol Prices," *Financial Times*, May 25, 2011.
12. Genesis, 41–47.
13. Telephone interview, March 28, 2011.
14. For a more detailed discussion of different factors behind today's food crises, see Derek Headey and Shenggen Fan, "Reflections on the Global Food Crisis," The International Food Policy Research Institute, November 2010.
15. Telephone interview, November 17, 2010.
16. Interview, Chicago, December 16, 2010.
17. Telephone interview, November 22, 2010.
18. Interview, Chicago, November 16, 2010.

Chapter 4: A Recipe for Famine

1. Ethiopia interviews were conducted October 11–25, 2008, unless otherwise noted. Portions of this chapter previously appeared in the Bloomberg News "Recipe for Famine" series: see Alan Bjerga, "Dead Children Linked to Aid Policy in Africa Favoring Americans," Bloomberg News, December 8, 2008.
2. Antoine Bouët and David Laborde Debucquet, "Economics of Export Taxation in a Context of Food Crisis: A Theoretical and CGE Approach Contribution," International Food Policy Research Institute (IFPRI) Discussion paper 00994, June 2010.
3. Kartik Goyal, "India Scraps Tender to Buy 350,000 Tons of Wheat on High Prices (Update 2)," Bloomberg News, December 24, 2007.
4. Thomas Kutty Abraham, "Pakistan to Import 300,000 tons of Wheat to Build Stockpiles," Bloomberg News, February 4, 2008.
5. Sofia News Agency, "Grain Shortage in Bulgaria After Ukraine Refuses Exports," February 13, 2008.
6. Tony C. Dreibus and Jeff Wilson, "Wheat Rebounds to Record after Dropping the Limit in Chicago," Bloomberg News, February 27, 2011.
7. Jacob Bunge, "MF Global Gets a Win on Rogue-Trading Insurance Claim," *Wall Street Journal*, October 21, 2010.
8. Bibhudatta Pradhan, "India Eases Ban on Rice Exports, Sets Benchmark Prices (Update 1)," Bloomberg News, October 25 2007.
9. Tom Slayton, "Rice Crisis Forensics: How Asian Governments Carelessly Set the World Rice Market on Fire," Center for Global Development, March 2009.
10. Will Martin and Kym Anderson, "Trade Distortions and Food Price Surges," World Bank and University of Adelaide, October 1, 2010.
11. Tom Slayton, "The 'Diplomatic Crop' or How the U.S. Provided Critical Leadership in Ending Rice Crisis." In *The Rice Crisis: Markets, Policies and Food Security*, ed. David Dawe, UN Food and Agriculture Organization, September 2010.

12. Christine Harper, "Goldman Beats Estimates on Prime Brokerage, Commodities Gains," Bloomberg News, June 17, 2008.
13. Christine Harper, " Morgan Stanley Profit Drops on Debt Losses, Trading," Bloomberg News, June 18, 2008.
14. Alan Bjerga, "CFTC Failing in Market Regulation, Growers and Traders Say," Bloomberg News, April 22, 2008.
15. United Nations ReliefWeb, "Ethiopia: Food Insecurity Revised Emergency Appeal No. MDRET005," 2008, http://reliefweb.int/sites/reliefweb.int/files/reliefweb_pdf/node-276918.pdf (accessed June 12, 2011).
16. Cotton Timberlake, "Wal-Mart's Sam's Club Restricts Purchase of Some Rice (Update 5), Bloomberg News, April 23, 2011.
17. Reinwald testimony before Congress's Joint Economic Committee on May 1, 2008, www.retailbakersofamerica.org/sites/default/files/REINWALD%20Testimony%20final.pdf (accessed December 18, 2010).
18. Dale Wetzel, "State Flour Mill Records a Loss of $12 Million in First Quarter," Associated Press, November 24, 2008.
19. Jeff Wilson, "Wall Street Grain Hoarding Brings Farmers, Consumers Near Ruin," Bloomberg News, April 28, 2008.
20. C. Levin and T. Coburn, "Excessive Speculation in the Wheat Market," Permanent Sub-Committee on Investigation, United States Senate, 2009.
21. USDA, "Food CPI and Expenditures: CPI for Food Forecasts," www.ers.usda.gov/briefing/cpifoodandexpenditures/data/cpiforecasts.htm (accessed June 12, 2011).
22. Kim Chipman and Peter Cook, "Obama Says Spurring Growth Would Let Fed Focus on Inflation," Bloomberg News, June 26, 2008.

Chapter 5: The View from Rome

1. Interview, telephone, February 1, 2011.
2. James Bone, "New UN Food Programme Head," *Times* (London), November 6, 2006.
3. State Department Ceremony for the George McGovern Leadership Award, awarded to Secretary of State Hillary Clinton, October 5, 2010.
4. Interview, Rome, January 23, 2011.
5. Adam Thomson, "'Tortilla Riots' Give Foretaste of Food Challenge," *Financial Times*, October 12, 2010.
6. William Bi, "China Restricts Grain Flour Exports to Boost Supply (Update 2)," Bloomberg News, January 1, 2008.
7. Pius Lukong, "Cameroon Revises Death Toll in Protests to 40, Minister Says," Bloomberg News, March 11, 2008.
8. Daniel Williams, "Egypt's Ruling Party Wins Election Even Before Votes Counted," Bloomberg News, April 9, 2008.

9. Ramola Talwar Badam, "Angry Consumers in India Protest Fuel Prices," Associated Press, June 6, 2008.

10. Joseph Guyler Delva and Jim Loney, "Haiti's Government Falls after Food Riots," Reuters, April 12, 2008.

11. Randeep Ramesh, "Bangladeshi Garment Workers Strike over Food Prices," *Guardian* (Manchester, UK), April 15, 2008.

12. UN News Centre, "Top UN Official Calls for Bolstered Global Governance System for World Food Security," June 6, 2009.

13. Interview, Bangkok, March 22, 2011.

14. Presentation, Washington, DC, May 24, 2011.

15. Interview, Rome, January 23, 2011.

16. Bill Varner, "Saudi Arabia Gives UN $500 Million to Pay for Food Aid Program," Bloomberg News, May 23, 2011.

17. World Food Program, "WFP Annual Report 2009."

18. Declaration of the High-Level Conference on World Food Security: The Challenges of Climate Change and Bioenergy, Rome, June 5, 2008.

19. Alan Bjerga, "Zoellick Sees Renewed Risk of Food Crisis in 2010 (Update 1)," November 24, 2009.

20. www.feedthefuture.gov/commitment.html (accessed May 12, 2011).

21. Keith Bradsher and Andres Martin, "World's Poor Pay Price as Crop Research Is Cut," *New York Times*, May 18, 2008.

22. Christopher Swann, "Gates Foundation to Boost Farm Aid 50% as Food Crisis Deepens," Bloomberg News, April 24, 2011.

23. United Nations, www.unmultimedia.org/tv/unifeed/d/9064.html (accessed May 12, 2011).

24. Feiwen Rong, "UBS to Exit Commodities Business, Excluding Precious Metals," Bloomberg News, October 3. 2008.

25. Chanyaporn Chanjaroen, "Pickens's BP Capital Says Equity Fund Withdrawal Rate at 65%," Bloomberg News, December 17, 2008.

26. Interview, Rome, January 23, 2011.

27. Telephone interview, November 24, 2009.

28. Richard Owen, "Hunger Crisis Pact Agreed as Biofuels Clash Set Aside," *Times* (London), June 6, 2008.

29. Javier Blas, "High Food Prices for 'Years to Come,'" *Financial Times*, June 5, 2008.

30. Klaus Deininger, Derek Byerlee, et al., *Rising Global Interest in Farmland: Can It Yield Sustainable and Equitable Benefits?* (Washington: World Bank, 2011).

31. "When Others are Grabbing Their Land: Evidence Is Piling Up against Acquisitions of Farmland in Poor Countries," *Economist*, May 5, 2011.

32. Oliver Ramaro and Antony Sguazzin, "Madagascar May Welcome Farm Ventures after Daewoo Cancellation," Bloomberg News, April 10, 2009.

33. "Brazil Tightens Land Acquisition by Foreigners: 'Speculators and Sovereign Funds,'" MercoPress, March 17, 2011.

34. Andrew Downie, "Food Inflation, Land Grabs Spur Latin America to Restrict Foreign Ownership," *Christian Science Monitor*, May 6, 2011.
35. Scott Baldauf, "Hunger and Food Security: Is Africa Selling the Farm?" *Christian Science Monitor*, February 6, 2011. See also Ashwin Parulkar, "African Land, Up for Grabs," *World Policy Journal* (Spring 2011).
36. Interview, State Minister for Agriculture Wonderad Mandefro, Addis Ababa, February 7, 2011.
37. Interview, Washington, May 24, 2011.
38. Transcript of Howard Buffett television interview with Betty Liu of Bloomberg News, February 25, 2011.
39. Silvia Aloisi, "UN Body Fails to Back 'Land Grabs' Code of Conduct," Reuters, October 15, 2010; William Davison, "Saudi Billionaire to Invest $2.5 Billion in Ethiopia Rice Farm," Bloomberg News, March 23, 2011.
40. Telephone interview, March 15, 2011.
41. Interview, Des Moines, Iowa, October 14, 2011.
42. Rudy Ruitenberg, "World Hunger to Decline for First Time in 15 Years (Update 1)," *Bloomberg Businessweek*, September 14, 2011.
43. Extended description of 2009 Rome summit taken from Karl Maier, "Food Summit Ends With Sweeping Pledges, Little Action on Hunger," Bloomberg News, November 18, 2009. For more details on Muammar Qaddafi's party habits, Reuters reported the Libyan leader had an online ad placed seeking "500 attractive girls between 18 and 35 years old, at least 1.70 metres (5 foot, 7 inches) tall, well-dressed but not in mini-skirts or low cut dresses." Women at one party were personally told by Qaddafi "that Jesus was not crucified but that 'someone who looked like him' was put to death in his place." This occurred when the world found Qaddafi more amusing than murderous.

Chapter 6: Hot Air

1. Ed Allen, Olga Liefert, William Liefert, and Gary Vocke, "Former Soviet Union to Play Larger Role in Meeting World Wheat Needs," *Amber Waves* (June 2010).
2. E. M. Collingham, *The Taste of War: World War Two and the Battle for Food* (London: Allen Lane, 2011).
3. Fred Katerere and Brian Latham, "Mozambique Scraps Higher Prices Increases after Riots (Update 1)," Bloomberg News, September 7, 2010.
4. Voice of America, "Cost of Wheat Rises as Russia Extends Export Ban," from *Connect the World*, broadcast transcript, September 3, 2010.
5. allAfrica.com, "Mozambique: Wheat Production Only Covers Five Per Cent of Needs," September 4, 2010, http://allafrica.com/stories/201009040228.html (accessed May 7, 2011).
6. Lulu Sinclair, "Death Rate Surges in Russian Heatwave," *SkyNews*, August 6, 2010.

7. Maria Kolesnikova and Luzi Ann Javier, "Wheat Soars to 23-Month High as Drought-Hit Russia Bans Exports," Bloomberg News, August 5, 2011.
8. Ola Galal, "Russia Grain-Export Ban to Affect Some Egypt Imports (Update 2)," Bloomberg News, August 5, 2010.
9. Elizabeth Campbell, "Egypt Buying of U.S. Crops Surged as Unrest Spurred Mubarak Exit," Bloomberg News, March 11, 2011.
10. Tony Dreibus, "Food Security Is Less of a Concern, UN Agency Says," Bloomberg News, October 12, 2010.
11. Kateryna Choursina and Daryna Krasnolutska, "Ukraine Will Lift Grain-Shipment Curbs after Seven Months (1)," Bloomberg News, May 25, 2011.
12. Eric Pooley and Philip Revzin, "World Feeding Itself Spurs Search Amid Global Feast and Famine," Bloomberg News, February 18, 2011.
13. Suki Cooper and Roxana Mohammadian Molina, "The Commodity Investor," *Barclays Capital* (April 2011).
14. Aya Takada, "Japan to Restrict Rice Planting Near Fukushima Nuclear Plant (3)," Bloomberg News, April 8, 2011.
15. William Neuman, "Vegetable Bandits Strike as Food Prices Soar," *New York Times*, April 15, 2011.
16. Rudy Ruitenberg, "World Food Import Bill in 2010 Will Top $1 Trillion, FAO Says," Bloomberg News, November 17, 2010.
17. Beatrice Khadige, "Riots Erupt across Algeria against Prices, Jobs," Agence France-Presse, January 6, 2011.
18. Salah Slimani, "Algerian Minister Says 3 Killed, 420 Wounded in Riots (Update 1)," Bloomberg News, January 9, 2011.
19. Michael Slackman and Mona El Naggar, "Tunisia Casts Shadow on Arab Meeting," *New York Times*, January 20, 2011.
20. Quaddafi also did not attend the African Union Summit in Addis Ababa later that month. His absence was noted, as his habit of staying in a tent outside a luxury hotel was always one of the summit's signature curiosities. Whether he was staying home because of Egyptian unrest was a hot topic of barroom speculation. The consensus was that no, he probably just didn't feel like coming this time. Why would Qaddafi be worried about revolution in Libya when his grip had been so strong for 42 years?
21. Sandrine Rastello, "Food Prices Pushed More Into Poverty, World Bank Says (Update 2)," Bloomberg News, February 15, 2011.
22. From USDA World Agricultural Supply and Demand Estimates, June 9, 2011.
23. Maria Kolesnikova and Marina Sysoyeva, "Wheat Planting Falls to 4-Year Low in Russia Amid Export Ban," Bloomberg News, March 7, 2011.
24. Howard Schneider, "China Food Choices Reshaping World Markets," *Washington Post*, May 22, 2011.
25. Tom Odula, "Kenya Food Taxes Cut as Four Die of Hunger," Associated Press, April 27, 2011.
26. Press Trust of India (New Delhi), "India's Coconut Exports Surge on Lanka Ban," February 22, 2011.

27. Isis Almeida, "Cocoa Advances to 32-Year High on Ivory Coast Supply Concern," Bloomberg News, March 4, 2011.
28. Supunnabul Suwannakij, "Myanmar to Resume Rice Exports after Harvest Starts, FAO Says," Bloomberg News, March 11, 2011.
29. Jimmy Bolanos, "Bean Trade Policy," Managua: U.S. Department of Agriculture, March 10, 2011.
30. Ivan Castro and Mica Rosenberg, "Nicaragua's Ortega Says Crisis Is God Punishing U.S.," Reuters, October 10, 2008.
31. Interview, Sebaco, Nicaragua, April 29, 2011.
32. Patrick Donohue, "WTO's Lamy Blames Export Restrictions for Food-Price Increases," Bloomberg News, January 22, 2011.
33. Fred Ojambo, "Uganda Police Fire Bullets, Tear Gas in Kampala Amid Riots," Bloomberg News, April 28, 2011.
34. Oxfam News Release, distributed April 11, 2011; http://media-newswire.com/release_1147701.html (accessed May 8, 2011).
35. Daniel Flynn, "Aid Flows Set Record in 2010 but Pace to Slow—OECD," Reuters, April 6, 2011.
36. Chris Giles, "G8 Accused of Cover-Up on Aid Targets," *Financial Times*, May 16, 2011.
37. Oxfam, "Growing a Better Future," June 2011.
38. Peggy Hollinger, and Javier Blas, "French Anger at Speculators Hits G20 Hopes," *Financial Times*, February 2, 2011.
39. Alan Bjerga, "U.S. Says Corn Supply to Be Tight Even with Record Crop (2)," Bloomberg News, February 24 2011.

Chapter 7: Promise

1. Renee Bonorchis and Nasreen Seria, "Nigerian Banks Winning Mobius with Asia-Like Growth in Africa," Bloomberg News, April 27, 2011.
2. www.transparency.org/policy_research/surveys_indices/cpi/2010/results (accessed May 8, 2011). Angola is tied with Equatorial Guinea at 10th from the bottom.
3. Interview, Angata Barakoi, Kenya, February 14, 2011.
4. Interview, Washington, June 2, 2011.
5. Piaui Cremaq, "The Miracle of the Cerrado: Brazil Has Revolutionized its Own Farms. Can It Do the Same for Others?" *Economist*, August 26, 2010.
6. Interview, Washington, DC, March 29, 2011.
7. Interview, Washington, DC, March 29, 2011.
8. Integrated Regional Information Network (IRIN), "NGOs pare down in face of financial crisis," October 27, 2008.
9. Calestous Juma, *The New Harvest: Agricultural Innovation in Africa* (New York: Oxford University Press, 2010).

10. "Ease of Doing Business" rankings as of June 2010 as compiled by the International Finance Corporation and the World Bank www.doingbusiness .org/rankings (accessed April 7, 2011).
11. www.afrik-news.com/article17839.html (accessed May 8, 2011).
12. Centre for Chinese Studies, Stellenbosch University (Stellenbosch, South Africa), "China's Interest and Activity in Africa's Construction and Infrastructure Sectors, 2006.
13. "China Vows to Increase Government Scholarships for African Students," Xinhua News Agency, April 26, 2011.
14. Hannah Edinger and Ron Sandrey, "The Relevance of Chinese Agricultural Technologies for African Smallholder Farmers: Agricultural Technology Research in China" (University of Stellenbosch Centre for Chinese Studies, Stennenbosch, South Africa, April 2009), 38.
15. "Trying to Pull Together: Africans Are Asking whether China Is Making Their Lunch or Eating It," *Economist*, April 20, 2011.
16. James R. Hagerty and Will Connors, "U.S. Companies Race to Catch Up in Africa," *Wall Street Journal*, June 6, 2011.
17. Economic Commission for Africa, "To Contribute to MDGs, African Agriculture Needs to Transform from Subsistence to Market Systems, says Dione," Press Release No. 04/2011.
18. Interview, Nairobi, February 16, 2011.
19. World Bank, "World Development Report 2008: Agriculture and Poverty Reduction" (2008).
20. Calestous Juma, *The New Harvest: Agricultural Innovation in Africa* (New York: Oxford University Press, 2010.)
21. Integrated Regional Information Networks (IRIN), "South Africa: Aid Agency to Be Launched," January 17, 2011.
22. Capability—another key concept in development elaborated by Amartya Sen. See Amartya Sen, "Equality of What?" The Tanner Lecture on Human Values, Stanford University, May 22, 1979.
23. United Nations, "World Population Prospects: The 2010 Revision," released May 3, 2011, http://esa.un.org/unpd/wpp/index.htm (accessed May 8, 2011).
24. Miriam Gathigah, "The Struggle for Women to Own Land," Inter Press Service, July 14, 2011.
25. "Growing a Better Future," Oxfam, June 2011.
26. Matt Richmond, "South Sudan Wins Independence in Shadow of Conlict, Poverty (2), Blooomberg News, July 9, 2011; David K. Deng, "The New Frontier: A Baseline Survey of Large-Scale Land-Based Investment in Southern Sudan," Norwegian People's Aid, March 2011.
27. Telephone interview, June 6, 2011.
28. Telephone interview, February 11, 2011.
29. Alan Bjerga, "Africa Needs Soil 'Revolution,' Howard Buffett Says (Update 1)," Bloomberg News, October 13, 2010.

30. Claude Ringler et al. *Climate Change Impacts on Food Security in Sub-Saharan Africa: Insights from Comprehensive Climate Changes Scenarios* (Washington, DC: IFPRI, 2010).
31. Ibid., p. 12.
32. Ibid.
33. Steve Karnowski, "Scientists Say 'Super' New Wheat Varieties Will Resist Virulent Fungus while Boosting Yields," Associated Press, June 9. Telephone interview, Ronnie Coffman, head of the Durable Rust Resistance in Wheat project at Cornell University, June 9.
34. Statements on the urgency of ending hunger found at www.g8italia2009. it/static/G8_Allegato/LAquila_Joint_Statement_on_Global_Food_ Security%5B1%5D,0.pdf, www.fao.org/DOCREP/MEETING/005/Y7106e/ Y7106E09.htm#TopOfPage, www.un.org/millennium/declaration/ares552e.htm, www2.ohchr.org/english/issues/food/standards.htm, www.un.org/en/documents/ udhr/index.shtml (accessed April 7, 2011).
35. Examples: The 1974 UN food summit created the International Fund for Agricultural Development, which has benefited millions of struggling farmers, and it set up the famine early warning system that's guided World Food Program famine response to this day. The Millennium Development Goals have helped coordinate antipoverty programs even as 2015 approaches and the odds of reaching them are remote in many nations. Food-security gatherings of the late 2000s have prompted a rethinking of food-aid policy that promises to redouble efforts to increase farm productivity, which is fundamental to feeding the world.
36. Oxfam America Media Release, May 6, 2011.
37. Rudy Ruitenberg, "Farming Needs $83 Billion a Year to Feed World in 2050, UN Says," Bloomberg News, October 8, 2008.
38. See William Easterly, *The White Man's Burden: Why the West's Efforts to Aid the Rest Have Done So Much Ill And So Little Good* (Cambridge: MIT Press, 2001); and Dambisa Moyo, *Dead Aid: Why Aid Is Not Working and How There Is Another Way for Africa* (London: Allen Lane, 2009).
39. Howard Buffett quote taken from e-mail, March 11, 2011.
40. Oxfam International, "Survival of the Fttest" (Oxfam Briefing Paper, Oxford, 2008).
41. Interview, Kenya, February 14, 2011.
42. Interview with Purchase for Progress coordinator Ken Davies, Rome, January 24, 2011.
43. Interview, Washington, May 16, 2011.

Chapter 8: The Price of a Cup of Coffee

1. All Ethiopia interviews, unless noted otherwise, were conducted between January 26 and February 9, 2011.
2. Telephone interview by Bloomberg's Leslie Patton, March 18, 2011.

3. Eleni Gabre-Madhin, "This Is My Ethiopian Story," Nazret.com, August 11, 2009; http://nazret.com/blog/index.php/2009/08/11/ethiopia_this_is_my_ethiopian_story_by_e (accessed May 16, 2011).

4. CIA: The World Factbook, www.cia.gov/library/publications/the-world-factbook/geos/et.html (accessed June 19, 2011).

5. Steve Bloomfield, "Mengistu Found Guilty of Ethiopian Genocide," *Independent* (London), December 13, 2006.

6. The Ibrahim Index, www.moibrahimfoundation.org/en/section/the-ibrahim-index (accessed June 13, 2011).

7. Freedom House Freedom of the Press 2011 Survey, http://freedomhouse.org/images/File/fop/2011/FOTP2011GlobalRegionalTables.pdf (accessed May 9, 2011).

8. "Africa's impressive growth," *Economist* online, January 6, 2011.

9. William Davison, "Ethiopia Approves Five-Year Growth Plan That Targets Farming," Bloomberg News, December 2, 2011.

10. "Quotation for the Day," *Ethiopian Herald*, February 5, 2011.

11. USAID/Ethiopia, "2002–2003 Drought Emergency, Mitigation and Response Plan for Ethiopia," October 22, 2002.

12. Eleni Z. Gabre-Madhin and Ian Goggin, "Does Ethiopia Need a Commodity Exchange? An Integrated Approach to Market Development," International Food Policy Research Institute, November 2005. Goggin, the chief executive officer of the Africa Commodity Exchange in Malawi, had previously been president of the Zimbabwe Agricultural Commodity Exchange.

13. "Ethiopia Commodity Exchange Authority Proclamation," Federal Negarit Gazeta of the Federal Democratic Republic of Ethiopia, September 4, 2007.

14. The International Food Policy Research Institute, news release, April 2008, www.ifpri.org/pressrelease/ethiopias-commodity-exchange-opens-its-doors?print (accessed May 9, 2011).

15. Gabre-Madhin interview, Washington, DC, July 19, 2011.

16. Telephone interview with Kristian Schach Moller, technical and legal advisor for the Agricultural Commodity Exchange for Africa, July 18, 2011.

17. "The History of Coffee," National Coffee Association of U.S.A., Inc., www.ncausa.org/i4a/pages/index.cfm?pageid=68 (accessed May 15, 2011).

18. Charis Gresser and Sophia Tickell, "Mugged: Poverty in Your Coffee Cup," Oxfam International, 2002.

19. E-mail from SCAA, April 22, 2011.

20. Interview, Washington, DC, July 19, 2011.

21. "ECX Direct Specialty Trade (DST)," January 4, 2010.

22. Interview, Chicago, December 14, 2010.

23. News from the ICO, www.ico.org (accessed May 9, 2011).

24. Jason McLure, "Ethiopia Halts Coffee Auctions, Moves to Exchange," Bloomberg News, November 28, 2008.

25. Shahidur Rashid, Alex Winter-Nelson; and Philip Garcia, "Purpose and Potential for Commodity Exchanges in African Economies," International Food Policy Research Institute, November 2010.
26. "Ethiopia's ECX Trades $6.7 Billion of Commodities," *Ethiopian Journal*, November 2, 2010.
27. Jason McLure, "Ethiopia May Prosecute Coffee Exporters Accused of Hoarding," Bloomberg News, April 14, 2009.
28. Jason McLure, "Ethiopia Warns Coffee Exporters against Crimes, Capital Reports," Bloomberg News, January 26, 2009.
29. Interview by Leslie Patton of Bloomberg News, March 8, 2011.
30. Interview conducted in Soddo, Ethiopia, January 31, 2011; follow-up interview conducted by Will Davison by telephone, July 20, 2011.
31. Interview, Washington, DC, July 20, 2011.
32. Interview, Addis Ababa, January 27, 2011.
33. E-mail, December 9, 2010.
34. Davison, William, "Ethiopia May Ban Coffee Exporters Caught Hoarding, Defaulting," Bloomberg News, May 11, 2011.
35. Interview, July 20, 2011.
36. Telephone interview, July 17, 2011.
37. Interview by Leslie Patton of Bloomberg News, August 11, 2011.

Chapter 9: A Better Banana

1. All interviews done by me in Kenya from February 9–18, 2011, unless otherwise noted.
2. Shabd S. Acharya and Mary G. Alton Mackey, "Socio-economic Impact Assessment of the Tissue Culture Banana Industry in Kenya" (Africa Harvest Biotech Foundation International; Nairobi, Kenya; Johannesburg, South Africa; Washington, DC, 2008).
3. Interview in Washington, April 27, 2011.
4. Jay Shankar, "Janus-Backed Jain Irrigation Plans to Build a Plant in Africa, Mundra Says," Bloomberg News, December 13, 2010.
5. Charlotte Hebebrand, "Leveraging Private Sector Investment in Developing Country Agrifood Systems" (Chicago Council on Global Affairs, May 2011).
6. For an extensive discussion of this, see Aneel Karnani, *Fighting Poverty Together: Rethinking Strategies for Business, Governments and Civil Society to Reduce Poverty* (New York: Palgrave Macmillan, 2011).
7. Duane Stanford, "Coca-Cola's Chief Kent Roams Africa as Last World to Conquer," Bloomberg News, October 28, 2010.
8. Telephone interview, March 8, 2011.
9. CIA Factbook, www.cia.gov/library/publications/the-world-factbook/geos/ ke.html and www.cia.gov/library/publications/the-world-factbook/geos/et.html (accessed June 14, 2011).

10. L. Meuleman, "Impact Study of the Market Information System of KACE in Kenya" (M.Sc. Thesis, Catholic University of Leuven, Faculty of Bioscience Engineering, W. de Croylaan 42, 3001 Leuven, Belgium, 2007).

11. Wangari Maathai, "Constituency Boundaries and Options," presented to the Interim Independent Boundaries Review Commission, Nyeri, Central Province, Kenya, November 4 2009, www.greenbeltmovement.org/a.php?id=443 (accessed May 6, 2011).

12. Freedom House 2011 Freedom of the Press Rankings, http://freedomhouse.org/images/File/fop/2011/FOTP2011GlobalRegionalTables.pdf (accessed May 6, 2011). Five African countries—Mali, Ghana, Cape Verde, Mauritius, and Sao Tome and Principe—are listed as free.

13. Muchiri Karanja, "Good Health Beats Money Anytime: Kenyans," *Nation* (Nairobi), February 19, 2011.

14. "Kenya Launches Chinese-Funded Road Construction Work," Xinhua, August 22, 2009, http://english.peopledaily.com.cn/90001/90776/90883/6736267.html (accessed April 23, 2011).

15. Mike Peed, "We Have No Bananas: Can Scientists Defeat a Devastating Blight?" *New Yorker*, January 10, 2011.

16. "Financial Times Ranks TechnoServe Among World's Top Five Non-Governmental Organizations," www.technoserve.org/resources/press-room/2007-press-releases/dc070507.html (accessed March 6, 2011).

17. International Institute of Tropical Agriculture, "First Ever Pan-Africa Banana Conference Opens in Kenya," October 5, 2008.

18. USDA Economic Research Service, "Fruit and Tree Nut Yearbook" dataset, at http://usda.mannlib.cornell.edu/MannUsda/viewStaticPage.do?url=http://usda.mannlib.cornell.edu/usda/ers/./89022/2009/index.html (accessed June 19, 2011).

19. "Army Starts Food Aid Operation," World Food Programme, August 13, 2009.

20. Sarah McGregor, "World Bank Cuts Kenya Growth Estimate on Drought (1)," Bloomberg News, June 2, 2011.

21. E. S. Njeru, J. G. Muthamia, and S. C. Abmoga, "Effects of Organic Soil Amendments in Nutrition of Banana Plants," *African Journal of Horticultural Science* Vol. 1 (2008).

22. Stockholm Environment Institute, "Economics of Climate Change in Kenya: Final Report Submitted in Advance of COP15," December 1, 2009.

23. "Growing a Better Future," Oxfam International, June 1, 2011.

24. E-mail from Gerald Muthomi, July 25, 2011.

25. ISAAA's executive summary for its "Global Status of Commercialized Biotech/GM Crops: 2010," www.isaaa.org/resources/publications/briefs/42/executivesummary/default.asp (accessed March 8, 2011).

26. See David Ewing Duncan, "Without a Genetic Fix, the Banana May Be History," *San Francisco Chronicle*, April 4, 2004; Linda Nordling, "Uganda prepares to plant transgenic bananas," *Nature*, October 1, 2010; Robert Uhlig, "Defenceless Banana 'Will Be Extinct in 10 Years,'" *Telegraph* (London), January 16, 2003.

27. Telephone interview, March 8, 2011.
28. Gerdien Meijerink and Myrtille Danse, "Riding the Wave: High Prices, Big Business? The Role of Multinationals in the International Grain Markets," 2009, LEI Wageningen UR.
29. Charlotte Hebebrand, "Leveraging Private Sector Investment in Developing Country Agrifood Systems," Chicago Council on Global Affairs, May 2011.
30. Interview, Washington, June 3, 2011.
31. Carli Lourens, "DuPont Unit Asks South Africa to Reconsider Halt to Pannar Deal," *Bloomberg Businessweek*, December 13, 2010.
32. Telephone interview, March 8, 2011.
33. "DuPont Leaders: Growth in Africa Gains Momentum," corporate news release, September 28, 2010 www2.dupont.com/Media_Center/en_US/daily_news/september/article20100928.html (accessed May 6, 2011).

Chapter 10: Thai Quality

1. Unless otherwise noted, all interviews conducted in Thailand, March 19–26, 2011.
2. Food and Agricultural Organization of the United Nations, *The State of Food Insecurity in the World: Addressing Food Insecurity in Protracted Crises* (Rome, Italy: FAO Electronic Publishing Policy and Support Branch Communication Division, 2010).
3. Me Posop story taken largely from Thailand Ministry of Culture, http://webhost.m-culture.go.th/culture01/en/index.php/articles/50-belief-and-religion/173-me-posopthe-rice-mother.html as (accessed March 27, 2011).
4. Interview conducted by Supunnabul Suwannakij of Bloomberg News, March 19, 2011.
5. Daniel Ten Kate, "Abhisit Takes Aim at Thaksin's Turf as 'Brutal' Thai Vote Nears," Bloomberg News, May 9, 2011; Danies Ten Kate, "Thaksin Looms in Thai Vote as Yingluck Lead Deters Investors," Bloomberg News, June 16, 2011.
6. Daniel Ten Kate, "Thai Army Warns Against 'Same' Poll Result, Royal Insults (1)," Bloomberg News, June 15, 2011.
7. Information supplied by Thai Rice Exporters Association.
8. From the International Rice Research Institute, http://irri.org/world-rice-statistics (accessed March 23, 2011).
9. Nguyen Van Bo interview done via telephone in Hanoi, March 31, 2011, by Bloomberg's Diep Ngoc Pham.
10. Amy Yee, "Organic Farming Finds a Growing Fan Base in India," *New York Times*, June 2, 2011.
11. Interview, Nicaragua, April 30, 2011.
12. Interview, Washington, May 3, 2011.
13. Interview, Washington, May 10, 2011.

14. *The Week*, "Bolivia's Quinoa Quandary," March 22, 2011. http://theweek.com/article/index/213390/bolivias-quinoa-quandary.
15. "Preliminary Observations and Conclusions," Office of the United Nations High Commissioner for Human Rights, Mandate of the Special Rapporteur on the Right to Food, Beijing, 23 December 2010.
16. Jeff Wilson, "China Pork Binge Driving Iowa-Sized Soy Imports on Shortages," Bloomberg News, April 11, 2011.
17. Tom Polansek, "China Bought U.S. Corn," *Wall Street Journal*, May 27, 2011.
18. Jeff Wilson, "Corn Jumps to Two-Week High as U.S. Export Sale May Be for China," Bloomberg News, March 25, 2011.
19. Steve Stroth, "U.S. Sells 840,000 Tons of Corn, Including 540,000 to China," Bloomberg News, July 7, 2011; Chuin-Wei Yap, "Can G20 Separate Wheat from Chaff with China Food Data?" *Wall Street Journal*, June 29, 2011.
20. Fred Gale and Kuo Huang, "Demand for Food Quantity and Quality in China" (U.S. Department of Agriculture Economic Research Report Number 32, January 2007).
21. Interview in Xi'an, China, November 1, 2005.
22. Supunnabul Suwannakij, "Thai Rice-Buying Plan Threatens Shipment Target, Exporters Say," Bloomberg News, June 20, 2011.
23. Interview by Supunnabul Suwannakij, July 7, 2011.

Chapter 11: Steps Up

1. Ivory Coast reporting taken from Alan Bjerga and Shruti Date Singh, "Texas Cotton's Subsidies Help Destroy Africa's Cheaper Farmers," Bloomberg News, October 29, 2007. Soro interview done by Pauline Dix of Bloomberg.
2. Claudia Carpenter, "Ivory Coast Contributed to Lack of Cotton Supply, Cotlook Says," Bloomberg News, March 1, 2011.
3. Soumaila T. Diarra, "Mali: Cotton and Food Security Closely Linked," allAfrica.com, January 17, 2011.
4. It is unlikely that every single person on earth will always be able to afford or have access to food, which is why emergency food aid programs, government and charitable nutrition assistance, etc. will remain necessary.
5. "Russia: Wheat Ban Worked," *Financial Times*, May 31, 2011.
6. Lester Brown, "Water Shortages Threaten Food Future in the Arab Middle East," The Permaculture Research Institute of Australia, May 4, 2011, http://permaculture.org.au/2011/05/04/water-shortages-threaten-food-future-in-the-arab-middle-east (accessed May 15, 2011).
7. Fumbuka Ng'wanakilala, "S. Korea to Farm Tanzania Site in Early 2011," Reuters, November 11, 2010.

8. Peter Warr, "Indonesia: Why Food Self-Sufficiency Is Different from Food Security," Development Policy Centre, April 28, 2011. http://devpolicy.org/indonesia-why-food-self-sufficiency-is-different-from-food-security (accessed May 15, 2011).

9. Jeffrey J. Reimer and Man Li, "Trade Costs and the Gains from Trade in Crop Agriculture," *American Journal of Agricultural Economics* 92, no. 4 (2010): 1024–1039.

10. Interview, Washington, April 25, 2011.

11. Ola Galal, "Egypt Buys First Russian Wheat Since Export Ban Was Imposed (1)," Bloomberg News, July 7, 2011; Isabel Gorst, "Russian Exporters Forced to Drop Grain Prices," *Financial Times*, July 4, 2011.

12. Pratik Parija, "Rice from India at $400 a Ton May Cut Global Prices, Group Says," Bloomberg News, July 20, 2011.

13. Mathabo Le Roux, "Japan, Swiss Want Limits to Food Export Bans," *BusinessDay* (Johannesburg, South Africa), May 6, 2011.

14. Jennifer M. Freedman, "WTO Targets Deal for Poor Nations as Top Priority in Doha Talks," Bloomberg News, May 31, 2011.

15. Jennifer M. Freedman, "Russia Moves Closer to WTO Membership With EU Deal (Update 4), December 7, 2010.

16. Unpublished (as of May 2011) study from the International Food & Agricultural Trade Policy Council.

17. Alan Bjerga, "Mad Cow Cost U.S. Beef Industry $11 Billion in Trade, ITC Says," Bloomberg News, October 10, 2008.

18. Linda R. Horton and Elisabeth Ann Wright, "Reconciling Food Safety with Import Facilitation Objectives: Helping Developing Country Producers Meet U.S. and EU Food Requirements Through Transatlantic Cooperation," International Food & Agriculture Trade Policy Council, June 2008.

19. Interview, Washington, April 26, 2011.

20. OECD data, compiled May 31, 2011.

21. Subsidy figures taken from Akin Adesina, "Africa's Food Crisis: Conditioning Trends and Global Development Policy" (International Association of Agricultural Economists Conference, Beijing, August 16, 2006).

22. Alan Bjerga, "Billionaires Receive Farm Payments; Means Tests Urged," Bloomberg News, June 11, 2007.

23. David Hencke and Rob Evans, "Royal Farms Get £1m from Taxpayers," *Guardian* (London), March 23, 2005; Mary Clare Jalonick, "Prince Charles Champions Organic Farming, Criticizes Big Ag Subsidies in DC Speech," Huffington Post, May 4, 2011.

24. Carla Simoes and Andre Soliani, "Brazil Won't Retaliate Against U.S. Over Cotton Aid (Update 2)," Bloomberg News, June 17, 2010.

25. Josiah Ryan, "Bipartisan Call to End 'Lunacy' of Brazil Cotton Payments," *The Hill*, February 18, 2011.

26. Alan Bjerga, "U.S. House Approves Amendment to Stop Brazil Cotton Payments," Bloomberg News, June 16, 2011.

27. Tim Josling, David Blandford, Jane Earley, "Biofuel and Biomass Subsidies in the U.S., EU and Brazil: Towards a Transparent System of Notification" (International Food & Agricultural Trade Policy Council, September 2010); Charlotte Hebebrand interview, Washington. May 12, 2011.

28. Interview, Des Moines, Iowa, October 14, 2009.

29. "World Development Report 2008: Agriculture for Development, World Bank."

30. Celia W. Dugger, "Ending Famine, Simply by Ignoring the Experts," *New York Times*, December 2, 2007.

31. Drew Hinshaw, "Senegal Achieves Rice Sustenance, Plans Exports, President Says," Bloomberg News, April 18, 2011.

32. "Malawi, Fertilizer Subsidies and the World Bank," World Bank, http://web.worldbank.org/wbsite/external/countries/africaext/malawiextn/0,,content MDK:21575335~pagePK:141137~piPK:141127~theSitePK:355870,00.html (accessed April 16, 2011).

33. Andrew Dorward and E. Chirwa, "The Malawi Agricultural Input Subsidy Programme: 2005–6 to 2008–9," *International Journal of Agricultural Sustainability* 9, no. 1 (2011): 232–247.

34. "Cotton Production Risk Sinking in Malawi," *Nyasia Times,* September 2, 2009.

35. Interview, Washington, DC, May 16, 2011.

36. E-mail from Land O' Lakes, July 20, 2011.

37. Tina Rosenberg, "Doing More Than Praying for Rain," *New York Times* Opinionator Blog, May 9, 2011.

38. See Calestous Juma, *The New Harvest: Agricultural Innovation in Africa* (New York: Oxford University Press, 2010), 19–21.

39. "Trade Facilitation," African Trade Policy Centre, June 2004.

Chapter 12: Harvest of Hope

1. Interview, May 24, 2011.

2. Donna Gordan Blankinship, "Gates Foundation Spends $1.7B on Farming in Africa," Associated Press, June 1, 2011.

3. David Malingha Doya, "African Agriculture Group May Get Islamic Development Bank Loan," Bloomberg News, April 5, 2011.

4. J. Ato Kobbie, "Why Africa Is 30 Years Backwards—AGRA Reveals," GhanaWeb, April 23, 2011.

5. Interview, Washington, May 19, 2011.

6. Mary Clare Jalonick, "Clinton: Too Much Ethanol Could Lead to Food Riots," Associated Press, February 24, 2011.

7. Growth Energy and Renewable Fuels Association e-mails, February 24, 2011.

8. "Bill Clinton's Corn Sense: The Former President Connects Ethanol to Rising Food Prices," *Wall Street Journal*, February 28, 2011.
9. Kim Chipman and Alan Bjerga, "Ethanol Politics Recast as Iowans Back End to U.S. Tax Subsidies," Bloomberg News, May 26, 2011.
10. Alan Bjerga, "Rising Corn Prices Threaten Meat Profits, Seaboard Says (1)," Bloomberg News, May 4, 2011.
11. Jim Efstathiou Jr., "World Biofuels Production Guidelines Set by G8-Led Group of Nations," Bloomberg News, May 23, 2011.
12. "Global Trends in Sustainable Energy Investment 2009," United Nations Environment Programme; "Global Trends in Renewable Energy Investment 2011," Bloomberg New Energy Finance, July 2011.
13. A very truncated selection of papers on speculation consulted for this section:

    Philip C. Abbott, Christopher Hurt, and Wallace E. Tyner, "What's Driving Food Prices: March 2009 Update" (Issue Report, Farm Foundation, 2011).

    J. Baffes, (World Bank) and T. Haniotis (European Commission), "Placing the 2006/08 Commodities Boom into Perspective" (World Bank Research Working Paper 5371, 2010).

    Oscar Calvo-Gonzalez, Rashmi Shankar, and Riccardo Trezzi, "Are Commodity Prices More Volatile Now? A Long-Run Perspective" (Policy Research Working Paper Series 5460, World Bank, 2010).

    Olivier De Schutter, "Food Commodities Speculation and Food Price Crises" (Briefing Note 02, U.N. Food and Agriculture Organization, 2010).

    C. Levin C. and T. Coburn, "Excessive Speculation in the Wheat Market" (Permanent Sub-Committee on Investigation, United States Senate, 2009).

    Michael C., Litt, "The Great Grain Robbery" (Core Strategy Series, Arrowhawk Capital Partners, 2010).

    S. H. Irwin and D. R. Sanders, "The Impact of Index and Swap Funds on Commodity Futures Markets: Preliminary Results" (OECD Food, Agriculture and Fisheries Working Papers, No. 27, OECD Publishing, 2010).

    Michael W. Masters, and Adam K. White, "The Accidental Hunt Brothers: How Institutional Investors are Driving Up Food and Energy Prices (2008), www.loe. org/images/content/080919/Act1.pdf (accessed July 18, 2011).

    Donald Mitchell, "A Note on Rising Food Prices" (Policy Research Working Paper Series 4682, World Bank, 2008).

    Ke Tang and Wei Xiong, "Index Investment and the Financialization of Commodities," www.princeton.edu/~wxiong/papers/commodity.pdf (accessed July 18, 2011).

    C. Peter Timmer, "Causes of High Food Prices" (Asian Development Bank Working Paper Series No. 128, 2008).

14. Telephone interview, March 2, 2011.

15. Asjylyn Loder and Phil Mattingly, "Wall Street Lobbyists Besiege CFTC to Shape Derivatives Rules," Bloomberg News, October 14, 2010.
16. Senate Agriculture Committee hearing, March 3, 2011.
17. Asjylyn Loder, "'Europe Won't Be Haven from New U.S. Trading Rules,' Bernier Says," Bloomberg News, November 2, 2010.
18. "Leaders See Threat to Growth from Commodity Price Swings (3)," Bloomberg News, April 14, 2011.
19. Steve Matthews and Silla Brush, "Fed's Givson Urges 'Consistent' Global Rules on Derivatives (1)," Bloomberg News, June 15, 2011.
20. Interview, Washington, May 25, 2011.
21. Robert Zoellick, "Free Markets Can Still Feed the World," Financial Times, January 5, 2011; U.S. Agency for International Development, "USAID Expands Global Emergency Food Aid Prepositioning System," agency news release, October 5, 2010.
22. Mark Drajem, "Cargill Urges Pacific Nations to Renounce Food Export Curbs," Bloomberg News, May 20, 2011; Petchanet Pratruangkrai, "Food Security, Relief Top Agenda," Nation (Bangkok), May 20, 2011; Rudy Ruitenberg and Tony Dreibus, "G-20 Agrees Agriculture Plan to Tackle Food-Price 'Plague' (1)," Blomberg News, June 23, 2011.
23. Jonathan Watts, "Fish Farming Is Answer to Increasing Global Meat Demands, Says Report," Guardian (London), June 14, 2011.
24. Interview, Washington, May 19, 2011.
25. Flavia Krause-Jackson, "Mother Tells UN's Ban How Son's Suicide Sparked Revolt (1)," Bloomberg News, March 23, 2011.

Acknowledgments

Writing a book is daunting for someone who has spent his career in newspapers and wire services, in that, when something changes or new information comes to light, you can't just go back to the published book and write another 500 words. The covers close and the moment is frozen, but with each day, actions and their consequences challenge our understanding of how to meet a basic responsibility, that of feeding the world.

Some of what's been written here may someday seem prescient, other parts less so. No one will agree with everything I've written, and often those disagreements will be backed by sound reasoning. My own knowledge and understanding of the topics explored here is growing and evolving—the book I set out to write one year ago isn't the one that was written, and one year from now it would be different as well. My hope is that this work makes its own small contribution to an important conversation that, collectively, creates better solutions to hunger and poverty on a pain-ridden, promising planet. Anyone who has questions, comments, or suggestions about this book or the issues it explores, please contact me at endlessappetites@gmail.com, one place where I'm hoping this conversation can continue. It is important not to lose urgency on food security, as undoubtedly the casino-set prices will dip again, people will declare the food crisis solved, and short attention spans will drift elsewhere—until the next shock causes even more suffering. Let's try to avoid that as much as possible. Thank you for your own thoughts and assistance, and for choosing to join me on these pages.

■ ■ ■

A single name on a book cover doesn't accurately reflect the essential contributions of others. Some people of note among the many who shaped this project:

Endless Appetites wouldn't have happened without leaders at Bloomberg News who supported this project. Steve Stroth first asked me if I wanted to write a book. Matt Winkler and Reto Gregori green-lighted the project.

Flynn McRoberts, Anne Reifenberg, Chris Power, and Larry Liebert helped maintain the balance between book and Bloomberg reporting. Robert Simison, Amanda Bennett, and Jeffrey Taylor were reporting guides during the 2008 "Recipe for Famine" project that in part created the opportunity to write this book. Stephen Isaacs was the liaison between Bloomberg News and Bloomberg Press, now an imprint of John Wiley & Sons, who expertly handled the relationship between the two. Stacey Fischkelta accommodated my urge to make up-to-the-minute revisions during production—to a point— and Emilie Herman demystified John Wiley & Sons and the publishing process throughout. Together with Pamela van Giessen, she made sure the book was actually a book, rather than 70,000 words of rambling. Although you may be the judge of that.

Colleagues, friends, and experts who agreed to read through portions of the book were fountains of insight and sources of support in what otherwise can be a very solitary pursuit. Susan Straight provided extensive reads from beginning to end, and Caron Gala's comments throughout were a key complement. Barbara Noe, Kirsten Winters, Devry Boughner, Jason McLure, Daniel Enoch, Asjylyn Loder, Tom Slayton, Roxana Saberi, Julia Oliver and Heather Yamour each added their own comments on individual chapters, which ranged from that of the expert to that of a blank-slate reader, and on whose suggestions I acted upon with varying degrees of effectiveness.

Jian Zhang, who compiled and created many of the figures in this book, helped in ways that were unexpected and necessary. Elizabeth Wolfe provided backup on key research. Also essential to this project, which included complex travel logistics on short notice, were Will Davison, Supunnabul Suwannaki, and Kassahun Addis. I will always owe Leslie Patton a cup of the world's best coffee, and Alison Fitzgerald, Rudy Ruitenberg, and Jerry Hagstrom all deserve appreciation for providing observations that helped carry me through this process, even though they probably didn't realize they were doing so at the time. This book was written between November 2010 and July 2011 in: the president's office of the National Press Club; a Caribou Coffee outside Baxter, Minnesota; Bloomberg bureaus in Chicago, Rome, New York, Nairobi, Bangkok, and Washington, D.C.; other locations in Nicaragua and Ethiopia; airport layovers in Dubai, Doha, Columbus, Ohio, and Fort Lauderdale, Florida; and rural roads throughout the developing world. Any bumps in this book are my responsibility; everyone listed above did their best to smooth them out.

July 10, 2011

About the Author

Alan Bjerga has made agriculture a focus of his writing since arriving in Washington, D.C., in 2001. His work on famine and the relationship between food markets and farm policy has garnered awards from the Overseas Press Club, the New York Press Club, the Kansas Press Association, the Society of American Business Editors and Writers, and the North American Agricultural Journalists. He won the North American Agricultural Journalists (NAAJ) Glenn Cunningham award, its top writing distinction, in 2005, and was the organization's president in 2010–2011. He also served as president of the National Press Club in Washington in 2010, hosting its televised speaker series and advocating for press freedom and more open government.

Bjerga holds a master's degree in mass communication from the University of Minnesota in Minneapolis and a bachelor's in history and English literature from Concordia College in Moorhead, Minnesota. He began his newspaper career at the St. Paul *Pioneer Press* in Minnesota. He reported for the Sioux Falls *Argus Leader* in South Dakota and the Wichita *Eagle* in Kansas before becoming that paper's correspondent in Washington for Knight Ridder, later McClatchy, Newspapers. He joined Bloomberg News in 2006.

In his spare time Bjerga stays outdoors and sings along with the radio. He lives in Alexandria, Virginia, with several well-cared-for house plants.

Index